☆☆☆☆☆

The UFO Files

The Report on

Unidentified Flying Objects

Cover & Graphic Design

Mattias Långström

Contact: oneofakindbooks@bhagwan.se

Introduction

This book is part of the "The UFO Files" series, based on my own, old favorite UFO books. It can be read individually or as part of the entire series.

In May 2019, The New York Times reported that American Navy fighter jets had several encounters with unexplained objects while conducting exercises off the eastern seaboard of the United States from the summer of 2014 to March 2015. On April 12, 2021, the Pentagon confirmed the authenticity of pictures and videos gathered by the Unidentified Aerial Phenomena Task Force (UAPTF), purportedly showing "pyramid shaped objects" hovering above the USS Russell in 2019, off the coast of California, with spokeswoman Susan Gough saying "I can confirm that the referenced photos and videos were taken by Navy personnel...

Unidentified lights and flying objects have been reported for much of human history. Skeptics including scientists, and organizations such as the Committee for Skeptical Inquiry, state that UFOs are conventional objects or phenomena, while "Ufologists" favour unconventional hypotheses. UFOs are a worldwide cultural phenomenon, appearing in fictional movies, television and other media. UFO reports continue to appear in news media. So, observations of aerial phenomena have been described throughout history and continue to be the subject of interest by skywatchers: — On April 14, 1561, residents of Nuremberg described the appearance of a large black triangular object. According to witnesses, there were also hundreds of spheres, cylinders and other odd-shaped objects that moved erratically overhead...

— In April 1897, thousands of people reported seeing "airships" in various parts of the United States. Many signed affidavits. Scores of people even reported talking to the pilots. Thomas Edison was asked his opinion, and said, "You can take it from me that it is a pure fake..."

— In 1946, more than 2,000 reports were collected, primarily by the Swedish military, of unidentified aerial objects over the Scandinavian nations, along with isolated reports from France, Portugal, Italy and Greece...

UFO is a fascinating subject that you can study in depth and constantly learn more about. The phrase UFO was coined as an acronym by Project Blue Book head Edward J. Ruppelt, but today UFO is widely used as a stand-in for extraterrestrial spacecraft-aircraft that people claim to have observed. Many UFOs are described as being flying saucers.

This interesting and fascinating book is based on The Report on Unidentified Flying Objects by Edward J. Ruppelt. It is actually more than a book; it is a report because it is the first time that anyone, either military or civilian, has brought together in one document all the facts about this fascinating subject...

Psychic Mattias Långström

FOREWORD

*This is a book about unidentified flying objects—
UFO's—"flying saucers." It is actually more than a book;
it is a report because it is the first time that anyone,
either military or civilian, has brought together in one
document all the facts about this fascinating subject.
With the exception of the style, this report is written
exactly the way I would have written it had I been officially asked to do so while I was chief of the Air Force's
project for investigating UFO reports—Project Blue
Book.*

*In many instances I have left out the names of the people
who reported seeing UFO's, or the names of certain
people who were associated with the project, just as
I would have done in an official report. For the same
reason I have changed the locale in which some of the
UFO sightings occurred. This is especially true in chapter
fifteen, the story of how some of our atomic scientists
detected radiation whenever UFO's were reported
near their "UFO-detection stations." This policy of not
identifying the "source," to borrow a term from military
intelligence, is insisted on by the Air Force so that the*

people who have co-operated with them will not get any unwanted publicity. Names are considered to be "classified information."

But the greatest care has been taken to make sure that the omission of names and changes in locale has in no way altered the basic facts because this report is based on the facts—all of the facts—nothing of significance has been left out.

It was only after considerable deliberation that I put this report together, because it had to be told accurately, with no holds barred. I finally decided to do it for two reasons. First, there is world-wide interest in flying saucers; people want to know the facts. But more often than not these facts have been obscured by secrecy and confusion, a situation that has led to wild speculation on one end of the scale and an almost dangerously blasé attitude on the other. It is only when all of the facts are laid out that a correct evaluation can be made.

Second, after spending two years investigating and analyzing UFO reports, after talking to the people who have seen UFO's—industrialists, pilots, engineers, generals, and just the plain man-on-the-street, and after discussing the subject with many very capable scientists, I felt that I was in a position to be able to put together the complete account of the Air Force's struggle with the flying saucer.

The report has been difficult to write because it involves something that doesn't officially exist. It is well known that ever since the first flying saucer was reported in June 1947 the Air Force has officially said that there is no proof that such a thing as an interplanetary spaceship exists. But what is not well known is that this conclusion is far from being unanimous among the military and their scientific advisers because of the one word, proof; so the UFO investigations continue.

The hassle over the word "proof" boils down to one question: What constitutes proof? Does a UFO have to land at the River Entrance to the Pentagon, near the Joint Chiefs of Staff offices? Or is it proof when a ground radar station detects a UFO, sends a jet to intercept it, the jet pilot sees it, and locks on with his radar, only to have the UFO streak away at a phenomenal speed? Is it proof when a jet pilot fires at a UFO and sticks to his story even under the threat of court-martial? Does this constitute proof?

The at times hotly debated answer to this question may be the answer to the question, "Do the UFO's really exist?" I'll give you the facts—all of the facts—you decide.

CHAPTER 1

Project Blue Book and the UFO Story

In the summer of 1952 a United States Air Force F-86 jet interceptor shot at a flying saucer.

This fact, like so many others that make up the full flying saucer story, has never before been told.

I know the full story about flying saucers and I know that it has never before been told because I organized and was chief of the Air Force's Project Blue Book, the special project set up to investigate and analyze uniden-tified flying object, or UFO, reports. (UFO is the official term that I created to replace the words "flying saucers.")

There is a fighter base in the United States which I used to visit frequently because, during 1951, 1952, and 1953, it got more than its share of good UFO reports.

The commanding officer of the fighter group, a full colo-nel and command pilot, believed that UFO's were real. The colonel believed in UFO's because he had a lot of faith in his pilots—and they had chased UFO's in their F-86's. He had seen UFO's on the scopes of his radar sets, and he knew radar.

*The colonel's intelligence officer, a captain, didn't exactly
believe that UFO's were real, but he did think that they
warranted careful investigation. The logic the intelligence officer used in investigating UFO reports—and in
getting answers to many of them—made me wish many
times that he worked for me on Project Blue Book.*

*One day the intelligence officer called me at my base in
Dayton, Ohio. He wanted to know if I was planning to
make a trip his way soon. When I told him I expected to
be in his area in about a week, he asked me to be sure to
look him up. There was no special hurry, he added, but
he had something very interesting to show me.*

*When we got wind of a good story, Project Blue Book
liked to start working on it at once, so I asked the
intelligence officer to tell me what he had. But nothing
doing. He didn't want to discuss it over the phone. He
even vetoed the idea of putting it into a secret wire. Such
extreme caution really stopped me, because anything
can be coded and put in a wire.*

*When I left Dayton about a week later I decided to go
straight to the fighter base, planning to arrive there
in midmorning. But while I was changing airlines my
reservations got fouled up, and I was faced with waiting
until evening to get to the base. I called the intelligence*

*officer and told him about the mix-up. He told me to
hang on right there and he would fly over and pick me
up in a T-33 jet.*

*As soon as we were in the air, on the return trip, I called
the intelligence officer on the interphone and asked him
what was going on. What did he have? Why all the
mystery? He tried to tell me, but the interphone wasn't
working too well and I couldn't understand what he was
saying. Finally he told me to wait until we returned to
his office and I could read the report myself.*

*Report! If he had a UFO report why hadn't he sent it in
to Project Blue Book as he usually did?*

*We landed at the fighter base, checked in our parachu-
tes, Mae Wests, and helmets, and drove over to his office.
There were several other people in the office, and they
greeted me with the usual question, "What's new on
the flying saucer front?" I talked with them for a while,
but was getting impatient to find out what was on the
intelligence officer's mind. I was just about to ask him
about the mysterious report when he took me to one side
and quietly asked me not to mention it until everybody
had gone.*

Once we were alone, the intelligence officer shut the

door, went over to his safe, and dug out a big, thick report. It was the standard Air Force reporting form that is used for all intelligence reports, including UFO reports. The intelligence officer told me that this was the only existing copy. He said that he had been told to destroy all copies, but had saved one for me to read.

With great curiosity, I took the report and started to read. What had happened at this fighter base?

About ten o'clock in the morning, one day a few weeks before, a radar near the base had picked up an unidentified target. It was an odd target in that it came in very fast—about 700 miles per hour—and then slowed down to about 100 miles per hour. The radar showed that it was located northeast of the airfield, over a sparsely settled area.

Unfortunately the radar station didn't have any height-finding equipment. The operators knew the direction of the target and its distance from the station but they didn't know its altitude. They reported the target, and two F-86's were scrambled.

The radar picked up the F-86's soon after they were airborne, and had begun to direct them into the target when the target started to fade on the radarscope. At the time several of the operators thought that this fade was caused by the target's losing altitude rapidly and getting below the radar's beam. Some of the other operators thought that it was a high-flying target and that it was fading just because it was so high.

In the debate which followed, the proponents of the high-flying theory won out, and the F-86's were told to go up to 40,000 feet. But before the aircraft could get to that altitude, the target had been completely lost on the radarscope.

The F-86's continued to search the area at 40,000 feet, but could see nothing. After a few minutes the aircraft ground controller called the F-86's and told one to come down to 20,000 feet, the other to 5,000 feet. and continue the search. The two jets made a quick letdown, with one pilot stopping at 20,000 feet and the other heading for the deck.

The second pilot, who was going down to 5,000 feet, was just beginning to pull out when he noticed a flash below and ahead of him. He flattened out his dive a little and headed toward the spot where he had seen the light. As he closed on the spot he suddenly noticed what he first thought was a weather balloon. A few seconds later he realized that it couldn't be a balloon because it was stay-

ing ahead of him. Quite an achievement for a balloon, since he had built up a lot of speed in his dive and now was flying almost straight and level at 3,000 feet and was traveling "at the Mach."

Again the pilot pushed the nose of the F-86 down and started after the object. He closed fairly fast, until he came to within an estimated 1,000 yards. Now he could get a good look at the object. Although it had looked like a balloon from above, a closer view showed that it was definitely round and flat—saucer-shaped. The pilot described it as being "like a doughnut without a hole."

As his rate of closure began to drop off, the pilot knew that the object was picking up speed. But he pulled in behind it and started to follow. Now he was right on the deck.

About this time the pilot began to get a little worried. What should he do? He tried to call his buddy, who was flying above him somewhere in the area at 20,000 feet. He called two or three times but could get no answer. Next he tried to call the ground controller but he was too low for his radio to carry that far. Once more he tried his buddy at 20,000 feet, but again no luck.

By now he had been following the object for about

two minutes and during this time had closed the gap between them to approximately 500 yards. But this was only momentary. Suddenly the object began to pull away, slowly at first, then faster. The pilot, realizing that he couldn't catch it, wondered what to do next.

When the object traveled out about 1,000 yards, the pilot suddenly made up his mind—he did the only thing that he could do to stop the UFO. It was like a David about to do battle with a Goliath, but he had to take a chance. Quickly charging his guns, he started shooting. . . . A moment later the object pulled up into a climb and in a few seconds it was gone. The pilot climbed to 10,000 feet, called the other F-86, and now was able to contact his buddy. They joined up and went back to their base.

As soon as he had landed and parked, the F-86 pilot went into operations to tell his story to his squadron commander. The mere fact that he had fired his guns was enough to require a detailed report, as a matter of routine. But the circumstances under which the guns actually were fired created a major disturbance at the fighter base that day.

After the squadron commander had heard his pilot's story, he called the group commander, the colonel, and the intelligence officer. They heard the pilot's story.

*For some obscure reason there was a "personality clash,"
the intelligence officer's term, between the pilot and the
squadron commander. This was obvious, according to
the report I was reading, because the squadron commander immediately began to tear the story apart and
accuse the pilot of "cracking up," or of just "shooting
his guns for the hell of it and using the wild story as a
cover-up."*

*Other pilots in the squadron, friends of the accused
pilot—including the intelligence officer and a flight
surgeon—were called in to "testify." All of these men
were aware of the fact that in certain instances a pilot
can "flip" for no good reason, but none of them said that
he had noticed any symptoms of mental crack-up in the
unhappy pilot.*

*None, except the squadron commander. He kept poun-
ding home his idea—that the pilot was "psycho"—and
used a few examples of what the report called "minor
incidents" to justify his stand.*

*Finally the pilot who had been flying with the "accused"
man was called in. He said that he had been monitoring
the tactical radio channel but that he hadn't heard any
calls from his buddy's low-flying F-86. The squadron
commander triumphantly jumped on this point, but the*

accused pilot tended to refute it by admitting he was so jumpy that he might not have been on the right channel. But when he was asked if he had checked or changed channels after he had lost the object and before he had finally contacted the other F-86, he couldn't remember.

So ended the pilot's story and his interrogation.

The intelligence officer wrote up his report of a UFO sighting, but at the last minute, just before sending it, he was told to hold it back. He was a little unhappy about this turn of events, so he went in to see why the group commander had decided to delay sending the report to Project Blue Book.

They talked over the possible reactions to the report. If it went out it would cause a lot of excitement, maybe unnecessarily. Yet, if the pilot actually had seen what he claimed, it was vitally important to get the report in to ATIC immediately. The group commander said that he would made his decision after a talk with his executive officer. They decided not to send the report and ordered it destroyed.

When I finished reading, the intelligence officer's first comment was, "What do you think?"

Since the evaluation of the report seemed to hinge upon conflicts between personalities I didn't know, I could venture no opinion, except that the incident made up the most fascinating UFO report I'd ever seen. So I batted the intelligence officer's question back to him.

"I know the people involved," he replied, "and I don't think the pilot was nuts. I can't give you the report, because Colonel —— told me to destroy it. But I did think you should know about it." Later he burned the report.

The problems involved in this report are typical. There are certain definite facts that can be gleaned from it; the pilot did see something and he did shoot at something, but no matter how thoroughly you investigate the incident that something can never be positively identified. It might have been a hallucination or it might have been some vehicle from outer space; no one will ever know. It was a UFO.

The UFO story started soon after June 24, 1947, when newspapers all over the United States carried the first flying saucer report. The story told how nine very bright, disk-shaped objects were seen by Kenneth Arnold, a Boise, Idaho, businessman, while he was flying his private plane near Mount Rainier, in the state of Washington. With journalistic license, reporters converted Arnold's description of the individual motion of each of the objects—like "a saucer skipping across water"—into "flying saucer," a name for the objects themselves. In the eight years that have passed since Arnold's memorable sighting, the term has become so common that it is now in Webster's Dictionary and is known today in most languages in the world.

For a while after the Arnold sighting the term "flying saucer" was used to describe all disk-shaped objects that were seen flashing through the sky at fantastic speeds. Before long, reports were made of objects other than disks, and these were also called flying saucers. Today the words are popularly applied to anything seen in the sky that cannot be identified as a common, everyday object.

Thus a flying saucer can be a formation of lights, a single light, a sphere, or any other shape; and it can be any color. Performancewise, flying saucers can hover, go fast or slow, go high or low, turn 90-degree corners, or disappear almost instantaneously.

Obviously the term "flying saucer" is misleading when applied to objects of every conceivable shape and per-formance. For this reason the military prefers the more general, if less colorful, name: unidentified flying objects. UFO (pronounced Yoo-foe) for short.

Officially the military uses the term "flying saucer" on only two occasions. First in an explanatory sense, as when briefing people who are unacquainted with the term "UFO": "UFO—you know—flying saucers." And second in a derogatory sense, for purposes of ridicule, as when it is observed, "He says he saw a flying saucer."

This second form of usage is the exclusive property of those persons who positively know that all UFO's are nonsense. Fortunately, for the sake of good manners if for no other reason, the ranks of this knowing category are constantly dwindling. One by one these people drop out, starting with the instant they see their first UFO.

Some weeks after the first UFO was seen on June 24, 1947, the Air Force established a project to investigate and analyze all UFO reports. The attitude toward this task varied from a state of near panic, early in the life of the project, to that of complete contempt for anyone who even mentioned the words "flying saucer."

This contemptuous attitude toward "flying saucer nuts" prevailed from mid-1949 to mid-1950. During that interval many of the people who were, or had been, associated with the project believed that the public was suffering from "war nerves."

Early in 1950 the project, for all practical purposes, was closed out; at least it rated only minimum effort. Those in power now reasoned that if you didn't mention the words "flying saucers" the people would forget them and the saucers would go away. But this reasoning was false, for instead of vanishing, the UFO reports got better and better.

Airline pilots, military pilots, generals, scientists, and dozens of other people were reporting UFO's, and in greater detail than in reports of the past. Radars, which were being built for air defense, began to pick up some very unusual targets, thus lending technical corroboration to the unsubstantiated claims of human observers.

As a result of the continuing accumulation of more impressive UFO reports, official interest stirred. Early in 1951 verbal orders came down from Major General Charles P. Cabell, then Director of Intelligence for Headquarters, U.S. Air Force, to make a study reviewing the UFO situation for Air Force Headquarters.

I had been back in the Air Force about six months when this happened. During the second world war I had been a B-29 bombardier and radar operator. I went to India, China, and later to the Pacific, with the original B-29 wing. I flew two DCF's, and some Air Medals' worth of missions, got out of the Air Force after the war, and went back to college. To keep my reserve status while I was in school, I flew as a navigator in an Air Force Reserve Troop Carrier Wing.

Not long after I received my degree in aeronautical engineering, the Korean War started, and I went back on active duty. I was assigned to the Air Technical Intelligence Center at Wright-Patterson Air Force Base, in Dayton, Ohio. ATIC is responsible for keeping track of all foreign aircraft and guided missiles. ATIC also had the UFO project.

I had just finished organizing a new intelligence group when General Cabell's order to review past UFO reports came down. Lieutenant Colonel Rosengarten, who recei-ved the order at ATIC, called me in and wanted to know if I'd take the job of making the review. I accepted.

When the review was finished, I went to the Pentagon and presented my findings to Major General Samford, who had replaced General Cabell as Director of Intelli-gence.

ATIC soon got the word to set up a completely new pro-ject for the investigation and analysis of UFO reports. Since I had made the review of past UFO reports I was the expert, and I got the new job. It was given the code name Project Blue Book, and I was in charge of it until late in 1953. During this time members of my staff and I traveled close to half a million miles. We investigated dozens of UFO reports, and read and analyzed several thousand more. These included every report ever received by the Air Force.

For the size of the task involved Project Blue Book was always understaffed, even though I did have ten people on my regular staff plus many paid consultants representing every field of science. All of us on Project Blue Book had Top Secret security clearances so that security was no block in our investigations. Behind this organization was a reporting network made up of every Air Force base intelligence officer and every Air Force radar station in the world, and the Air Defense Command's Ground Observer Corps. This reporting net sent Project Blue Book reports on every conceivable type of UFO, by every conceivable type of person.

What did these people actually see when they reported that they had observed a UFO? Putting aside truly unidentifiable flying objects for the present, this question has several answers.

In many instances it has been positively proved that

people have reported balloons, airplanes, stars, and many other common objects as UFO's. The people who make such reports don't recognize these common objects because something in their surroundings temporarily assumes an unfamiliar appearance.

Unusual lighting conditions are a common cause of such illusions. A balloon will glow like a "ball of fire" just at sunset. Or an airplane that is not visible to the naked eye suddenly starts to reflect the sun's rays and appears to be a "silver ball." Pilots in F-94 jet interceptors chase Venus in the daytime and fight with balloons at night, and people in Los Angeles see weird lights.

On October 8, 1954, many Los Angeles newspapers and newscasters carried an item about a group of flying saucers, bright lights, flying in a V formation. The lights had been seen from many locations over Southern California. Pilots saw them while bringing their airplanes into Los Angeles International Airport, Air Force pilots flying out of Long Beach saw them, two CBS reporters in Hollywood gave an eyewitness account, and countless people called police and civil defense officials. All of them excitedly reported lights they could not identify. The next day the Air Force identified the UFO's; they were Air Force airplanes, KC-97 aerial tankers, refueling B-47 jet bombers in flight. The reason for the weird effect that startled so many Southern Californians was that when the refueling is taking place a floodlight on the bottom of the tanker airplane lights up the bomber that is being refueled. The airplanes were flying high, and slowly, so no sound was heard; only the bright floodlights could be seen. Since most people, even other pilots, have never seen a night aerial refueling operation and could not identify the odd lights they saw, the lights became UFO's.

In other instances common everyday objects look like UFO's because of some odd quirk in the human mind. A star or planet that has been in the sky every day of the observer's life suddenly "takes off at high speed on a highly erratic flight path." Or a vapor trail from a high-flying jet—seen a hundred times before by the observer—becomes a flying saucer.

Some psychologists explain such aberrations as being akin to the crowd behavior mechanism at work in the "bobby-sox craze." Teen-agers don't know why they squeal and swoon when their current fetish sways and croons. Yet everybody else is squealing, so they squeal too. Maybe that great comedian, Jimmy Durante, has the answer: "Everybody wants to get into the act." I am convinced that a certain percen tage of UFO reports come from people who see flying saucers because others report seeing them.

But this "will to see" may have deeper roots, almost religious implications, for some people. Consciously or unconsciously, they want UFO's to be real and to come from outer space. These individuals, frightened perhaps by threats of atomic destruction, or lesser fears—who knows what—act as if nothing that men can do can save the earth. Instead, they seek salvation from outer space, on the forlorn premise that flying saucer men, by their very existence, are wiser and more advanced than we. Such people may reason that a race of men capable of interplanetary travel have lived well into, or through, an atomic age. They have survived and they can tell us their secret of survival. Maybe the threat of an atomic war unified their planet and allowed them to divert their war effort to one of social and technical advancement. To such people a searchlight on a cloud or a bright star is an interplanetary spaceship.

If all the UFO reports that the Air Force has received in the past eight years could be put in this "psychological quirk" category, Project Blue Book would never have been organized. It is another class of reports that causes the Air Force to remain interested in UFO's. This class of reports are called "Unknowns."

In determining the identity of a UFO, the project based its method of operation on a well-known psychological premise. This premise is that to get a reaction from one

*of the senses there must be a stimulus. If you think you
see a UFO you must have seen something. Pure hallucinations are extremely rare.*

*For anything flying in the air the stimulus could be
anything that is normally seen in the air. Balloons,
airplanes, and astronomical bodies are the commoner
stimuli. Birds and insects are common also, but usually
are seen at such close range that they are nearly always
recognized. Infrequently observed things, such as sundogs, mirages, huge fireballs, and a host of other unusual
flying objects, are also known stimuli.*

*On Project Blue Book our problem was to identify these
stimuli. We had methods for checking the location, at
any time, of every balloon launched anywhere in the
United States. To a certain degree the same was true
for airplanes. The UFO observer's estimate of where
the object was located in the sky helped us to identify
astronomical bodies. Huge files of UFO characteristics,
along with up-to-the-minute weather data, and advice
from specialists, permitted us to identify such things as
sun-dogs, paper caught in updrafts, huge meteors, etc.*

*This determination of the stimuli that triggered UFO
sightings, while not an insurmountable task, was a long,
tedious process. The identification of known objects was*

routine, and caused no excitement. The excitement and serious interest occurred when we received UFO reports in which the observer was reliable and the stimuli could not be identified. These were the reports that challenged the project and caused me to spend hours briefing top U.S. officials. These were the reports that we called "Unknowns."

Of the several thousand UFO reports that the Air Force has received since 1947, some 15 to 20 per cent fall into this category called unknown. This means that the observer was not affected by any determinable psychological quirks and that after exhaustive investigation the object that was reported could not be identified. To be classed as an unknown, a UFO report also had to be "good," meaning that it had to come from a competent observer and had to contain a reasonable amount of data.

Reports are often seen in the newspapers that say: "Mrs. Henry Jones, of 5464 South Elm, said that 10:00 A.M. she was shaking her dust mop out of the bedroom window when she saw a flying saucer"; or "Henry Armstrong was driving between Grundy Center and Rienbeck last night when he saw a light. Henry thinks it was a flying saucer." This is not a good UFO report.

This type of UFO report, if it was received by Project Blue Book, was stamped "Insufficient Data for Evaluation" and dropped into the dead file, where it became a mere statistic.

Next to the "Insufficient Data" file was a file marked "C.P." This meant crackpot. Into this file went all reports from people who had talked with flying saucer crews, who had inspected flying saucers that had landed in the United States, who had ridden in flying saucers, or who were members of flying saucer crews. By Project Blue Book standards, these were not "good" UFO reports either.

But here is a "good" UFO report with an "unknown" conclusion:

On July 24, 1952, two Air Force colonels, flying a B-25, took off from Hamilton Air Force Base, near San Francisco, for Colorado Springs, Colorado. The day was clear, not a cloud in the sky.

The colonels had crossed the Sierra Nevada between Sacramento and Reno and were flying east at 11,000 feet on "Green 3," the aerial highway to Salt Lake City. At 3:40 P.M. they were over the Carson Sink area of Nevada, when one of the colonels noticed three objects ahead of them and a little to their right. The objects looked like three F-86's flying a tight V formation. If they were F-86's they should have been lower, according to civil air regulations, but on a clear day some pilots don't watch their altitude too closely.

In a matter of seconds the three aircraft were close enough to the B-25 to be clearly seen. They were not F-86's. They were three bright silver, delta wing craft with no tails and no pilot's canopies. The only thing that broke the sharply defined, clean upper surface of the triangular wing was a definite ridge that ran from the nose to the tail.

In another second the three deltas made a slight left bank and shot by the B-25 at terrific speed. The colonels estimated that the speed was at least three times that of an F-86. They got a good look at the three deltas as the unusual craft passed within 400 to 800 yards of the B-25.

When they landed at Colorado Springs, the two colonels called the intelligence people at Air Defense Command Headquarters to make a UFO report. The suggestion was offered that they might have seen three F-86's. The colonels promptly replied that if the objects had been F-86's they would have easily been recognized as such.

The colonels knew what F-86's looked like.

Air Defense Command relayed the report to Project Blue Book. An investigation was started at once.

Flight Service, which clears all military aircraft flights, was contacted and asked about the location of aircraft near the Carson Sink area at 3:40 P.M. They had no record of the presence of aircraft in that area.

Since the colonels had mentioned delta wing aircraft, and both the Air Force and the Navy had a few of this type, we double-checked. The Navy's deltas were all on the east coast, at least all of the silver ones were. A few deltas painted the traditional navy blue were on the west coast, but not near Carson Sink. The Air Force's one delta was temporarily grounded. Since balloons once in a while can appear to have an odd shape, all balloon flights were checked for both standard weather balloons and the big 100-foot-diameter research balloons. Nothing was found.

A quick check on the two colonels revealed that both of them were command pilots and that each had several thousand hours of flying time. They were stationed at the Pentagon. Their highly classified assignments were such that they would be in a position to recogni-

*ze anything that the United States knows to be flying
anywhere in the world.*

*Both men had friends who had "seen flying saucers"
at some time, but both had openly voiced their skepti-
cism. Now, from what the colonels said when they were
interviewed after landing at Colorado Springs, they had
changed their opinions.*

*Nobody knows what the two colonels saw over Carson
Sink. However, it is always possible to speculate. Maybe
they just thought they were close enough to the three
objects to see them plainly. The objects might have been
three F-86's: maybe Flight Service lost the records. It
could be that the three F-86's had taken off to fly in
the local area of their base but had decided to do some
illegal sight-seeing. Flight Service would have no record
of a flight like this. Maybe both of the colonels had
hallucinations.*

*There is a certain mathematical probability that any
one of the above speculative answers is correct—correct
for this one case. If you try this type of speculation on
hundreds of sightings with "unknown" answers, the probability that the speculative answers are correct rapidly
approaches zero.*

Maybe the colonels actually did see what they thought they did, a type of craft completely foreign to them.

Another good UFO report provides an incident in which there is hardly room for any speculation of this type. The conclusion is more simply, "Unknown," period.

On January 20, 1952, at seven-twenty in the evening, two master sergeants, both intelligence specialists, were walking down a street on the Fairchild Air Force Base, close to Spokane, Washington.

Suddenly both men noticed a large, bluish-white, spherical-shaped object approaching from the east. They stopped and watched the object carefully, because several of these UFO's had been reported by pilots from the air base over the past few months. The sergeants had written up the reports on these earlier sightings.

The object was traveling at a moderately fast speed on a horizontal path. As it passed to the north of their position and disappeared in the west, the sergeants noted that it had a long blue tail. At no time did they hear any sound. They noted certain landmarks that the object had crossed and estimated the time taken in passing these landmarks. The next day they went out and measured the angles between these landmarks in order to include them in their report.

When we got the report at ATIC, our first reaction was that the master sergeants had seen a large meteor. From the evidence I had written off, as meteors, all previous similar UFO reports from this air base.

The sergeants' report, however, contained one bit of information that completely changed the previous picture. At the time of the sighting there had been a solid 6,000-foot-thick overcast at 4,700 feet. And meteors don't go that low.

A few quick calculations gave a rather fantastic answer. If the object was just at the base of the clouds it would have been 10,000 feet from the two observers and traveling 1,400 miles per hour.

But regardless of the speed, the story was still fantastic. The object was no jet airplane because there was no sound. It was not a searchlight because there were none on the air base. It was not an automobile spotlight because a spotlight will not produce the type of light the sergeants described. As a double check, however, both men were questioned on this point. They stated firmly that they had seen hundreds of searchlights and spotlights playing on clouds, and that this was not what they saw.

Beyond these limited possibilities the sergeants' UFO discourages fruitful speculation. The object remains unidentified.

The UFO reports made by the two colonels and the two master sergeants are typical of hundreds of other good UFO reports which carry the verdict, "Conclusion unknown."

Some of these UFO reports have been publicized, but many have not. Very little information pertaining to UFO's was withheld from the press—if the press knew of the occurrence of specific sightings. Our policy on releasing information was to answer only direct questions from the press. If the press didn't know about a given UFO incident, they naturally couldn't ask questions about it. Consequently such stories were never released. In other instances, when the particulars of a UFO sighting were released, they were only the bare facts about what was reported. Any additional information that might have been developed during later investigations and analyses was not released.

There is a great deal of interest in UFO's and the interest shows no signs of diminishing. Since the first flying saucer skipped across the sky in the summer of 1947, thousands of words on this subject have appeared in every newspaper and most magazines in the United States. During a six-month period in 1952 alone 148 of the nation's leading newspapers carried a total of over 16,000 items about flying saucers.

During July 1952 reports of flying saucers sighted over Washington, D.C., cheated the Democratic National Convention out of precious headline space.

The subject of flying saucers, which has generated more unscientific behavior than any other topic of modern times, has been debated at the meetings of professional scientific societies, causing scientific tempers to flare where unemotional objectivity is supposed to reign supreme.

Yet these thousands of written words and millions of spoken words—all attesting to the general interest— have generated more heat than light. Out of this avalanche of print and talk, the full, factual, true story of UFO's has emerged only on rare occasions. The general public, for its interest in UFO's, has been paid off in misinformation.

Many civilian groups must have sensed this, for while I was chief of Project Blue Book I had dozens of requests to speak on the subject of UFO's. These civilian requests had to be turned down because of security regulations.

I did give many official briefings, however, behind closed doors, to certain groups associated with the government—all of them upon request.

The subject of UFO's was added to a regular series of intelligence briefings given to students at the Air Force's Command and Staff School, and to classes at the Air Force's Intelligence School.

I gave briefings to the technical staff at the Atomic Energy Commission's Los Alamos laboratory, where the first atomic bomb was built. The theater where this briefing took place wouldn't hold all of the people who tried to get in, so the briefing was recorded and replayed many times. The same thing happened at AEC's Sandia Base, near Albuquerque.

Many groups in the Pentagon and the Office of Naval Research requested UFO briefings. Civilian groups, made up of some of the nation's top scientists and industrialists, and formed to study special military problems, worked in a UFO briefing. Top Air Force commanders were given periodic briefings.

Every briefing I gave was followed by a discussion that lasted anywhere from one to four hours.

In addition to these, Project Blue Book published a classified monthly report on UFO activity. Requests to be put on distribution for this report were so numerous that the distribution had to be restricted to major Air Force Command Headquarters.

This interest was not caused by any revolutionary information that was revealed in the briefings or reports. It stemmed only from a desire to get the facts about an interesting subject.

Many aspects of the UFO problem were covered in these official briefings. I would give details of many of the better reports we received, our conclusions about them, and how those conclusions were reached. If we had identified a UFO, the audience was told how the identification was made. If we concluded that the answer to a UFO sighting was "Unknown," the audience learned why we were convinced it was unknown.

Among the better sightings that were described fully to interested government groups were: the complete story of the Lubbock Lights, including the possible sighting of the same V-shaped light formations at other locations on the same night; the story of a group of scientists who detected mysterious nuclear radiation when UFO's were sighted; and all of the facts behind such famous cases as the Mantell Incident, the Florida scoutmaster who was burned by a "flying saucer," and headline-capturing sightings at Washington, D.C.

I showed them what few photographs we had, the majority of which everyone has seen, since they have been widely published in magazines and newspapers. Our collection of photographs was always a disappointment as far as positive proof was concerned because, in a sense, if you've seen one you've seen them all. We had no clear pictures of a saucer, just an assortment of blurs, blotches, and streaks of light.

The briefings included a description of how Project Blue Book operated and a survey of the results of the many studies that were made of the mass of UFO data we had collected. Also covered were our interviews with a dozen North American astronomers, the story of the unexplained green fireballs of New Mexico, and an account of how a committee of six distinguished United States scientists spent many hours attempting to answer the question, "Are the UFO's from outer space?"

Unfortunately the general public was never able to hear these briefings. For a long time, contrary to present thinking in military circles, I have believed that the public also is entitled to know the details of what was covered in these briefings (less, of course, the few items pertaining to radar that were classified "Secret," and the names of certain people). But withholding these will not alter the facts in any way.

A lot has already been written on the subject of UFO's, but none of it presents the true, complete story. Previous forays into the UFO field have been based on inadequate information and have been warped to fit the personal biases of the individual writers. Well meaning though these authors may be, the degree to which their books have misinformed the public is incalculable.

It is high time that we let the people know.

The following chapters present the true and complete UFO story, based on what I learned about UFO's while I was chief of Project Blue Book, the Air Force's project for the investigation and analysis of UFO reports. Here is the same information that I gave to Secretary of the Air Force, Thomas K. Finletter, to the Air Force commanders, to scientists and industrialists. This is what the Air Force knows about unidentified flying objects.

You may not agree with some of the official ideas or conclusions—neither did a lot of people I briefed—but this is the story.

CHAPTER 2

The Era of Confusion Begins

On September 23, 1947, the chief of the Air Technical Intelligence Center, one of the Air Force's most highly specialized intelligence units, sent a letter to the Commanding General of the then Army Air Forces.

The letter was in answer to the Commanding General's verbal request to make a preliminary study of the reports of unidentified flying objects. The letter said that after a preliminary study of UFO reports, ATIC concluded that, to quote from the letter, "the reported phenomena were real." The letter strongly urged that a permanent project be established at ATIC to investigate and analyze future UFO reports. It requested a priority for the project, a registered code name, and an over-all security classification. ATIC's request was granted and Project Sign, the forerunner of Project Grudge and Project Blue Book, was launched. It was given a 2A priority, 1A being the highest priority an Air Force project could have. With this the Air Force dipped into the most prolonged and widespread controversy it has ever, or may ever, encounter. The Air Force grabbed the proverbial bear by the tail and to this day it hasn't been able to let loose.

The letter to the Commanding General of the Army Air Forces from the chief of ATIC had used the word "phenomena." History has shown that this was not a too well-chosen word. But on September 23, 1947, when the letter was written, ATIC's intelligence specialists were confident that within a few months or a year they would have the answer to the question, "What are UFO's?" The question, "Do UFO's exist?" was never mentioned. The only problem that confronted the people at ATIC was, "Were the UFO's of Russian or interplanetary origin?" Either case called for a serious, secrecy-shrouded project. Only top people at ATIC were assigned to Project Sign.

Although a formal project for UFO investigation wasn't set up until September 1947, the Air Force had been vitally interested in UFO reports ever since June 24, 1947, the day Kenneth Arnold made the original UFO report.

As Arnold's story of what he saw that day has been handed down by the bards of saucerism, the true facts have been warped, twisted, and changed. Even some points in Arnold's own account of his sighting as published in his book, The Coming of the Saucers, do not jibe with what the official files say he told the Air Force in 1947. Since this incident was the original UFO sighting, I used to get many inquiries about it from the press and at briefings. To get the true and accurate story of what did happen to Kenneth Arnold on June 24, 1947, I had to go back through old newspaper files, official reports, and talk to people who had worked on Project Sign. By cross-checking these data and talking to people who had heard Arnold tell about his UFO sighting soon after it happened, I finally came up with what I believe is the accurate story.

Arnold had taken off from Chehalis, Washington, intending to fly to Yakima, Washington. About 3:00 P.M. he arrived in the vicinity of Mount Rainier. There was a Marine Corps C-46 transport plane lost in the Mount Rainier area, so Arnold decided to fly around awhile and look for it. He was looking down at the ground when suddenly he noticed a series of bright flashes off to his left. He looked for the source of the flashes and saw a string of nine very bright disk-shaped objects, which he estimated to be 45 to 50 feet in length. They were traveling from north to south across the nose of his airplane. They were flying in a reversed echelon (i.e., lead object high with the rest stepped down), and as they flew along they weaved in and out between the mountain peaks, once passing behind one of the peaks. Each individual object had a skipping motion described by Arnold as a "saucer skipping across water."

During the time that the objects were in sight, Arnold had clocked their speed. He had marked his position

*and their position on the map and again noted the time.
When he landed he sketched in the flight path that the
objects had flown and computed their speed, almost
1,700 miles per hour. He estimated that they had been
20 to 25 miles away and had traveled 47 miles in 102
seconds.*

*I found that there was a lot of speculation on this report.
Two factions at ATIC had joined up behind two lines
of reasoning. One side said that Arnold had seen plain,
everyday jet airplanes flying in formation. This side's
argument was based on the physical limitations of the
human eye, visual acuity, the eye's ability to see a small,
distant object. Tests, they showed, had proved that a
person with normal vision can't "see" an object that
subtends an angle of less than 0.2 second of arc. For example, a basketball can't be seen at a distance of several
miles but if you move the basketball closer and closer,
at some point you will be able to see it. At this point the
angle between the top and bottom of the ball and your
eye will be about 0.2 of a second of arc. This was applied
to Arnold's sighting. The "Arnold-saw-airplanes" faction
maintained that since Arnold said that the objects were
45 to 50 feet long they would have had to be much closer
than he had estimated or he couldn't even have seen
them at all. Since they were much closer than he estimated, Arnold's timed speed was all wrong and instead of*

going 1,700 miles per hour the objects were traveling at a speed closer to 400 miles per hour, the speed of a jet. There was no reason to believe they weren't jets. The jets appeared to have a skipping motion because Arnold had looked at them through layers of warm and cold air, like heat waves coming from a hot pavement that cause an object to shimmer.

The other side didn't buy this idea at all. They based their argument on the fact that Arnold knew where the objects were when he timed them.

After all, he was an old mountain pilot and was as familiar with the area around the Cascade Mountains as he was with his own living room. To cinch this point the fact that the objects had passed behind a mountain peak was brought up. This positively established the distance the objects were from Arnold and confirmed his calculated 1,700-miles-per-hour speed. Besides, no airplane can weave in and out between mountain peaks in the short time that Arnold was watching them. The visual acuity factor only strengthened the "Arnold-saw-a-flying-saucer" faction's theory that what he'd seen was a spaceship. If he could see the objects 20 to 25 miles away, they must have been about 210 feet long instead of the poorly estimated 45 to 50 feet.

In 1947 this was a fantastic story, but now it is just another UFO report marked "Unknown." It is typical in that if the facts are accurate, if Arnold actually did see the UFO's go behind a mountain peak, and if he knew his exact position at the time, the UFO problem cannot be lightly sloughed off; but there are always "ifs" in UFO reports. This is the type of report that led Major General John A. Samford, Director of Intelligence for Headquarters, Air Force, to make the following comment during a press conference in July 1952: "However, there have remained a percentage of this total [of all UFO reports received by the Air Force], about 20 per cent of the reports, that have come from credible observers of relatively incredible things. We keep on being concerned about them."

In warping, twisting, and changing the Arnold incident, the writers of saucer lore haven't been content to confine themselves to the incident itself; they have dragged in the crashed Marine Corps' C-46. They intimate that the same flying saucers that Arnold saw shot down the C-46, grabbed up the bodies of the passengers and crew, and now have them pickled at the University of Venus Medical School. As proof they apply the same illogical reasoning that they apply to most everything. The military never released photos of the bodies of the dead men, therefore there were no bodies. There were photographs and there were bodies. In consideration of the families of air crewmen and passengers, photos of air crashes showing dead bodies are never released.

Arnold himself seems to be the reason for a lot of the excitement that heralded flying saucers. Stories of odd incidents that occur in this world are continually being reported by newspapers, but never on the scale of the first UFO report. Occasional stories of the "Himalayan snowmen," or the "Malayan monsters," rate only a few inches or a column on the back pages of newspapers. Arnold's story, if it didn't make the headlines, at least made the front page. I had the reason for this explained to me one day when I was investigating a series of UFO reports in California in the spring of 1952.

I was making my headquarters at an air base where a fighter-bomber wing was stationed. Through a mutual friend I met one of the fighter-bomber pilots who had known Arnold. In civilian life the pilot was a newspaper reporter and had worked on the original Arnold story. He told me that when the story first broke all the newspaper editors in the area were thoroughly convinced that the incident was a hoax, and that they intended to write the story as such. The more they dug into the facts, however, and into Arnold's reputation, the more it appeared that he was telling the truth. Besides having an unquestionable character, he was an excellent mountain pilot, and mountain pilots are a breed of men who know every nook and cranny of the mountains in their area, The most fantastic part of Arnold's story had been the 1,700-miles-per-hour speed computed from Arnold's timing the objects between two landmarks. "When Arnold told us how he computed the speed," my chance acquaintance told me, "we all put a lot of faith in his story." He went on to say that when the editors found out that they were wrong about the hoax, they did a complete about-face, and were very much impressed by the story. This enthusiasm spread, and since the Air Force so quickly denied ownership of the objects, all of the facts built up into a story so unique that papers all over the world gave it front-page space.

There was an old theory that maybe Arnold had seen wind whipping snow along the mountain ridges, so I asked about this. 1 got a flat "Impossible." My expert on the early Arnold era said, "I've lived in the Pacific Northwest many years and have flown in the area for hundreds of hours. It's impossible to get powder snow low in the mountains in June. Personally, I believe Arnold saw some kind of aircraft and they weren't from this earth." He went on to tell me about two other very similar sightings that had happened the day after Arnold saw the nine disks. He knew the people who made these sigh-

tings and said that they weren't the kind to go off "half cocked." He offered to get a T-6 and fly me up to Boise to talk to them since they had never made a report to the military, but I had to return to Dayton so I declined.

Within a few days of Arnold's sighting, others began to come in. On June 28 an Air Force pilot in an F-51 was flying near Lake Mead, Nevada. when he saw a formation of five or six circular objects off his right wing. This was about three-fifteen in the afternoon.

That night at nine-twenty, four Air Force officers, two pilots, and two intelligence officers from Maxwell AFB in Montgomery, Alabama, saw a bright light traveling across the sky. It was first seen just above the horizon, and as it traveled toward the observers it "zigzagged," with bursts of high speed. When it was directly overhead it made a sharp 90-degree turn and was lost from view as it traveled south.

Other reports came in. In Milwaukee a lady saw ten go over her house "like blue blazes," heading south. A school bus driver in Clarion, Iowa, saw an object streak across the sky. In a few seconds twelve more followed the first one. White Sands Proving Ground in New Mexico chalked up the first of the many sightings that this location would produce when several people riding in an automobile saw a pulsating light travel from horizon to horizon in thirty seconds. A Chicago housewife saw one "with legs."

The week of July 4, 1947, set a record for reports that was not broken until 1952. The center of activity was the Portland, Oregon, area. At 11:00 A.M. a carload of people driving near Redmond saw four disk-shaped objects streaking past Mount Jefferson. At 1:05 P.M. a policeman was in the parking lot behind the Portland City Police Headquarters when he noticed some pigeons suddenly began to flutter around as if they were scared. He looked up and saw five large disk-shaped objects, two going south and three going east. They were traveling at a high rate of speed and seemed to be oscillating about their lateral axis. Minutes later two other policemen, both ex-pilots, reported three of the same things flying in trail. Before long the harbor patrol called into headquarters. A crew of four patrolmen had seen three to six of the disks, "shaped like chrome hub caps," traveling very fast. They also oscillated as they flew. Then the citizens of Portland began to see them. A man saw one going east and two going north. At four-thirty a woman called in and had just seen one that looked like "a new dime flipping around." Another man reported two, one going southeast, one northeast. From Milwaukie, Oregon, three were reported going northwest. In Vancouver,

Washington, sheriff's deputies saw twenty to thirty.

The first photo was taken on July 4 in Seattle. After much publicity it turned out to be a weather balloon.

That night a United Airlines crew flying near Emmett, Idaho, saw five. The pilot's report read:

Five "somethings," which were thin and smooth on the bottom and rough-appearing on top, were seen silhouetted against the sunset shortly after the plane took off from Boise at 8:04 P.M. We saw them clearly. We followed them in a northeasterly direction for about 45 miles. They finally disappeared. We were unable to tell whether they outsped us or disintegrated. We can't say whether they were "smearlike," oval, or anything else but whatever they were they were not aircraft, clouds or smoke.

Civilians did not have a corner on the market. On July 6 a staff sergeant in Birmingham, Alabama, saw several "dim, glowing lights" speeding across the sky and photographed one of them. Also on the sixth the crew of an Air Force B-25 saw a bright, disk-shaped object "low at nine o'clock." This is one of the few reports of an object lower than the aircraft. At Fairfield-Suisun AFB in California a pilot saw something travel three quarters of the way across the sky in a few seconds. It, too, was oscillating on its lateral axis.

According to the old hands at ATIC, the first sighting that really made the Air Force take a deep interest in UFO's occurred on July 8 at Muroc Air Base (now Edwards AFB), the supersecret Air Force test center in the Mojave Desert of California. At 10:10 A.M. a test pilot was running up the engine of the then new XP-84 in preparation for a test flight. He happened to look up and to the north he saw what first appeared to be a weather balloon traveling in a westerly direction. After watching it a few seconds, he changed his mind. He had been briefed on the high-altitude winds, and the object he saw was going against the wind. Had it been the size of a normal aircraft, the test pilot estimated that it would have been at 10,000 to 12,000 feet and traveling 200 to 225 miles per hour. He described the object as being spherically shaped and yellowish white in color.

Ten minutes before this several other officers and airmen had seen three objects. They were similar except they had more of a silver color. They were also heading in a westerly direction.

Two hours later a crew of technicians on Rogers Dry Lake, adjacent to Muroc Air Base, observed another

UFO. Their report went as follows:

On the 8 July 1947 at 11:50 we were sitting in an observation truck located in Area #3, Rogers Dry Lake. We were gazing upward toward a formation of two P-82's and an A-26 aircraft flying at 20,000 feet. They were preparing to carry out a seat-ejection experiment. We observed a round object, white aluminum color, which at first resembled a parachute canopy. Our first impression was that a premature ejection of the seat and dummy had occurred but this was not the case. The object was lower than 20,000 feet, and was falling at three times the rate observed for the test parachute, which ejected thirty seconds after we first saw the object. As the object fell it drifted slightly north of due west against the prevailing wind. The speed, horizontal motion, could not be determined, but it appeared to be slower than the maximum velocity F-80 aircraft.

As this object descended through a low enough level to permit observation of its lateral silhouette, it presented a distinct oval-shaped outline, with two projections on the upper surface which might have been thick fins or nobs. These crossed each other at intervals, suggesting either rotation or oscillation of slow type.

No smoke, flames, propeller arcs, engine noise, or other

plausible or visible means of propulsion were noted. The color was silver, resembling an aluminum-painted fabric, and did not appear as dense as a parachute canopy.

When the object dropped to a level such that it came into line of vision of the mountain tops, it was lost to the vision of the observers.

It is estimated that the object was in sight about 90 seconds. Of the five people sitting in the observation truck, four observed this object.

The following is our opinion about this object:

It was man-made, as evidenced by the outline and functional appearance.

Seeing this was not a hallucination or other fancies of sense.

Exactly four hours later the pilot of an F-51 was flying at 20,000 feet about 40 miles south of Muroc Air Base when he sighted a "flat object of a light-reflecting nature." He reported that it had no vertical fin or wings. When he first saw it, the object was above him and he tried to climb up to it, but his F-51 would not climb high enough. All air bases in the area were contacted but they had no aircraft in the area.

By the end of July 1947 the UFO security lid was down tight. The few members of the press who did inquire about what the Air Force was doing got the same treatment that you would get today if you inquired about the number of thermonuclear weapons stock-piled in the U.S.'s atomic arsenal. No one, outside of a few high-ranking officers in the Pentagon, knew what the people in the barbed-wire enclosed Quonset huts that housed the Air Technical Intelligence Center were thinking or doing.

The memos and correspondence that Project Blue Book inherited from the old UFO projects told the story of the early flying saucer era. These memos and pieces of correspondence showed that the UFO situation was considered to be serious; in fact, very serious. The paper work of that period also indicated the confusion that surrounded the investigation; confusion almost to the point of panic. The brass wanted an answer, quickly, and people were taking off in all directions. Everyone's theory was as good as the next and each person with any weight at ATIC was plugging and investigating his own theory. The ideas as to the origin of the UFO's fell into two main categories, earthly and non-earthly. In the earthly category the Russians led, with the U.S. Navy and their XF-5-U-1, the "Flying Flapjack," pulling a not too close second. The desire to cover all leads was graphically pointed up to be a personal handwritten note I found in a file. It was from ATIC's chief to a civilian intelligence specialist. It said, "Are you positive that the Navy junked the XF-5-U-1 project?" The non-earthly category ran the gamut of theories, with space animals trailing interplanetary craft about the same distance the Navy was behind the Russians.

This confused speculating lasted only a few weeks. Then the investigation narrowed down to the Soviets and took off on a much more methodical course of action.

When World War II ended, the Germans had several radical types of aircraft and guided missiles under development. The majority of these projects were in the most preliminary stages but they were the only known craft that could even approach the performance of the objects reported by UFO observers. Like the Allies, after World War II the Soviets had obtained complete sets of data on the latest German developments. This, coupled with rumors that the Soviets were frantically developing the German ideas, caused no small degree of alarm. As more UFO's were observed near the Air Force's Muroc Test Center, the Army's White Sands Proving Ground, and atomic bomb plants, ATIC's efforts became more concentrated.

Wires were sent to intelligence agents in Germany requesting that they find out exactly how much progress had been made on the various German projects.

The last possibility, of course, was that the Soviets had discovered some completely new aerodynamic concept that would give saucer performance.

While ATIC technical analysts were scouring the United States for data on the German projects and the intelligence agents in Germany were seeking out the data they had been asked for, UFO reports continued to flood the country. The Pacific Northwest still led with the most sightings, but every state in the Union was reporting a few flying saucers.

At first there was no co-ordinated effort to collect data on the UFO reports. Leads would come from radio reports or newspaper items. Military intelligence agencies outside of ATIC were hesitant to investigate on their own initiative because, as is so typical of the military, they lacked specific orders. When no orders were forthcoming, they took this to mean that the military had no interest in the UFO's. But before long this placid attitude changed, and changed drastically. Classified orders came down to investigate all UFO sightings. Get every detail and send it direct to ATIC at Wright Field. The order carried no explanation as to why the information was wanted. This lack of an explanation and the fact that the information was to be sent directly to a high-powered intelligence group within Air Force Headquarters stirred the imagination of every potential cloak-and-dagger man in the military intelligence system. Intelligence people in the field who had previously been free with opinions now clammed up tight.

The era of confusion was progressing.

Early statements to the press, which shaped the opinion of the public, didn't reduce the confusion factor. While ATIC was grimly expending maximum effort in a serious study, "certain high-placed officials" were officially chuckling at the mention of UFO's.

In July 1947 an International News Service wire story quoted the public relations officer at Wright Field as saying, "So far we haven't found anything to confirm that saucers exist. We don't think they are guided missiles." He went on to say, "As things are now, they appear to be either a phenomenon or a figment of somebody's imagination."

A few weeks later a lieutenant colonel who was Assistant to the Chief of Staff of the Fourth Air Force was widely quoted as saying, "There is no basis for belief in flying saucers in the Tacoma area [referring to a UFO sighting in the area of Tacoma, Washington], or any other area."

The "experts," in their stories of saucer lore, have said that these brushoffs of the UFO sightings were intentional smoke screens to cover the facts by adding confusion. This is not true; it was merely a lack of coordination. But had the Air Force tried to throw up a screen of confusion, they couldn't have done a better job.

When the lieutenant colonel from the Fourth Air Force made his widely publicized denunciation of saucer believers he specifically mentioned a UFO report from the Tacoma, Washington, area.

The report of the investigation of this incident, the Maury Island Mystery, was one of the most detailed reports of the early UFO era. The report that we had in our files had been pieced together by Air Force Intelligence and other agencies because the two intelligence officers who started the investigation couldn't finish it. They were dead.

For the Air Force the story started on July 31, 1947, when Lieutenant Frank Brown, an intelligence agent at Hamilton AFB, California, received a long-distance phone call. The caller was a man whom I'll call Simpson, who had met Brown when Brown investigated an earlier UFO sighting, and he had a hot lead on another UFO incident. He had just talked to two Tacoma Harbor patrolmen. One of them had seen six UFO's hover over his patrol boat and spew out chunks of odd metal. Simpson had some of the pieces of the metal.

The story sounded good to Lieutenant Brown, so he reported it to his chief. His chief OK'd a trip and within an hour Lieutenant Brown and Captain Davidson were flying to Tacoma in an Air Force B-25. When they arrived they met Simpson and an airline pilot friend of his in Simpson's hotel room. After the usual round of introductions Simpson told Brown and Davidson that he had received a letter from a Chicago publisher asking him, Simpson, to investigate this case. The publisher had paid him $200 and wanted an exclusive on the story, but things were getting too hot, Simpson wanted the military to take over.

Simpson went on to say that he had heard about the experience off Maury Island but that he wanted Brown and Davidson to hear it firsthand.

[paragraph continues]He had called the two harbor patrolmen and they were on their way to the hotel. They arrived and they told their story.

I'll call these two men Jackson and Richards although these aren't their real names. In June 1947, Jackson said, his crew, his son, and the son's dog were on his patrol boat patrolling near Maury Island, an island in Puget Sound, about 3 miles from Tacoma. It was a gray day, with a solid cloud deck down at about 2,500 feet. Suddenly everyone on the boat noticed six "doughnut-shaped" objects, just under the clouds, headed toward the boat. They came closer and closer, and when they were about 500 feet over the boat they stopped. One of the doughnut-shaped objects seemed to be in trouble as the other five were hovering around it. They were close, and everybody got a good look. The UFO's were about 100 feet in diameter, with the "hole in the doughnut" being about 25 feet in diameter. They were a silver color and made absolutely no noise. Each object had large portholes around the edge.

As the five UFO's circled the sixth, Jackson recalled, one of them came in and appeared to make contact with the disabled craft. The two objects maintained contact for a few minutes, then began to separate. While this was going on, Jackson was taking photos. Just as they began to separate, there was a dull "thud" and the next second the UFO began to spew out sheets of very light metal from the hole in the center. As these were fluttering to the water, the UFO began to throw out a harder, rocklike material. Some of it landed on the beach of

Maury Island. Jackson took his crew and headed toward the beach of Maury Island, but not before the boat was damaged, his son's arm had been injured, and the dog killed. As they reached the island they looked up and saw that the UFO's were leaving the area at high speed. The harbor patrolman went on to tell how he scooped up several chunks of the metal from the beach and boarded the patrol boat. He tried to use his radio to summon aid, but for some unusual reason the interference was so bad he couldn't even call the three miles to his headquarters in Tacoma. When they docked at Tacoma, Jackson got first aid for his son and then reported to his superior officer, Richards, who, Jackson added to his story, didn't believe the tale. He didn't believe it until he went out to the island himself and saw the metal. Jackson's trouble wasn't over. The next morning a mysterious visitor told Jackson to forget what he'd seen.

Later that same day the photos were developed. They showed the six objects, but the film was badly spotted and fogged, as if the film had been exposed to some kind of radiation.

Then Simpson told about his brush with mysterious callers. He said that Jackson was not alone as far as mysterious callers were concerned, the Tacoma newspapers had been getting calls from an anonymous tipster telling exactly what was going on in Simpson's hotel room. This was a very curious situation because no one except Simpson, the airline pilot, and the two harbor patrolmen knew what was taking place. The room had even been thoroughly searched for hidden microphones.

That is the way the story stood a few hours after Lieutenant Brown and Captain Davidson arrived in Tacoma.

After asking Jackson and Richards a few questions, the two. intelligence agents left, reluctant even to take any of the fragments. As some writers who have since written about this incident have said, Brown and Davidson seemed to be anxious to leave and afraid to touch the fragments of the UFO, as if they knew something more about them. The two officers went to McChord AFB, near Tacoma, where their B-25 was parked, held a conference with the intelligence officer at McChord, and took off for their home base, Hamilton. When they left McChord they had a good idea as to the identity of the UFO's. Fortunately they told the McChord intelligence officer what they had determined from their interview.

In a few hours the two officers were dead. The B-25 crashed near Kelso, Washington. The crew chief and a passenger had parachuted to safety. The newspapers hinted that the airplane was sabotaged and that it was carrying highly classified material. Authorities at McChord AFB confirmed this latter point, the airplane was carrying classified material.

In a few days the newspaper publicity on the crash died down, and the Maury Island Mystery was never publicly solved.

Later reports say that the two harbor patrolmen mysteriously disappeared soon after the fatal crash.

They should have disappeared, into Puget Sound. The whole Maury Island Mystery was a hoax. The first, possibly the second-best, and the dirtiest hoax in the UFO history. One passage in the detailed official report of the Maury Island Mystery says:

Both —— (the two harbor patrolmen) admitted that the rock fragments had nothing to do with flying saucers. The whole thing was a hoax. They had sent in the rock fragments [to a magazine publisher] as a joke. —— One of the patrolmen wrote to —— [the publisher] stating that the rock could have been part of a flying saucer. He had said the rock came from a flying saucer because that's what —— [the publisher] wanted him to say.

The publisher, mentioned above, who, one of the two hoaxers said, wanted him to say that the rock fragments had come from a flying saucer, is the same one who paid the man I called Simpson $200 to investigate the case.

The report goes on to explain more details of the incident. Neither one of the two men could ever produce the photos. They "misplaced" them, they said. One of them, I forget which, was the mysterious informer who called the newspapers to report the conversations that were going on in the hotel room. Jackson's mysterious visitor didn't exist. Neither of the men was a harbor patrolman, they merely owned a couple of beat-up old boats that they used to salvage floating lumber from Puget Sound. The airplane crash was one of those unfortunate things. An engine caught on fire, burned off, and just before the two pilots could get out, the wing and tail tore off, making it impossible for them to escape. The two dead officers from Hamilton AFB smelled a hoax, accounting for their short interview and hesitancy in bothering to take the "fragments." They confirmed their convictions when they talked to the intelligence officer at McChord. It had already been established, through an informer, that the fragments were what Brown and Davidson thought, slag. The classified material on the B-25 was a file of reports the two officers offered to take back to Hamilton and had nothing to do with the Maury Island Mystery, or better, the Maury Island Hoax.

Simpson and his airline pilot friend weren't told about the hoax for one reason. As soon as it was discovered that they had been "taken," thoroughly, and were not a party to the hoax, no one wanted to embarrass them.

The majority of the writers of saucer lore have played this sighting to the hilt, pointing out as their main premise the fact that the story must be true because the government never openly exposed or prosecuted either of the two hoaxers. This is a logical premise, but a false one. The reason for the thorough investigation of the Maury Island Hoax was that the government had thought seriously of prosecuting the men. At the last minute it was decided, after talking to the two men, that the hoax was a harmless joke that had mushroomed, and that the loss of two lives and a B-25 could not be directly blamed on the two men. The story wasn't even printed because at the time of the incident, even though in this case the press knew about it, the facts were classed as evidence. By the time the facts were released they were yesterday's news. And nothing is deader than yesterday's news.

As 1947 drew to a close, the Air Force's Project Sign had outgrown its initial panic and had settled down to a routine operation. Every intelligence report dealing with the Germans' World War II aeronautical research had been studied to find out if the Russians could have developed any of the late German designs into flying saucers. Aerodynamicists at ATIC and at Wright Field's Aircraft Laboratory computed the maximum performance that could be expected from the German designs. The designers of the aircraft themselves were contacted. "Could the Russians develop a flying saucer from their designs?" The answer was, "No, there was no conceivable way any aircraft could perform that would match the reported maneuvers of the UFO's." The Air Force's Aeromedical Laboratory concurred. If the aircraft could be built, the human body couldn't stand the violent maneuvers that were reported. The aircraft-structures people seconded this, no material known could stand the loads of the reported maneuvers and heat of the high speeds.

Still convinced that the UFO's were real objects, the people at ATIC began to change their thinking. Those who were convinced that the UFO's were of Soviet origin now began to eye outer space, not because there was any evidence that the UFO's did come from outer space but because they were convinced that UFO's existed and only some unknown race with a highly developed state of technology could build such vehicles. As far as the effect on the human body was concerned, why couldn't these people, whoever they might be, stand these horrible maneuver forces? Why judge them by earthly standards?

I found a memo to this effect was in the old Project Sign files.

Project Sign ended 1947 with a new problem. How do you collect interplanetary intelligence? During World War II the organization that was ATIC's forerunner, the Air Matériel Command's secret "T-2," had developed highly effective means of wringing out every possible bit of information about the technical aspects of enemy aircraft. ATIC knew these methods, but how could this be applied to spaceships? The problem was tackled with organized confusion.

If the confusion in the minds of Air Force people was organized the confusion in the minds of the public was not. Publicized statements regarding the UFO were conflicting.

A widely printed newspaper release, quoting an unnamed Air Force official in the Pentagon, said:

The "flying saucers" are one of three things:

1. Solar reflections on low-hanging clouds.
2. Small meteors that break up, their crystals catching the rays of the sun.
3. Icing conditions could have formed large hailstones and they might have flattened out and glided.

A follow-up, which quoted several scientists, said in essence that the unnamed Air Force official was crazy. Nobody even heard of crystallized meteors, or huge, flat hailstones, and the solar-reflection theory was absurd.

Life, Time, Newsweek, and many other news magazines carried articles about the UFO's. Some were written with tongue in cheek, others were not. All the articles mentioned the Air Force's mass-hysterical induced hallucinations. But a Veterans' Administration psychiatrist publicly pooh-poohed this. "Too many people are seeing things," he said.

It was widely suggested that all the UFO's were meteors. Two Chicago astronomers queered this. Dr. Gerard Kuiper, director of the University of Chicago observatory, was quoted as flatly saying the UFO's couldn't be meteors. "They are probably man-made," he told the Associated Press. Dr. Oliver Lee, director of Northwestern University's observatory, agreed with Dr. Kuiper and he threw in an additional confusion factor that had been in the back of many people's minds. Maybe they were our own aircraft.

The government had been denying that UFO's belonged to the U.S. from the first, but Dr. Vannevar Bush, the world-famous scientist, and Dr. Merle Tuve, inventor

*of the proximity fuse, added their weight. "Impossible,"
they said.*

*All of this time unnamed Air Force officials were disclaiming serious interest in the UFO subject. Yet every time
a newspaper reporter went out to interview a person
who had seen a UFO, intelligence agents had already
been flown in, gotten the detailed story complete with
sketches of the UFO, and sped back to their base to send
the report to Project Sign. Many people had supposedly
been "warned" not to talk too much. The Air Force was
mighty interested in hallucinations.*

*Thus 1947 ended with various-sized question marks
in the mind of the public. If you followed flying saucers
closely the question mark was big, if you just noted the
UFO story titles in the papers it was smaller, but it was
there and it was growing. Probably none of the people,
military or civilian, who had made the public statements were at all qualified to do so but they had done it,
their comments had been printed, and their comments
had been read. Their comments formed the question
mark.*

CHAPTER 3

The Classics

*1948 was only one hour and twenty-five minutes old
when a gentleman from Abilene, Texas, made the first
UFO report of the year. What he saw, "a fan-shaped
glow" in the sky, was insignificant as far as UFO reports
go, but it ushered in a year that was to bring feverish
activity to Project Sign.*

*With the Soviets practically eliminated as a UFO source,
the idea of interplanetary spaceships was becoming more
popular. During 1948 the people in ATIC were openly discussing the possibility of interplanetary visitors
without others tapping their heads and looking smug.
During 1948 the novelty of UFO's had worn off for the
press and every John and Jane Doe who saw one didn't
make the front pages as in 1947. Editors were becoming
hardened, only a few of the best reports got any space.
Only "The Classics" rated headlines. "The Classics" were
three historic reports that were the highlights of 1948.
They are called "The Classics," a name given them by
the Project Blue Book staff, because: (1) they are classic
examples of how the true facts of a UFO report can be
twisted and warped by some writers to prove their point,*

(2) they are the most highly publicized reports of this early era of the UFO's, and (3) they "proved" to ATIC's intelligence specialists that UFO's were real.

The apparent lack of interest in UFO reports by the press was not a true indication of the situation. I later found out, from talking to writers, that all during 1948 the interest in UFO's was running high. The Air Force Press Desk in the Pentagon was continually being asked what progress was being made in the UFO investigation. The answer was, "Give us time. This job can't be done in a week." The press respected this and was giving them time. But every writer worth his salt has contacts, those "usually reliable sources" you read about, and these contacts were talking. All during 1948 contacts in the Pentagon were telling how UFO reports were rolling in at the rate of several per day and how ATIC UFO investigation teams were flying out of Dayton to investigate them. They were telling how another Air Force investigative organization had been called in to lighten ATIC's load and allow ATIC to concentrate on the analysis of the reports. The writers knew this was true because they had crossed paths with these men whom they had mistakenly identified as FBI agents. The FBI was never officially interested in UFO sightings. The writers' contacts in the airline industry told about the UFO talk from V.P.'s down to the ramp boys. Dozens of good, solid, reliable, experienced airline pilots were seeing UFO's. All of this led to one conclusion: whatever the Air Force had to say, when it was ready to talk, would be newsworthy. But the Air Force wasn't ready to talk.

Project Sign personnel were just getting settled down to work after the New Year's holiday when the "ghost rockets" came back to the Scandinavian countries of Europe. Air attachés in Sweden, Denmark, and Norway fired wires to ATIC telling about the reports. Wires went back asking for more information.

The "ghost rockets," so tagged by the newspapers, had first been seen in the summer of 1946, a year before the first UFO sighting in the U.S. There were many different descriptions for the reported objects. They were usually seen in the hours of darkness and almost always traveling at extremely high speeds. They were shaped like a ball or projectile, were a bright green, white, red, or yellow and sometimes made sounds. Like their American cousins, they were always so far away that no details could be seen. For no good reason, other than speculation and circulation, the newspapers had soon begun to refer authoritatively to these "ghost rockets" as guided missiles, and implied that they were from Russia. Peenemünde, the great German missile development center and birthplace of the V-1 and V-2 guided missiles, came in for its share of suspicion since it was held by the Russians. By the end of the summer of 1946 the reports were widespread, coming from Denmark, Norway, Spain, Greece, French Morocco, Portugal, and Turkey. In 1947, after no definite conclusions as to identity of the "rockets" had been established, the reports died out. Now in early January 1948 they broke out again. But Project Sign personnel were too busy to worry about European UFO reports, they were busy at home. A National Guard pilot had just been killed chasing a UFO.

On January 7 all of the late papers in the U.S. carried headlines similar to those in the Louisville Courier: "F-51 and Capt. Mantell Destroyed Chasing Flying Saucer." This was Volume I of "The Classics," the Mantell Incident.

At one-fifteen on that afternoon the control tower operators at Godman AFB, outside Louisville, Kentucky, received a telephone call from the Kentucky State Highway Patrol. The patrol wanted to know if Godman Tower knew anything about any unusual aircraft in the vicinity. Several people from Maysville, Kentucky, a small town 80 miles east of Louisville, had reported seeing a strange aircraft. Godman knew that they had nothing in the vicinity so they called Flight Service at Wright-Patterson AFB. In a few minutes Flight Service called back. Their air Traffic control board showed no flights in the area. About twenty minutes later the state police called again. This time people from the towns of Owensboro and Irvington, Kentucky, west of Louisville, were reporting a strange craft. The report from these two towns was a little more complete. The townspeople had described the object to the state police as being "circular, about 250 to 300 feet in diameter," and moving westward at a "pretty good clip." Godman Tower checked Flight Service again. Nothing. All this time the tower operators had been looking for the reported object. They theorized that since the UFO had had to pass north of Godman to get from Maysville to Owensboro it might come back.

At one forty-five they saw it, or something like it. Later, in his official report, the assistant tower operator said that he had seen the object for several minutes before he called his chief's attention to it. He said that he had been reluctant to "make a flying saucer report." As soon as the two men in the tower had assured themselves that the UFO they saw was not an airplane or a weather balloon, they called Flight Operations. They wanted the operations officer to see the UFO. Before long word of the sighting had gotten around to key personnel on the base, and several officers, besides the base operations officer and the base intelligence officer, were in the tower.

*All of them looked at the UFO through the tower's 6
× 50 binoculars and decided they couldn't identify it.
About this time Colonel Hix, the base commander,
arrived. He looked and he was baffled. At two-thirty,
they reported, they were discussing what should be done
when four F-51's came into view, approaching the base
from the south.*

*The tower called the flight leader, Captain Mantell, and
asked him to take a look at the object and try to identify
it. One F-51 in the flight was running low on fuel, so
he asked permission to go on to his base. Mantell took
his two remaining wing men, made a turn, and started
after the UFO. The people in Godman Tower were directing him as none of the pilots could see the object at this
time. They gave Mantell an initial heading toward the
south and the flight was last seen heading in the general
direction of the UFO.*

*By the time the F-5 l's had climbed to 10,000 feet, the
two wing men later reported, Mantell had pulled out
ahead of them and they could just barely see him. At
two forty-five Mantell called the tower and said, "I see
something above and ahead of me and I'm still climbing." All the people in the tower heard Mantell say this
and they heard one of the wing men call back and ask,
"What the hell are we looking for?" The tower immedi-*

ately called Mantell and asked him for a description of what he saw. Odd as it may seem, no one can remember exactly what he answered. Saucer historians have credited him with saying, "I've sighted the thing. It looks metallic and it's tremendous in size. . . . Now it's starting to climb." Then in a few seconds he is supposed to have called and said, "It's above me and I'm gaining on it. I'm going to 20,000 feet." Everyone in the tower agreed on this one last bit of the transmission, "I'm going to 20,000 feet," but didn't agree on the first part, about the UFO's being metallic and tremendous.

The two wing men were now at 15,000 feet and trying frantically to call Mantell. He had climbed far above them by this time and was out of sight. Since none of them had any oxygen they were worried about Mantell. Their calls were not answered. Mantell never talked to anyone again. The two wing men leveled off at 15,000 feet, made another fruitless effort to call Mantell, and started to come back down. As they passed Godman Tower on their way to their base, one of them said something to the effect that all he had seen was a reflection on his canopy.

When they landed at their base, Standiford Field, just north of Godman, one pilot had his F-51 refueled and serviced with oxygen, and took off to search the area again. He didn't see anything.

At three-fifty the tower lost sight of the UFO. A few minutes later they got word that Mantell had crashed and was dead.

Several hours later, at 7:20 P.M., airfield towers all over the Midwest sent in frantic reports of another UFO. In all about a dozen airfield towers reported the UFO as being low on the southwestern horizon and disappearing after about twenty minutes. The writers of saucer lore say this UFO was what Mantell was chasing when he died; the Air Force says this UFO was Venus.

The people on Project Sign worked fast on the Mantell Incident. Contemplating a flood of queries from the press as soon as they heard about the crash, they realized that they had to get a quick answer. Venus had been the target of a chase by an Air Force F-51 several weeks before and there were similarities between this sighting and the Mantell Incident. So almost before the rescue crews had reached the crash, the word "Venus" went out. This satisfied the editors, and so it stood for about a year; Mantell had unfortunately been killed trying to reach the planet Venus.

To the press, the nonchalant, offhand manner with which the sighting was written off by the Air Force public relations officer showed great confidence in the conclusion, Venus, but behind the barbed-wire fence that encircled ATIC the nonchalant attitude didn't exist among the intelligence analysts. One man had already left for Louisville and the rest were doing some tall speculating. The story about the tower-to-air talk, "It looks metallic and it's tremendous in size," spread fast. Rumor had it that the tower had carried on a running conversation with the pilots and that there was more information than was so far known. Rumor also had it that this conversation had been recorded. Unfortunately neither of these rumors was true.

Over a period of several weeks the file on the Mantell Incident grew in size until it was the most thoroughly investigated sighting of that time, at least the file was the thickest.

About a year later the Air Force released its official report on the incident. To use a trite term, it was a masterpiece in the art of "weasel wording." It said that the UFO might have been Venus or it could have been a balloon. Maybe two balloons. It probably was Venus except that this is doubtful because Venus was too dim to be seen in the afternoon. This jolted writers who had been following the UFO story. Only a few weeks before, The Saturday Evening Post had published a two-part story entitled "What You Can Believe about Flying Saucers." The story had official sanction and had quoted the Venus theory as a positive solution. To clear up the situation, several writers were allowed to interview a major in the Pentagon, who was the Air Force's Pentagon "expert" on UFO's. The major was asked directly about the conclusion of the Mantel] Incident, and he flatly stated that it was Venus. The writers pointed out the official Air Force analysis. The major's answer was, "They checked again and it was Venus." He didn't know who "they" were, where they had checked, or what they had checked, but it was Venus. The writers then asked, "If there was a later report they had made why wasn't it used as a conclusion?" "Was it available?" The answer to the last question was "No," and the lid snapped back down. This interview gave the definite impression that the Air Force was unsuccessfully trying to cover up some very important information, using Venus as a front. Nothing excites a newspaper or magazine writer more than to think he has stumbled onto a big story and that someone is trying to cover it up. Many writers thought this after the interview with the major, and many still think it. You can't really blame them, either.

In early 1952 I got a telephone call on ATIC's direct line to the Pentagon. It was a colonel in the Director of Intelligence's office. The Office of Public Information had been getting a number of queries about all of the confusion over the Mantell Incident. What was the answer?

I dug out the file. In 1949 all of the original material on the incident had been microfilmed, but something had been spilled on the film. Many sections were so badly faded they were illegible. As I had to do with many of the older sightings that were now history, I collected what I could from the file, filling in the blanks by talking to people who had been at ATIC during the early UFO era. Many of these people were still around, "Red" Honnacker, George Towles, Al Deyarmond, Nick Post, and many others. Most of them were civilians, the military had been transferred out by this time.

Some of the press clippings in the file mentioned the Pentagon major and his concrete proof of Venus. I couldn't find this concrete proof in the file so I asked around about the major. The major, I found, was an officer in the Pentagon who had at one time written a short intelligence summary about UFO's. He had never been stationed at ATIC, nor was he especially well versed on the UFO problem. When the word of the press conference regarding the Mantell Incident came down, a UFO expert was needed. The major, because of his short intelligence summary on UFO's, became the "expert." He had evidently conjured up "they" and "their later report" to support his Venus answer because the writers at the press conference had him in a corner. I looked farther.

Fortunately the man who had done the most extensive

work on the incident, Dr. J. Allen Hynek, head of the Ohio State University Astronomy Department, could be contacted. I called Dr. Hynek and arranged to meet him the next day.

Dr. Hynek was one of the most impressive scientists I met while working on the UFO project, and I met a good many. He didn't do two things that some of them did: give you the answer before he knew the question; or immediately begin to expound on his accomplishments in the field of science. I arrived at Ohio State just before lunch, and Dr. Hynek invited me to eat with him at the faculty club. He wanted to refer to some notes he had on the Mantell Incident and they were in his office, so we discussed UFO's in general during lunch.

Back in his office he started to review the Mantell Incident. He had been responsible for the weasel-worded report that the Air Force released in late 1949, and he apologized for it. Had he known that it was going to cause so much confusion, he said, he would have been more specific. He thought the incident was a dead issue. The reason that Venus had been such a strong suspect was that it was in almost the same spot in the sky as the UFO. Dr. Hynek referred to his notes and told me that at 3:00 P.M., Venus had been south southwest of Godman and 33 degrees above the southern horizon. At 3:00 P.M. the people in the tower estimated the UFO to be southwest of Godman and at an elevation of about 45 degrees. Allowing for human error in estimating directions and angles, this was close. I agreed. There was one big flaw in the theory, however. Venus wasn't bright enough to be seen. He had computed the brilliance of the planet, and on the day in question it was only six times as bright as the surrounding sky. Then he explained what this meant. Six times may sound like a lot, but it isn't. When you start looking for a pinpoint of light only six times as bright as the surrounding sky, it's almost impossible to find it, even on a clear day.

Dr. Hynek said that he didn't think that the UFO was Venus.

I later found out that although it was a relatively clear day there was considerable haze.

I asked him about some of the other possibilities. He repeated the balloon, canopy-reflection, and sundog theories but he refused to comment on them since, as he said, he was an astrophysicist and would care to comment only on the astrophysical aspects of the sightings.

I drove back to Dayton convinced that the UFO wasn't Venus. Dr. Hynek had said Venus would have been a pinpoint of light. The people in the tower had been posi-tive of their descriptions, their statements brought that out. They couldn't agree on a description, they called the UFO "a parachute," "an ice cream cone tipped with red," "round and white," "huge and silver or metallic," "a small white object," "one fourth the size of the full moon," but all the descriptions plainly indicated a large ' object. None of the descriptions could even vaguely be called a pinpoint of light.

This aspect of a definite shape seemed to eliminate the sundog theory too. Sundogs, or parhelia, as they are technically known, are caused by ice particles reflecting a diffused light. This would not give a sharp outline. I also recalled two instances where Air Force pilots had chased sundogs. In both instances when the aircraft began to climb, the sundog disappeared. This was because the angle of reflection changed as the

airplane climbed several thousand feet. These sundog-caused UFO's also had fuzzy edges.

I had always heard a lot of wild speculation about the condition of Mantell's crashed F-51, so I wired for a copy of the accident report. It arrived several days after my visit with Dr. Hynek. The report said that the F-51 had lost a wing due to excessive speed in a dive after Mantell had "blacked out" due to the lack of oxygen. Mantell's body had not burned, not disintegrated, and was not *full of holes; the wreck was not radioactive, nor was it magnetized.*

One very important and pertinent question remained. Why did Mantell, an experienced pilot, try to go to 20,000 feet when he didn't even have an oxygen mask? If he had run out of oxygen, it would have been different. Every pilot and crewman has it pounded into him, "Do not, under any circumstances, go above 15,000 feet without oxygen." In high-altitude indoctrination during World War II, I made several trips up to 30,000 feet in a pressure chamber. To demonstrate anoxia we would leave our oxygen masks off until we became dizzy. A few of the more hardy souls could get to 15,000 feet, but nobody ever got over 17,000. Possibly Mantell thought he could climb up to 20,000 in a hurry and get back down before he got anoxia and blacked out, but this would be a foolish chance. This point was covered in the sighting report. A long-time friend of Mantell's went on record as saying that he'd flown with him several years and knew him personally. He couldn't conceive of Mantell's even thinking about disregarding his lack of oxygen. Mantell was one of the most cautious pilots he knew. "The only thing I can think," he commented, "was that he was after something that he believed to be more important than his life or his family."

My next step was to try to find out what Mantell's wing men had seen or thought but this was a blind alley. All of this evidence was in the ruined portion of the microfilm, even their names were missing. The only reference I could find to them was a vague passage indicating they hadn't seen anything.

I concentrated on the canopy-reflection theory. It is widely believed that many flying saucers appear to pilots who are actually chasing a reflection on their canopy. I checked over all the reports we had on file. I couldn't find one that had been written off for this reason. I dug back into my own flying experience and talked to a dozen pilots. All of us had momentarily been startled by a reflection on the aircraft's canopy or wing, but in a second or two it had been obvious that it was a reflection. Mantell chased the object for at least fifteen to twenty minutes, and it is inconceivable that he wouldn't realize in that length of time that he was chasing a reflection.

About the only theory left to check was that the object might have been one of the big, 100-foot-diameter, "skyhook" balloons. I rechecked the descriptions of the UFO made by the people in the tower. The first man to sight the object called it a parachute; others said ice cream cone, round, etc. All of these descriptions fit a balloon. Buried deep in the file were two more references to balloons that I had previously missed. Not long after the object had disappeared from view at Godman AFB, a man from Madisonville, Kentucky, called Flight Service in Dayton. He had seen an object traveling southeast. He had looked at it through a telescope and it was a balloon. At four forty-five an astronomer living north of Nashville, Tennessee, called in. He had also seen a UFO, looked at it through a telescope, and it was a balloon.

In the thousands of words of testimony and evidence taken on the Mantell Incident this was the only reference to balloons. I had purposely not paid too much attention to this possibility because I was sure that it had been thoroughly checked back in 1948. Now I wasn't sure. I talked with one of the people who had been in on the Mantell investigation. The possibility of a balloon's causing the sighting had been mentioned but hadn't been followed up for two reasons. Number one was that everybody at ATIC was convinced that the object Mantell was after was a spaceship and that this was the only course they had pursued. When the sighting grew older and no spaceship proof could be found, everybody jumped on the Venus band wagon, as this theory had "already been established." It was an easy way out. The second reason was that a quick check had been made on weather balloons and none were in the area. The big skyhook balloon project was highly classified at that time, and since they were all convinced that the object was of interplanetary origin (a minority wanted to give the Russians credit), they didn't want to bother to buck the red tape of security to get data on skyhook flights.

The group who supervise the contracts for all the skyhook research flights for the Air Force are located at Wright Field, so I called them. They had no records on flights in 1948 but they did think that the big balloons were being launched from Clinton County AFB in southern Ohio at that time. They offered to get the records of the winds on January 7 and see what flight path a balloon launched in southwestern Ohio would have taken. In a few days they had the data for me. Unfortunately the times of the first sightings, from the towns outside Louisville, were not exact but it was possible to partially reconstruct the sequence of events. The winds were such that a skyhook balloon launched from Clinton County AFB could be seen from the town east of Godman AFB, the town from which the first UFO was reported to the Kentucky State Police. It is not unusual to be able to see a large balloon for 50 to 60 miles. The balloon could have traveled west for a while, climbing as it moved with the strong east winds that were blowing that day and picking up speed as the winds got stronger at altitude. In twenty minutes it could have been in a position where it could be seen from Owensboro and Irvington, Kentucky, the two towns west of Godman. The second reports to the state police had come from these two towns. Still climbing, the balloon would have reached a level where a strong wind was blowing in a southerly direction. The jet-stream winds were not being plotted in 1948 but the weather chart shows strong indications of a southerly bend in the jet stream for this day. Jet stream or not, the balloon would have moved rapidly south, still climbing. At a point somewhere south or southwest of Godman it would have climbed through the southerly-moving winds to a calm belt at about 60,000 feet. At this level it would slowly drift south or southeast. A skyhook balloon can be seen at 60,000. When first seen by the people in Godman Tower, the UFO was south of the air base. It was relatively close and looked "like a parachute," which a balloon does. During the two hours that it was in sight, the observers reported that it seemed to hover, yet each observer estimated the time he looked at the object through the binoculars and timewise the descriptions ran "huge," "small," "one fourth the size of a full moon," "one tenth the size of a full moon." Whatever the UFO was, it was slowly moving away. As the balloon continued to drift in a southerly direction it would have picked up stronger winds, and could have easily been seen by the astronomers in Madisonville, Kentucky, and north of Nashville an hour after it disappeared from view at Godman.

Somewhere in the archives of the Air Force or the Navy

there are records that will show whether or not a balloon was launched from Clinton County AFB, Ohio, on January 7, 1948. I never could find these records. People who were working with the early skyhook projects "remember" operating out of Clinton County AFB in 1947 but refuse to be pinned down to a January 7 flight. Maybe, they said.

The Mantell Incident is the same old UFO jigsaw puzzle. By assuming the shape of one piece, a balloon launched from southwestern Ohio, the whole picture neatly falls together. It shows a huge balloon that Captain Thomas Mantell died trying to reach. He didn't know that he was chasing a balloon because he had never heard of a huge, 100-foot-diameter skyhook balloon, let alone seen one. Leave out the one piece of the jigsaw puzzle and the picture is a UFO, "metallic and tremendous in size."

It could have been a balloon. This is the answer I phoned back to the Pentagon.

During January and February of 1948 the reports of "ghost rockets" continued to come from air attachés in foreign countries near the Baltic Sea. People in North Jutland, Norway, Denmark, Sweden, and Germany reported "balls of fire traveling slowly across the sky." The reports were very sketchy and incomplete, most of them accounts from newspapers. In a few days the UFO's were being seen all over Europe and South America. Foreign reports hit a peak in the latter part of February and U.S. newspapers began to pick up the stories.

The Swedish Defense Staff supposedly conducted a comprehensive study of the incidents and concluded that they were all explainable in terms of astronomical phenomena. Since this was UFO history, I made several attempts to get some detailed and official information on this report and the sightings, but I was never successful.

The ghost rockets left in March, as mysteriously as they had arrived.

All during the spring of 1948 good reports continued to come in. Some were just run-of-the-mill but a large percentage of them were good, coming from people whose reliability couldn't be questioned. For example, three scientists reported that for thirty seconds they had watched a round object streak across the sky in a highly erratic flight path near the Army's secret White Sands Proving Ground. And on May 28 the crew of an Air Force C-47 had three UFO's barrel in from "twelve o'clock high" to buzz their transport.

On July 21 a curious report was received from the

Netherlands. The day before several persons reported seeing a UFO through high broken clouds over The Hague. The object was rocket-shaped, with two rows of windows along the side. It was a poor report, very sketchy and incomplete, and it probably would have been forgotten except that four nights later a similar UFO almost collided with an Eastern Airlines DC-3. This near collision is Volume II of "The Classics."

On the evening of July 24, 1948, an Eastern Airlines DC-3 took off from Houston, Texas. It was on a scheduled trip to Atlanta, with intermediate stops in between. The pilots were Clarence S. Chiles and John B. Whitted. At about 2:45 A.M., when the flight was 20 miles southwest of Montgomery, the captain, Chiles, saw a light dead ahead and closing fast. His first reaction, he later reported to an ATIC investigation team, was that it was a jet, but in an instant he realized that even a jet couldn't close as fast as this light was closing. Chiles said he reached over, gave Whitted, the other pilot, a quick tap on the arm, and pointed. The UFO was now almost on top of them. Chiles racked the DC-3 into a tight left turn. Just as the UFO flashed by about 700 feet to the right, the DC-3 hit turbulent air. Whitted looked back just as the UFO pulled up in a steep climb.

Both the pilots had gotten a good look at the UFO and were able to give a good description to the Air Force *intelligence people. It was a B-29 fuselage. The underside had a "deep blue glow." There were "two rows of windows from which bright lights glowed," and a "50-foot trail of orange-red flame" shot out the back.*

Only one passenger was looking out of the window at the time. The ATIC investigators talked to him. He said he saw a "strange, eerie streak of light, very intense," but that was all, no details. He said that it all happened before he could adjust his eyes to the darkness.

Minutes later a crew chief at Robins Air Force Base in Macon, Georgia, reported seeing an extremely bright light pass overhead, traveling at a high speed. A few days later another report from the night of July 24 came in. A pilot, flying near the Virginia-North Carolina state line, reported that he had seen a "bright shooting star" in the direction of Montgomery, Alabama, at about the exact time the Eastern Airlines DC-3 was "buzzed."

According to the old timers at ATIC, this report shook them worse than the Mantell Incident. This was the first time two reliable sources had been really close enough to anything resembling a UFO to get a good look and live to tell about it. A quick check on a map showed that the UFO that nearly collided with the airliner would have passed almost over Macon, Georgia, after passing the DC-3. It had been turning toward Macon when last seen. The story of the crew chief at Robins AFB, 200 miles away, seemed to confirm the sighting, not to mention the report from near the Virginia-North Carolina state line.

In intelligence, if you have something to say about some vital problem you write a report that is known as an "Estimate of the Situation." A few days after the DC-3 was buzzed, the people at ATIC decided that the time had arrived to make an Estimate of the Situation. The situation was the UFO's; the estimate was that they were interplanetary!

It was a rather thick document with a black cover and it was printed on legal-sized paper. Stamped across the front were the words TOP SECRET.

It contained the Air Force's analysis of many of the incidents I have told you about plus many similar ones. All of them had come from scientists, pilots, and other equally credible observers, and each one was an unknown.

The document pointed out that the reports hadn't actually started with the Arnold Incident. Belated reports from a weather observer in Richmond, Virginia, who observed a "silver disk" through his theodolite telescope; an F-47 pilot and three pilots in his formation who saw a "silver flying wing," and the English "ghost airplanes" that had been picked up on radar early in 1947 proved this point. Although reports on them were not received until after the Arnold sighting, these incidents all had taken place earlier.

When the estimate was completed, typed, and approved, it started up through channels to higher-command echelons. It drew considerable comment but no one stopped it on its way up.

A matter of days after the Estimate of the Situation was signed, sealed. and sent on its way, the third big sighting of 1948, Volume III of "The Classics," took place. The date was October 1, and the place was Fargo. North Dakota; it was the famous Gorman Incident, in which a pilot fought a "duel of death" with a UFO.

The pilot was George F. Gorman, a twenty-five-year-old second lieutenant in the North Dakota Air National Guard.

It was eight-thirty in the evening and Gorman was coming into Fargo from a cross-country flight. He flew around Fargo for a while and about nine o'clock decided to land. He called the control tower for landing instructions and was told that a Piper Cub was in the area. He saw the Cub below him. All of a sudden what appeared to be the taillight of another airplane passed him on his

*right. He called the tower and complained but they assu-
red him that no other aircraft except the Cub were in the
area. Gorman could still see the light so he decided to
find out what it was. He pushed the*

*F-51 over into a turn and cut in toward the light. He
could plainly see the Cub outlined against the city lights
below, but he could see no outline of a body near the
mysterious light. He gave the '51 more power and closed
to within a 1,000 yards, close enough to estimate that
the light was 6 to 8 inches in diameter, was sharply outlined, and was blinking on and off. Suddenly the light
became steady as it apparently put on power; it pulled
into a sharp left bank and made a pass at the tower. The
light zoomed up with the F-51 in hot pursuit. At 7,000
feet it made a turn. Gorman followed and tried to cut
inside the light's turn to get closer to it but he couldn't
do it. The light made another turn, and this time the '51
closed on a collision course. The UFO appeared to try to
ram the '51, and Gorman had to dive to get out of the
way. The UFO passed over the '51's canopy with only
a few feet to spare. Again both the F-51 and the object
turned and closed on each other head on, and again
the pilot had to dive out to prevent a collision. All of a
sudden the light began to climb and disappeared.*

"I had the distinct impression that its maneuvers were

controlled by thought or reason," Gorman later told ATIC investigators.

Four other observers at Fargo partially corroborated his story, an oculist, Dr. A. D. Cannon, the Cub's pilot, and his passenger, Einar Neilson. They saw a light "moving fast," but did not witness all the maneuvers that Gorman reported. Two CAA employees on the ground saw a light move over the field once.

Project Sign investigators rushed to Fargo. They had wired ahead to ground the plane. They wanted to check it over before it flew again. When they arrived, only a matter of hours after the incident, they went over the airplane, from the prop spinner to the rudder trim tab, with a Geiger counter. A chart in the official report shows where every Geiger counter reading was taken. For comparison they took readings on a similar airplane that hadn't been flown for several days. Gorman's airplane was more radioactive. They rushed around, got sworn statements from the tower operators and oculist, and flew back to Dayton.

In the file on the Gorman Incident I found an old memo reporting the meeting that was held upon the ATIC team's return from Fargo. The memo concluded that some weird things were taking place.

The historians of the UFO agree. Donald Keyhoe, a retired Marine Corps major and a professional writer, author of The Flying Saucers Are Real and Flying Saucers from Outer Space, needles the Air Force about

the Gorman Incident, pointing out how, after feebly hinting that the light could have been a lighted weather balloon, they dropped it like a hot UFO. Some person by the name of Wilkins, in an equally authoritative book, says that the Gorman Incident "stumped" the Air Force. Other assorted historians point out that normally the UFO's are peaceful, Gorman and Mantell just got too inquisitive, "they" just weren't ready to be observed closely. If the Air Force hadn't slapped down the security lid, these writers might not have reached this conclusion. There have been other and more lurid "duels of death."

On June 21, 1952, at 10:58 P.M., a Ground Observer Corps spotter reported that a slow-moving craft was nearing the AEC's Oak Ridge Laboratory, an area so secret that it is prohibited to aircraft. The spotter called the light into his filter center and the filter center relayed the message to the ground control intercept radar. They had a target. But before they could do more than confirm the GOC spotter's report, the target faded from the radarscope.

An F-47 aircraft on combat air patrol in the area was vectored in visually, spotted a light, and closed on it. They "fought" from 10,000 to 27,000 feet, and several times the object made what seemed to be ramming attacks. The light was described as white, 6 to 8 inches in diameter, and blinking until it put on power. The pilot could see no silhouette around the light. The similarity to the Fargo case was striking.

On the night of December 10, 1952, near another atomic installation, the Hanford plant in Washington, the pilot and radar observer of a patrolling F-94 spotted a light while flying at 26,000 feet. The crew called their ground control station and were told that no planes were known to be in the area. They closed on the object and saw a large, round, white "thing" with a dim reddish light coming from two "windows." They lost visual contact, but got a radar lock-on. They reported that when they attempted to close on it again it would reverse direction and dive away. Several times the plane altered course itself because collision seemed imminent.

In each of these instances, as well as in the case narrated next, the sources of the stories were trained airmen with excellent reputations. They were sincerely baffled by what they had seen. They had no conceivable motive for falsifying or "dressing up" their reports.

The other dogfight occurred September 24, 1952, between a Navy pilot of a TBM and a light over Cuba.

The pilot had just finished making some practice passes for night fighters when he spotted an orange light to the east of his plane. He checked on aircraft in the area, learned that the object was unidentified, and started after it. Here is his report, written immediately after he landed:

As it [the light] approached the city from the east it started a left turn. I started to intercept. During the first part of the chase the closest I got to the light was 8 to 10 miles. At this time it appeared to be as large as an SNJ and had a greenish tail that looked to be five to six times as long as the light's diameter. This tail was seen several times in the next 10 minutes in periods of from 5 to 30 seconds each. As I reached 10,000 feet it appeared to be at 15,000 feet and in a left turn. It took 40 degrees of bank to keep the nose of my plane on the light. At this time I estimated the light to be in a 10-to-15-mile orbit.

At 12,000 feet I stopped climbing, but the light was still climbing faster than I was. I then reversed my turn from left to right and the light also reversed. As I was not gaining distance, I held a steady course south trying to estimate a perpendicular between the light and myself. The light was moving north, so I turned north. As I *turned, the light appeared to move west, then south over the base. I again tried to intercept but the light appeared to climb rapidly at a 60-degree angle. It climbed to 35,000 feet, then started a rapid descent.*

Prior to this, while the light was still at approximately 15,000 feet, I deliberately placed it between the moon and myself three times to try to identify a solid body. I and my two crewmen all had a good view of the light as it passed the moon. We could see no solid body. We considered the fact that it might be an aerologist's balloon, but we did not see a silhouette. Also, we would have rapidly caught up with and passed a balloon.

During its descent, the light appeared to slow down at about 10,000 feet, at which time I made three runs on it. Two were on a 90-degree collision course, and the light traveled at tremendous speed across my bow. On the third run I was so close that the light blanked out the airfield below me. Suddenly it started a dive and I followed, losing it at 1,500 feet.

In this incident the UFO was a balloon.

The following night a lighted balloon was sent up and the pilot was ordered up to compare his experiences. He duplicated his dogfight—illusions and all. The Navy furnished us with a long analysis of the affair, explaining how the pilot had been fooled.

In the case involving the ground observer and the F-47 near the atomic installation, we plotted the winds and calculated that a lighted balloon was right at the spot where the pilot encountered the light.

In the other instance, the "white object with two windows," we found that a skyhook balloon had been plotted at the exact site of the "battle."

Gorman fought a lighted balloon too. An analysis of the sighting by the Air Weather Service sent to ATIC in a letter dated January 24, 1949, proved it. The radioactive F-51 was decontaminated by a memo from a Wright Field laboratory explaining that a recently flown airplane will be more radioactive than one that has been on the ground for several days. An airplane at 20,000 to 30,000 feet picks up more cosmic rays than one shielded by the earth's ever present haze.

Why can't experienced pilots recognize a balloon when they see one? If they are flying at night, odd things can happen to their vision. There is the problem of vertigo as well as disorientation brought on by flying without points of reference. Night fighters have told dozens of stories of being fooled by lights.

One night during World War II we had just dumped a load of bombs on a target when a "night fighter" started to make a pass at us. Everyone in the cockpit saw the fighter's red-hot exhaust stack as he bore down on us. I cut loose with six caliber-.50 machine guns. Fortunately I missed the "night fighter"—if I'd have shot it I'd have fouled up the astronomers but good because the "night fighter" was Venus.

While the people on Project Sign were pondering over Lieutenant Gorman's dogfight with the UFO—at the time they weren't even considering the balloon angle— the Top Secret Estimate of the Situation was working its way up into the higher echelons of the Air Force. It got to the late General Hoyt S. Vandenberg, then Chief of Staff, before it was batted back down. The general wouldn't buy interplanetary vehicles. The report lacked proof. A group from ATIC went to the Pentagon to bolster their position but had no luck, the Chief of Staff just couldn't be convinced.

The estimate died a quick death. Some months later it was completely declassified and relegated to the incinerator. A few copies, one of which I saw, were kept as mementos of the golden days of the UFO's. The top Air Force command's refusal to buy the interplanetary theory didn't have any immediate effect upon the morale of Project Sign because the reports were getting better.

A belated report that is more of a collectors' item than a good UFO sighting came into ATIC in the fall of 1948. It was from Moscow. Someone, I could never find out exactly who, reported a huge "smudge-like" object in the sky.

Then radar came into the picture. For months the anti-saucer factions had been pointing their fingers at the lack of radar reports, saying, "If they exist, why don't they show up on radarscopes?" When they showed up on radarscopes, the UFO won some converts.

On October 15 an F-61, a World War II "Black Widow" night fighter. was on patrol over Japan when it picked up an unidentified target on its radar. The target was flying between 5,000 and 6,000 feet and traveling about 200 miles per hour. When the F-61 tried to intercept it would get to within 12,000 feet of the UFO only to have it accelerate to an estimated 1,200 miles per hour, leaving the F-61 far behind before slowing down again. The F-61 crew made six attempts to close on the UFO. On one pass, the crew said, they did get close enough to see its silhouette. It was 20 to 30 feet long and looked "like a rifle bullet."

Toward the end of November a wire came into Project Sign from Germany. It was the first report where a UFO was seen and simultaneously picked up on radar. This type of report, the first of many to come, is one of the better types of UFO reports. The wire said:

At 2200 hours, local time, 23 November 1948, Capt. —— saw an object in the air directly east of this base. It was at an unknown altitude. It looked like a reddish star and was moving in a southerly direction across Munich, turning slightly to the southwest then the southeast. The speed could have been between 200 to 600 mph, the actual speed could not be estimated, not knowing the height. Capt. —— called base operations and they called the radar station. Radar reported that they had seen nothing on their scope but would check again. Radar then called operations to report that they did have a target at 27,000 feet, some 30 miles south of Munich, traveling at 900 mph. Capt. —— reported that the object that he saw was now in that area. A few minutes later radar called again to say that the target had climbed to 50,000 feet, and was circling 40 miles south of Munich.

Capt. —— is an experienced pilot now flying F-80's and is considered to be completely reliable. The sighting was verified by Capt. ——, also an F-80 pilot.

The possibility that this was a balloon was checked but the answer from Air Weather Service was "not a balloon." No aircraft were in the area. Nothing we know of, except possibly experimental aircraft, which are not in Germany, can climb 23,000 feet in a matter of minutes and travel 900 miles per hour.

By the end of 1948, Project Sign had received several hundred UFO reports. Of these, 167 had been saved as good reports. About three dozen were "Unknown." Even though the UFO reports were getting better and more numerous, the enthusiasm over the interplanetary idea was cooling off. The same people who had fought to go to Godman AFB to talk to Colonel Hix and his UFO observers in January now had to be prodded when a sighting needed investigating. More and more work was being pushed off onto the other investigative organization that was helping ATIC. The kickback on the Top Secret Estimate of the Situation was beginning to dampen a lot of enthusiasms. It was definitely a bear market for UFO's.

A bull market was on the way, however. Early 1949 was to bring "little lights" and green fireballs.

The "little lights" were UFO's, but the green fireballs were real.

CHAPTER 4

Green Fireballs, Project Twinkle, Little Lights, and Grudge

*At exactly midnight on September 18, 1954, my telepho-
ne rang. It was Jim Phalen, a friend of mine from the
Long Beach Press-Telegram, and he had a "good flying
saucer report," hot off the wires. He read it to me. The
lead line was: "Thousands of people saw a huge fireball
light up dark New Mexico skies tonight."*

*The story went on to tell about how a "blinding green"
fireball the size of a full moon had silently streaked
southeast across Colorado and northern New Mexico
at eight-forty that night. Thousands of people had seen
the fireball. It had passed right over a crowded football
stadium at Santa Fe, New Mexico, and people in Denver
said it "turned night into day." The crew of a TWA
airliner flying into Albuquerque from Amarillo, Texas,
saw it. Every police and newspaper switchboard in the
two-state area was jammed with calls.*

*One of the calls was from a man inquiring if anything
unusual had happened recently. When he was informed
about the mysterious fireball he heaved an audible sigh
of relief, "Thanks," he said, "I was afraid I'd gotten some
bad bourbon." And he hung up.*

Dr. Lincoln La Paz, world-famous authority on meteorites and head of the University of New Mexico's Institute of Meteoritics, apparently took the occurrence calmly. The wire story said he had told a reporter that he would plot its course, try to determine where it landed, and go out and try to find it. "But," he said, "I don't expect to find anything."

When Jim Phalen had read the rest of the report he asked, "What was it?"

"It sounds to me like the green fireballs are back," I answered.

"What the devil are green fireballs?"

What the devil are green fireballs? I'd like to know. So would a lot of other people.

The green fireballs streaked into UFO history late in November 1948, when people around Albuquerque, New Mexico, began to report seeing mysterious "green flares" at night. The first reports mentioned only a "green streak in the sky," low on the horizon. From the description the Air Force Intelligence people at Kirtland AFB in Albuquerque and the Project Sign people at ATIC wrote the objects off as flares. After all, thousands of GI's had probably been discharged with a duffel bag full of "liberated" Very pistols and flares.

But as days passed the reports got better. They seemed to indicate that the "flares" were getting larger and more people were reporting seeing them. It was doubtful if this "growth" was psychological because there had been no publicity—so the Air Force decided to reconsider the "flare" answer. They were in the process of doing this on the night of December 5, 1948, a memorable night in the green fireball chapter of UFO history.

At 9:27 P.M. on December 5, an Air Force C-47 transport was flying at 18,000 feet 10 miles east of Albuquerque. The pilot was a Captain Goede. Suddenly the crew, Captain Goede, his co-pilot, and his engineer were startled by a green ball of fire flashing across the sky ahead of them. It looked something like a huge meteor except that it was a bright green color and it didn't arch downward, as meteors usually do. The green-colored ball of fire had started low, from near the eastern slopes of the Sandia Mountains, arched upward a little, then seemed to level out. And it was too big for a meteor, at least it was larger than any meteor that anyone in the C-47 had ever seen before. After a hasty discussion the crew decided that they'd better tell somebody about it, especially since they had seen an identical object twenty-two minutes before near Las Vegas, New Mexico.

Captain Goede picked up his microphone and called the control tower at Kirtland AFB and reported what he and his crew had seen. The tower relayed the message to the local intelligence people.

A few minutes later the captain of Pioneer Airlines Flight 63 called Kirtland Tower. At 9:35 P.M. he had also seen a green ball of fire just east of Las Vegas, New Mexico. He was on his way to Albuquerque and would make a full report when he landed.

When he taxied his DC-3 up to the passenger ramp at Kirtland a few minutes later, several intelligence officers were waiting for him. He reported that at 9:35 P.M. he was on a westerly heading, approaching Las Vegas from the east, when he and his co-pilot saw what they first thought was a "shooting star." It was ahead and a little above them. But, the captain said, it took them only a split second to realize that whatever they saw was too low and had too flat a trajectory to be a meteor. As they watched, the object seemed to approach their airplane head on, changing color from orange red to green. As it became bigger and bigger, the captain said, he thought sure it was going to collide with them so he racked the DC-3 up in a tight turn. As the green ball of fire got abreast of them it began to fall toward the ground, getting dimmer and dimmer until it disappeared. Just before he swerved the DC-3, the fireball was as big, or bigger, than a full moon.

The intelligence officers asked a few more questions and went back to their office. More reports, which had been phoned in from all over northern New Mexico, were waiting for them. By morning a full-fledged investigation was under way.

No matter what these green fireballs were, the military was getting a little edgy. They might be common meteorites, psychologically enlarged flares, or true UFO's, but whatever they were they were playing around in one of the most sensitive security areas in the United States. Within 100 miles of Albuquerque were two installations that were the backbone of the atomic bomb program, Los Alamos and Sandia Base. Scattered throughout the countryside were other installations vital to the defense of the U.S.: radar stations, fighter-interceptor bases, and the other mysterious areas that had been blocked off by high chain-link fences.

Since the green fireballs bore some resemblance to meteors or meteorites, the Kirtland intelligence officers called in Dr. Lincoln La Paz. Dr. La Paz said that he would be glad to help, so the officers explained the strange series of events to him. True, he said, the description of the fireballs did sound as if they might be meteorites—except for a few points. One way to be sure was to try to plot the flight path of the green fireballs the same way he had so successfully plotted the flight path of meteorites in the past. From this flight path he could determine where they would have hit the earth—if they were meteorites. They would search this area, and if they found parts of a meteorite they would have the answer to the green fireball riddle.

The fireball activity on the night of December 5 was made to order for plotting flight paths. The good reports of that night included carefully noted locations, the directions in which the green objects were seen, their heights above the horizon, and the times when they were observed. So early the next morning Dr. La Paz and a crew of intelligence officers were scouring northern New Mexico. They started out by talking to the people who had made reports but soon found out that dozens of other people had also seen the fireballs. By closely checking the time of the observations, they determined that eight separate fireballs had been seen. One was evidently more spectacular and was seen by the most people. Everyone in northern New Mexico had seen it going from west to east, so Dr. La Paz and his crew worked eastward across New Mexico to the west border of Texas, talking to dozens of people. After many sleepless hours they finally plotted where it should have struck the earth. They searched the area but found nothing. They

*went back over the area time and time again—nothing.
As Dr. La Paz later told me, this was the first time that
he seriously doubted the green fireballs were meteorites.*

*Within a few more days the fireballs were appearing
almost nightly. The intelligence officers from Kirtland
decided that maybe they could get a good look at one of
them, so on the night of December 8 two officers took
off in an airplane just before dark and began to cruise
around north of Albuquerque. They had a carefully
worked out plan where each man would observe certain
details if they saw one of the green fireballs. At 6:33 P.M.
they saw one. This is their report:*

*At 6:33 P.M. while flying at an indicated altitude of
11,500 feet, a strange phenomenon was observed. Exact
position of the aircraft at time of the observation was 20
miles east of the Las Vegas, N.M., radio range station.
The aircraft was on a compass course of 90 degrees.
Capt. —— was pilot and I was acting as copilot. I first
observed the object and a split second later the pilot
saw it. It was 2,000 feet higher than the plane, and was
approaching the plane at a rapid rate of speed from 30
degrees to the left of our course. The object was similar
in appearance to a burning green flare, the kind that is
commonly used in the Air Force. However, the light was
much more intense and the object appeared conside-*

*rably larger than a normal flare. The trajectory of the
object, when first sighted, was almost flat and parallel to
the earth. The phenomenon lasted about 2 seconds. At
the end of this time the object seemed to begin to burn
out and the trajectory then dropped off rapidly. The
phenomenon was of such intensity as to be visible from
the very moment it ignited.*

*Back at Wright-Patterson AFB, ATIC was getting a
blow-by-blow account of the fireball activity but they
were taking no direct part in the investigation. Their
main interest was to review all incoming UFO reports
and see if the green fireball reports were actually unique
to the Albuquerque area. They were. Although a good
many UFO reports were coming in from other parts of
the U.S., none fit the description of the green fireballs.*

*All during December 1948 and January 1949 the green
fireballs continued to invade the New Mexico skies.
Everyone, including the intelligence officers at Kirtland
AFB, Air Defense Command people, Dr. La Paz, and
some of the most distinguished scientists at Los Alamos
had seen at least one.*

*In mid-February 1949 a conference was called at Los
Alamos to determine what should be done to further
pursue the investigation. The Air Force, Project Sign,
the intelligence people at Kirtland, and other interested*

parties had done everything they could think of and still no answer.

Such notable scientists as Dr. Joseph Kaplan, a world-renowned authority on the physics of the upper atmosphere, Dr. Edward Teller, of H-bomb fame, and of course Dr. La Paz, attended, along with a lot of military brass and scientists from Los Alamos.

This was one conference where there was no need to discuss whether or not this special type of UFO, the green fireball, existed. Almost everyone at the meeting had seen one. The purpose of the conference was to decide whether the fireballs were natural or man-made and how to find out more about them.

As happens in any conference, opinions were divided. Some people thought the green fireballs were natural fireballs. The proponents of the natural meteor, or meteorite, theory presented facts that they had dug out of astronomical journals. Greenish-colored meteors, although not common, had been observed on many occasions. The flat trajectory, which seemed to be so important in proving that the green fireballs were extraterrestrial, was also nothing new. When viewed from certain angles, a meteor can appear to have a flat trajectory. The reason that so many had been seen during

December of 1948 and January of 1949 was that the weather had been unusually clear all over the Southwest during this period.

Dr. La Paz led the group who believed that the green fireballs were not meteors or meteorites. His argument was derived from the facts that he had gained after many days of research and working with Air Force intelligence teams. He stuck to the points that (1) the trajectory was too flat, (2) the color was too green, and (3) he couldn't locate any fragments even though he had found the spots where they should have hit the earth if they were meteorites.

People who were at that meeting have told me that Dr. La Paz's theory was very interesting and that each point was carefully considered. But evidently it wasn't conclusive enough because when the conference broke up, after two days, it was decided that the green fireballs were a natural phenomenon of some kind. It was recommended that this phase of the UFO investigation be given to the Air Force's Cambridge Research Laboratory, since it is the function of this group to study natural phenomena, and that Cambridge set up a project to attempt to photograph the green fireballs and measure their speed, altitude, and size.

In the late summer of 1949, Cambridge established Project Twinkle to solve the mystery. The project called for establishing three cinetheodolite stations near White Sands, New Mexico. A cinetheodolite is similar to a 35-mm. movie camera except when you take a photograph of an object you also get a photograph of three dials that show the time the photo was taken, the azimuth angle, and the elevation angle of the camera.

If two or more cameras photograph the same object, it is possible to obtain a very accurate measurement of the photographed object's altitude, speed, and size.

Project Twinkle was a bust. Absolutely nothing was photographed. Of the three cameras that were planned for the project, only one was available. This one camera was continually being moved from place to place. If several reports came from a certain area, the camera crew would load up their equipment and move to that area, always arriving too late. Any duck hunter can tell you that this is the wrong tactic; if you want to shoot any ducks pick a good place and stay put, let the ducks come to you.

The people trying to operate Project Twinkle were having financial and morale trouble. To do a good job they needed more and better equipment and more people,

*but Air Force budget cuts precluded this. Moral support
was free but they didn't get this either.*

*When the Korean War started, Project Twinkle silently
died, along with official interest in green fireballs.*

*When I organized Project Blue Book in the summer
of 1951 I'd never heard of a green fireball. We had a
few files marked "Los Alamos Conference," "Fireballs,"
"Project Twinkle," etc., but I didn't pay any attention to
them.*

*Then one day I was at a meeting in Los Angeles with
several other officers from ATIC, and was introduced to
Dr. Joseph Kaplan. When he found we were from ATIC,
his first question was, "What ever happened to the green
fireballs?" None of us had ever heard of them, so he
quickly gave us the story. He and I ended up discussing
green fireballs. He mentioned Dr. La Paz and his opinion that the green fireballs might be man-made, and
although he respected La Paz's professional ability, he
just wasn't convinced. But he did strongly urge me to get
in touch with Dr. La Paz and hear his side of the story.*

*When I returned to ATIC I spent several days digging
into our collection of green fireball reports. All of these
reports covered a period from early December 1948 to*

1949. As far as Blue Book's files were concerned, there hadn't been a green fireball report for a year and a half. I read over the report on Project Twinkle and the few notes we had on the Los Alamos Conference, and decided that the next time I went to Albuquerque I'd contact Dr. La Paz. I did go to Albuquerque several times but my visits were always short and I was always in a hurry so I didn't get to see him.

It was six or eight months later before the subject of green fireballs came up again. I was eating lunch with a group of people at the AEC's Los Alamos Laboratory when one of the group mentioned the mysterious kelly-green balls of fire. The strictly unofficial bull-session-type discussion that followed took up the entire lunch hour and several hours of the afternoon. It was an interesting discussion because these people, all scientists and technicians from the lab, had a few educated guesses as to what they might be. All of them had seen a green fireball, some of them had seen several.

One of the men, a private pilot, had encountered a fireball one night while he was flying his Navion north of Santa Fe and he had a vivid way of explaining what he'd seen. "Take a soft ball and paint it with some kind of fluorescent paint that will glow a bright green in the dark," I remember his saying, "then have someone take the ball out about 100 feet in front of you and about 10 feet above you. Have him throw the ball right at your face, as hard as he can throw it. That's what a green fireball looks like."

The speculation about what the green fireballs were ran through the usual spectrum of answers, a new type of natural phenomenon, a secret U.S. development, and psychologically enlarged meteors. When the possibility of the green fireballs' being associated with interplanetary vehicles came up, the whole group got serious. They had been doing a lot of thinking about this, they said, and they had a theory.

The green fireballs, they theorized, could be some type of unmanned test vehicle that was being projected into our atmosphere from a "spaceship" hovering several hundred miles above the earth. Two years ago I would have been amazed to hear a group of reputable scientists make such a startling statement. Now, however, I took it as a matter of course. I'd heard the same type of statement many times before from equally qualified groups.

Turn the tables, they said, suppose that we are going to try to go to a far planet. There would be three phases to the trip: out through the earth's atmosphere, through space, and the re-entry into the atmosphere of the planet we're planning to land on. The first two phases would admittedly present formidable problems, but the last phase, the re-entry phase, would be the most critical. Coming in from outer space, the craft would, for all practical purposes, be similar to a meteorite except that it would be powered and not free-falling. You would have myriad problems associated with aerodynamic heating, high aerodynamic loadings, and very probably a host of other problems that no one can now conceive of. Certain of these problems could be partially solved by laboratory experimentation, but nothing can replace flight testing, and the results obtained by flight tests in our atmosphere would not be valid in another type of atmosphere. The most logical way to overcome this difficulty would be to build our interplanetary vehicle, go to the planet that we were interested in landing on, and hover several hundred miles up. From this altitude we could send instrumented test vehicles down to the planet. If we didn't want the inhabitants of the planet, if it were inhabited, to know what we were doing we could put destruction devices in the test vehicle, or arrange the test so that the test vehicles would just plain burn up at a certain point due to aerodynamic heating.

They continued, each man injecting his ideas. Maybe the green fireballs are test vehicles—somebody else's. The regular UFO reports might be explained by the fact that the manned vehicles were venturing down to within 100,000 or 200,000 feet of the earth, or to the altitude at which atmosphere re-entry begins to get critical.

I had to go down to the airstrip to get a CARCO Airlines plane back to Albuquerque so I didn't have time to ask a lot of questions that came into my mind. I did get to make one comment. From the conversations, I assumed that these people didn't think the green fireballs were any kind of a natural phenomenon. Not exactly, they said, but so far the evidence that said they were a natural phenomenon was vastly outweighed by the evidence that said they weren't.

During the kidney-jolting trip down the valley from Los Alamos to Albuquerque in one of the CARCO Airlines' Bonanzas, I decided that I'd stay over an extra day and talk to Dr. La Paz.

He knew every detail there was to know about the green fireballs. He confirmed my findings, that the genuine green fireballs were no longer being seen. He said that he'd received hundreds of reports, especially after he'd written several articles about the mysterious fireballs, but that all of the reported objects were just greenish-colored, common, everyday meteors.

Dr. La Paz said that some people, including Dr. Joseph Kaplan and Dr. Edward Teller, thought that the green fireballs were natural meteors. He didn't think so, however, for several reasons. First the color was so much different. To illustrate his point, Dr. La Paz opened his desk drawer and took out a well-worn chart of the color spectrum. He checked off two shades of green; one a pale, almost yellowish green and the other a much more distinct vivid green. He pointed to the bright green and told me that this was the color of the green fireballs. He'd taken this chart with him when he went out to talk to people who had seen the green fireballs and everyone had picked this one color. The pale green, he explained, was the color reported in the cases of documented green meteors.

Then there were other points of dissimilarity between a meteor and the green fireballs. The trajectory of the fireballs was too flat. Dr. La Paz explained that a meteor doesn't necessarily have to arch down across the sky, its trajectory can appear to be flat, but not as flat as that of the green fireballs. Then there was the size. Almost always such descriptive words as "terrifying," "as big as the moon," and "blinding" had been used to describe the fireballs. Meteors just aren't this big and bright.

No—Dr. La Paz didn't think that they were meteors.

Dr. La Paz didn't believe that they were meteorites either.

A meteorite is accompanied by sound and shock waves that break windows and stampede cattle. Yet in every case of a green fireball sighting the observers reported that they did not hear any sound.

But the biggest mystery of all was the fact that no particles of a green fireball had ever been found. If they were meteorites, Dr. La Paz was positive that he would have found one. He'd missed very few times in the cases of known meteorites. He pulled a map out of his file to show me what he meant. It was a map that he had used to plot the spot where a meteorite had hit the earth. I believe it was in Kansas. The map had been prepared from information he had obtained from dozens of people who had seen the meteorite come flaming toward the earth. At each spot where an observer was standing he'd drawn in the observer's line of sight to the meteorite. From the dozens of observers he had obtained dozens of lines of sight. The lines all converged to give Dr. La Paz a plot of the meteorite's downward trajectory. Then he had been able to plot the spot where it had struck the earth. He and his crew went to the marked area, probed the ground with long steel poles, and found the meteorite.

This was just one case that he showed me. He had records of many more similar successful expeditions in his file.

Then he showed me some other maps. The plotted lines looked identical to the ones on the map I'd just seen. Dr. La Paz had used the same techniques on these plots and had marked an area where he wanted to search. He had searched the area many times but he had never found anything.

These were plots of the path of a green fireball.

When Dr. La Paz had finished, I had one last question, "What do you think they are?"

He weighed the question for a few seconds—then he said that all he cared to say was that he didn't think that they were a natural phenomenon. He thought that maybe someday one would hit the earth and the mystery would be solved. He hoped that they were a natural phenomenon.

After my talk with Dr. La Paz I can well understand his apparent calmness on the night of September 18, 1954, when the newspaper reporter called him to find out if he planned to investigate this latest green fireball report. He was speaking from experience, not indifference, when he said, "But I don't expect to find anything."

If the green fireballs are back, I hope that Dr. La Paz gets an answer this time.

The story of the UFO now goes back to late January 1949, the time when the Air Force was in the midst of the green fireball mystery. In another part of the country another odd series of events was taking place. The center of activity was a highly secret area that can't be named, and the recipient of the UFO's, which were formations of little lights, was the U.S. Army.

The series of incidents started when military patrols who were protecting the area began to report seeing formations of lights flying through the night sky. At first the lights were reported every three or four nights, but inside of two weeks the frequency had stepped up. Before long they were a nightly occurrence. Some patrols reported that they had seen three or four formations in one night. The sightings weren't restricted to the men on patrol. One night, just at dusk, during retreat, the entire garrison watched a formation pass directly over the post parade ground.

As usual with UFO reports, the descriptions of the lights varied but the majority of the observers reported

*a V formation of three lights. As the formation moved
through the sky, the lights changed in color from a bluish
white to orange and back to bluish white. This color
cycle took about two seconds. The lights usually traveled
from west to east and made no sound. They didn't
streak across the sky like a meteor, but they were "going
faster than a jet." The lights were "a little bigger than the
biggest star." Once in a while the GI's would get binoculars on them but they couldn't see any more details. The
lights just looked bigger.*

*From the time of the first sighting, reports of the little
lights were being sent to the Air Force through Army
Intelligence channels. The reports were getting to ATIC,
but the green fireball activity was taking top billing and
no comments went back to the Army about their little
lights. According to an Army G-2 major to whom I talked in the Pentagon, this silence was taken to mean that
no action, other than sending in reports, was necessary
on the part of the Army.*

*But after about two weeks of nightly sightings and no
apparent action by the Air Force, the commander of the
installation decided to take the initiative and set a trap.
His staff worked out a plan in record time. Special UFO
patrols would be sent out into the security area and
they would be furnished with sighting equipment. This*

could be the equipment that they normally used for fire control. Each patrol would be sent to a specific location and would set up a command post. Operating out of the command post, at points where the sky could be observed, would be sighting teams. Each team had sighting equipment to measure the elevation and azimuth angle of the UFO. Four men were to be on each team, an instrument man, a timer, a recorder, and a radio operator. All the UFO patrols would be assigned special radio frequencies.

The operating procedure would be that when one sighting team spotted a UFO the radio operator would call out his team's location, the location of the UFO in the sky, and the direction it was going. All of the other teams from his patrol would thus know when to look for the UFO and begin to sight on it. While the radio man was reporting, the instrument man on the team would line up the UFO and begin to call out the angles of elevation and azimuth. The timer would call out the time., the recorder would write all of this down. The command post, upon hearing the report of the UFO, would call the next patrol and tell them. They too would try to pick it up.

Here was an excellent opportunity to get some concrete data on at least one type of UFO. It was something that should have been done from the start. Speeds, altitudes,

*and sizes that are estimated just by looking at a UFO
are miserably inaccurate. But if you could accurately
establish that some type of object was traveling 30,000
miles an hour—or even 3,000 miles an hour—through
our atmosphere, the UFO story would be the biggest
story since the Creation.*

*The plan seemed foolproof and had the full support of
every man who was to participate. For the first time
in history every GI wanted to get on the patrols. The
plan was quickly written up as a field order, approved,
and mimeographed. Since the Air Force had the prime
responsibility for the UFO investigation, it was decided
that the plan should be quickly co-ordinated with the
Air Force, so a copy was rushed to them. Time was
critical because every group of nightly reports might be
the last. Everything was ready to roll the minute the Air
Force said "Go."*

*The Air Force didn't O.K. the plan. I don't know where
the plan was killed, or who killed it, but it was killed. Its
death caused two reactions.*

*Many people thought that the plan was killed so that too
many people wouldn't find out the truth about UFO's.
Others thought somebody was just plain stupid. Neither
was true. The answer was simply that the official attitu-*

de toward UFO's had drastically changed in the past few months. They didn't exist, they couldn't exist. It was the belief at ATIC that the one last mystery, the green fireballs, had been solved a few days before at Los Alamos. The fireballs were meteors and Project Twinkle would prove it. Any further investigation by the Army would be a waste of time and effort.

This drastic change in official attitude is as difficult to explain as it was difficult for many people who knew what was going on inside Project Sign to believe. I use the words "official attitude" because at this time UFO's had become as controversial a subject as they are today. All through intelligence circles people had chosen sides and the

two UFO factions that exist today were born.

On one side was the faction that still believed in flying saucers. These people, come hell or high water, were hanging on to their original ideas. Some thought that the UFO's were interplanetary spaceships. Others weren't quite as bold and just believed that a good deal more should be known about the UFO's before they were so completely written off. These people weren't a bunch of nuts or crackpots either. They ranged down through the ranks from generals and top-grade civilians. On the outside their views were backed up by civilian scientists.

On the other side were those who didn't believe in flying saucers. At one time many of them had been believers. When the UFO reports were pouring in back in 1947 and 1948, they were just as sure that the UFO's were real as the people they were now scoffing at. But they had changed their minds. Some of them had changed their minds because they had seriously studied the UFO reports and just couldn't see any evidence that the UFO's were real. But many of them could see the "I don't believe" band wagon pulling out in front and just jumped on.

This change in the operating policy of the UFO project was so pronounced that I, like so many other people, wondered if there was a hidden reason for the change. Was it actually an attempt to go underground—to make the project more secretive? Was it an effort to cover up the fact that UFO's were proven to be interplanetary and that this should be withheld from the public at all cost to prevent a mass panic? The UFO files are full of references to the near mass panic of October 30, 1938, when Orson Welles presented his now famous "The War of the Worlds" broadcast.

This period of "mind changing" bothered me. Here were people deciding that there was nothing to this UFO business right at a time when the reports seemed to be getting better. From what I could see, if there was any mind changing to be done it should have been the other way, skeptics should have been changing to believers.

Maybe I was just playing the front man to a big cover-up. I didn't like it because if somebody up above me knew that UFO's were really spacecraft, I could make a big fool out of myself if the truth came out. I checked into this thoroughly. I spent a lot of time talking to people who had worked on Project Grudge.

The anti-saucer faction was born because of an old psychological trait, people don't like to be losers. To be a loser makes one feel inferior and incompetent. On September 23, 1947, when the chief of ATIC sent a letter to the Commanding General of the Army Air Forces stating that UFO's were real, intelligence committed themselves. They had to prove it. They tried for a year and a half with no success. Officers on top began to get anxious and the press began to get anxious. They wanted an answer. Intelligence had tried one answer, the then Top Secret Estimate of the Situation that "proved" that UFO's were real, but it was kicked back. The people on the UFO project began to think maybe the brass didn't consider them too sharp so they tried a new hypothesis: UFO's don't exist. In no time they found that this was easier to prove and it got recognition. Before if an especially interesting UFO report came in and the

Pentagon wanted an answer, all they'd get was an "It could be real but we can't prove it." Now such a request got a quick, snappy "It was a balloon," and feathers were stuck in caps from ATIC up to the Pentagon. Everybody felt fine.

In early 1949 the term "new look" was well known. The new look in women's fashions was the lower hemlines, in automobiles it was longer lines. In UFO circles the new look was cuss 'em.

The new look in UFO's was officially acknowledged on February 11, 1949, when an order was written that changed the name of the UFO project from Project Sign to Project Grudge. The order was supposedly written because the classified name, Project Sign, had been compromised. This was always my official answer to any questions about the name change. I'd go further and say that the names of the projects, first Sign, then Grudge, had no significance. This wasn't true, they did have significance, a lot of it.

CHAPTER 5

The Dark Ages

*The order of February 11, 1949, that changed the name
of Project Sign to Project Grudge had not directed any
change in the operating policy of the project. It had,
in fact, pointed out that the project was to continue to
investigate and evaluate reports of sightings of unidentified flying objects. In doing this, standard intelligence
procedures would be used. This normally means the
unbiased evaluation of intelligence data. But it doesn't
take a great deal of study of the old UFO files to see that
standard intelligence procedures were no longer being
used by Project Grudge. Everything was being evaluated on the premise that UFO's couldn't exist. No matter
what you see or hear, don't believe it.*

*New people took over Project Grudge. ATIC's top in-
telligence specialists who had been so eager to work on
Project Sign were no longer working on Project Grudge.
Some of them had drastically and hurriedly changed
their minds about UFO's when they thought that the
Pentagon was no longer sympathetic to the UFO cause.
They were now directing their talents toward more
socially acceptable projects. Other charter members of*

Project Sign had been "purged." These were the people who had refused to change their original opinions about UFO's.

With the new name and the new personnel came the new objective, get rid of the UFO's. It was never specified this way in writing but it didn't take much effort to see that this was the goal of Project Grudge. This unwritten objective was reflected in every memo, report, and directive.

To reach their objective Project Grudge launched into a campaign that opened a new age in the history of the UFO. If a comparative age in world history can be chosen, the Dark Ages would be most appropriate. Webster's Dictionary defines the Dark Ages as a period of "intellectual stagnation."

To one who is intimately familiar with UFO history it is clear that Project Grudge had a two-phase program of UFO annihilation. The first phase consisted of explaining every UFO report. The second phase was to tell the public how the Air Force had solved all the sightings. This, Project Grudge reasoned, would put an end to UFO reports.

Phase one had been started by the people of Project Sign. They realized that a great many reports were caused by people seeing balloons or such astronomical bodies as planets, meteors, or stars. They also realized that before they could get to the heart of the UFO problems they had to sift out this type of report. To do this they had called on outside help. Air Weather Service had been asked to screen the reports and check those that sounded like balloons against their records of balloon flights. Dr. J. Allen Hynek, distinguished astrophysicist and head of Ohio State University's Astronomy Department, had been given a contract to sort out those reports that could be blamed on stars, planets, meteors, etc. By early March the Air Weather Service and Dr. Hynek had some positive identifications. According to the old records, with these solutions and those that Sign and Grudge had already found, about 50 per cent of the reported UFO's could now be positively identified as hoaxes, balloons, planets, sundogs, etc. It was now time to start phase two, the publicity campaign.

For many months reporters and writers had been trying to reach behind the security wall and get the UFO story from the horse's mouth, but no luck. Some of them were still trying but they were having no success because they were making the mistake of letting it slip that they didn't believe that airline pilots, military pilots, scientists, and just all around solid citizens were having "hallucinations," perpetrating "hoaxes," or being deceived by the "misidentification of common objects." The people of Project Grudge weren't looking for this type of writer, they wanted a writer who would listen to them and write their story. As a public relations officer later told me, "We had a devil of a time. All of the writers who were after saucer stories had made their own investigations of sightings and we couldn't convince them they were wrong."

Before long, however, the right man came along. He was Sidney Shallet, a writer for The Saturday Evening Post. He seemed to have the prerequisites that were desired, so his visit to ATIC was cleared through the Pentagon. Harry Haberer, a crack Air Force public relations man, was assigned the job of seeing that Shallet got his story. I have heard many times, from both military personnel and civilians, that the Air Force told Shallet exactly what to say in his article—play down the UFO's—don't write anything that even hints that there might be something foreign in our skies. I don't believe that this is the case. I think that he just wrote the UFO story as it was told to him, told to him by Project Grudge.

Shallet's article, which appeared in two parts in the April 30 and May 7, 1949, issues of The Saturday Evening Post, is important in the history of the UFO and in understanding the UFO problem because it had *considerable effect on public opinion. Many people had, with varying degrees of interest, been wondering about the UFO's for over a year and a half. Very few had any definite opinions one way or the other. The feeling seemed to be that the Air Force is working on the problem and when they get the answer we'll know. There had been a few brief, ambiguous press releases from the Air Force but these meant nothing. Consequently when Shallet's article appeared in the Post it was widely read. It contained facts, and the facts had come from Air Force Intelligence. This was the Air Force officially reporting on UFO's for the first time.*

The article was typical of the many flying saucer stories that were to follow in the later years of UFO history, all written from material obtained from the Air Force. Shallet's article casually admitted that a few UFO sightings couldn't be explained, but the reader didn't have much chance to think about this fact because 99 per cent of the story was devoted to the anti-saucer side of the problem. It was the typical negative approach. I know that the negative approach is typical of the way that material is handed out by the Air Force because I was continually being told to "tell them about the sighting reports we've solved—don't mention the unknowns." I was never ordered to tell this, but it was a strong suggestion and in the military when higher headquarters suggests, you do.

*Shallet's article started out by psychologically conditio-
ning the reader by using such phrases as "the great flying
saucer scare," "rich, full-blown screwiness," "fearsome
freaks," and so forth. By the time the reader gets to the
meat of the article he feels like a rich, full-blown jerk for
ever even thinking about UFO's.*

*He pointed out how the "furor" about UFO reports got
so great that the Air Force was "forced" to investigate the
reports reluctantly. He didn't mention that two months
after the first UFO report ATIC had asked for Project
Sign since they believed that UFO's did exist. Nor did it
mention the once Top Secret Estimate of the Situation
that also concluded that UFO's were real. In no way did
the article reflect the excitement and anxiety of the age
of Project Sign when secret conferences preceded and
followed every trip to investigate a UFO report. This was
the Air Force being "forced" into reluctantly investigating the UFO reports.*

*Laced through the story were the details of several UFO
sightings; some new and some old, as far as the public
was concerned. The original UFO report by Kenneth
Arnold couldn't be explained. Arnold, however, had
sold his story to Fate magazine and in the same issue of
Fate were stories with such titles as "Behind the Etheric
Veil" and "Invisible Beings Walk the Earth," suggesting*

that Arnold's story might fall into the same category. The sightings where the Air Force had the answer had detailed explanations. The ones that were unknowns were mentioned, but only in passing.

Many famous names were quoted. The late General Hoyt S. Vandenberg, then Chief of Staff of the Air Force, had seen a flying saucer but it was just a reflection on the windshield of his B-17. General Lauris Norstad's UFO was a reflection of a star on a cloud, and General Curtis E. Le May found out that one out of six UFO's was a balloon; Colonel McCoy, then chief of ATIC, had seen lots of UFO's. All were reflections from distant airplanes. In other words, nobody who is anybody in the Air Force believes in flying saucers.

Figures in the top echelons of the military had spoken.

A few hoaxes and crackpot reports rounded out Mr. Shallet's article.

The reaction to the article wasn't what the Air Force and ATIC expected. They had thought that the public would read the article and toss it, and all thoughts of UFO's, into the trash can. But they didn't. Within a few days the frequency of UFO reports hit an all-time high. People, both military and civilian, evidently didn't much care what Generals Vandenberg, Norstad, Le May, or Colonel McCoy thought; they didn't believe what they were seeing were hallucinations, reflections, or balloons. What they were seeing were UFO's, whatever UFO's might be.

I heard many times from ex-Project Grudge people that Shallet had "crossed" them, he'd vaguely mentioned that there might be a case for the UFO. This made him pro-saucer.

A few days after the last installment of the Post article the Air Force gave out a long and detailed press release completely debunking UFO's, but this had no effect. It only seemed to add to the confusion.

The one thing that Shallet's article accomplished was to plant a seed of doubt in many people's minds. Was the Air Force telling the truth about UFO's? The public and a large percentage of the military didn't know what was going on behind ATIC's barbed-wire fence but they did know that a lot of reliable people had seen UFO's. Airline pilots are considered responsible people—airline pilots had seen UFO's. Experienced military pilots and ground officers are responsible people—they'd seen UFO's. Scientists, doctors, lawyers, merchants, and plain old Joe Doakes had seen UFO's, and their friends knew that they were responsible people. Somehow these facts and the tone of the Post article didn't quite jibe, and when things don't jibe, people get suspicious.

In those people who had a good idea of what was going on behind ATIC's barbed wire, the newspaper reporters and writers with the "usually reliable sources," the Post article planted a bigger seed of doubt. Why the sudden change in policy they wondered? If UFO's were so serious a few months ago, why the sudden debunking? Maybe Shallet's story was a put-up job for the Air Force. Maybe the security had been tightened. Their sources of information were reporting that many people in the military did not quite buy the Shallet article. The seed of doubt began to grow, and some of these writers began to start "independent investigations" to get the "true" story. Research takes time, so during the summer and fall of 1949 there wasn't much apparent UFO activity.

As the writers began to poke around for their own facts, Project Grudge lapsed more and more into a period of almost complete inactivity. Good UFO reports continued to come in at the rate of about ten per month but they weren't being verified or investigated. Most of them were being discarded. There are few, if any, UFO reports for the middle and latter part of 1949 in the ATIC files. Only the logbook, showing incoming reports, gives any idea of the activity of this period. The meager effort that was being made was going into a report that evaluated old UFO reports, those received prior to the spring of 1949. Project Grudge thought that they were writing a final report on the UFO's.

From the small bits of correspondence and memos that were in the ATIC files, it was apparent that Project Grudge thought that the UFO was on its way out. Any writers inquiring about UFO activity were referred to the debunking press release given out just after the Post article had been published. There was no more to say. Project Grudge thought they were winning the UFO battle; the writers thought that they were covering up a terrific news story—the story that the Air Force knew what flying saucers were and weren't telling.

By late fall 1949 the material for several UFO stories had been collected by writers who had been traveling all over the United States talking to people who had seen UFO's. By early winter the material had been worked up into UFO stories. In December the presses began to roll. True magazine "scooped" the world with their story that UFO's were from outer space.

The True article, entitled, "The Flying Saucers Are Real," was written by Donald Keyhoe. The article opened with a hard punch. In the first paragraph Keyhoe concluded that after eight months of extensive research he had found evidence that the earth was being closely scrutinized by intelligent beings. Their vehicles were the so-called flying saucers. Then he proceeded to prove his point. His argument was built around the three classics: the Mantell, the Chiles-Whitted, and the Gorman incidents. He took each sighting, detailed the "facts," ripped the official Air Force conclusions to shreds, and presented his own analysis. He threw in a varied assortment of technical facts that gave the article a distinct, authoritative flavor. This, combined with the fact that True had the name for printing the truth, hit the reading public like an 8-inch howitzer. Hours after it appeared in subscribers' mailboxes and on the newsstands, radio and TV commentators and newspapers were giving it a big play. UFO's were back in business, to stay. True was in business too. It is rumored among magazine publishers that Don Keyhoe's article in True was one of the most widely read and widely discussed magazine articles in history.

The Air Force had inadvertently helped Keyhoe—in fact, they made his story a success. He and several other writers had contacted the Air Force asking for information for their magazine articles. But, knowing that the articles were pro-saucer, the writers were unceremoniously sloughed off. Keyhoe carried his fight right to the top, to General Sory Smith, Director of the Office of Public Information, but still no dice—the Air Force wasn't divulging any more than they had already told. Keyhoe construed this to mean tight security, the tightest type of security. Keyhoe had one more approach, however. He was an ex-Annapolis graduate, and among his classmates were such people as Admiral Delmar Fahrney, then a top figure in the Navy guided missile program and Admiral Calvin Bolster, the Director of the Office of Naval Research. He went to see them but they couldn't help him. He knew that this meant the real UFO story was big and that it could be only one thing—interplanetary spaceships or earthly weapons—and his contacts denied they were earthly weapons. He played this security angle in his True article and in a later book, and it gave the story the needed punch.

But the Air Force wasn't trying to cover up. It was just that they didn't want Keyhoe or any other saucer fans in their hair. They couldn't be bothered. They didn't believe in flying saucers and couldn't feature anybody else believing. Believing, to the people in ATIC in 1949, meant even raising the possibility that there might be something to the reports.

The Air Force had a plan to counter the Keyhoe article, or any other story that might appear. The plan origina-

ted at ATIC. It called for a general officer to hold a short press conference, flash his stars, and speak the magic words "hoaxes, hallucinations, and the misidentification of known objects," True, Keyhoe and the rest would go broke trying to peddle their magazines. The True article did come out, the general spoke, the public laughed, and Keyhoe and True got rich. Only the other magazines that had planned to run UFO stories, and that were scooped by True, lost out. Their stories were killed—they would have been an anti-climax to Keyhoe's potboiler.

The Air Force's short press conference was followed by a press release. On December 27, 1949, it was announced that Project Grudge had been closed out and the final report on UFO's would be released to the press in a few days. When it was released it caused widespread interest because, supposedly, this was all that the Air Force knew about UFO's. Once again, instead of throwing large amounts of cold water on the UFO's, it only caused more confusion.

The report was officially titled "Unidentified Flying Objects—Project Grudge," Technical Report No. 102-AC-49/15-100. But it was widely referred to as the Grudge Report.

The Grudge Report was a typical military report. There

was the body of the report, which contained the short discussion, conclusions, and recommendations. Then there were several appendixes that were supposed to substantiate the conclusions and recommendations made in the report.

One of the appendixes was the final report of Dr. J. Allen Hynek, Project Grudge's contract astronomer. Dr. Hynek and his staff had studied 237 of the best UFO reports. They had spent several months analyzing each report. By searching through astronomical journals and checking the location of various celestial bodies, they found that some UFO's could be explained. Of the 237 reports he and his staff examined, 32 per cent could be explained astronomically.

The Air Force Air Weather Service and the Air Force Cambridge Research Laboratory had sifted the reports for UFO's that might have been balloons. These two organizations had data on the flights of both the regular weather balloons and the huge, high-flying skyhooks. They wrote off 12 per cent of the 237 UFO reports under study as balloons.

This left 56 per cent still unknown. By weeding out the hoaxes, the reports that were too nebulous to evaluate, and reports that could well be misidentified airplanes,

Project Grudge disposed of another 33 per cent of the reports. This left 23 per cent that fell in the "unknown" category.

There were more appendixes. The Rand Corporation, one of the most unpublicized yet highly competent contractors to the Air Force, looked over the reports and made the statement, "We have found nothing which would seriously controvert simple rational explanations of the various phenomena in terms of balloons, conventional aircraft, planets, meteors, bits of paper, optical illusions, practical jokers, psychopathological reporters, and the like." But Rand's comment didn't help a great deal because they didn't come up with any solutions to any of the 23 per cent unknown.

The Psychology Branch of the Air Force's Aeromedical Laboratory took a pass at the psychological angles. They said, "there are sufficient psychological explanations for the reports of unidentified objects to provide plausible explanations for reports not otherwise explainable." They pointed out that some people have "spots in front of their eyes" due to minute solid particles that float about in the fluids of the eye and cast shadows on the retina. Then they pointed out that some people are just plain nuts. Many people who read the Grudge Report took these two points to mean that all UFO observers either had spots in front of their eyes or were nuts. They broke the reports down statistically. The people who wrote the report found that over 70 per cent of the people making sightings reported a light-colored object. (This I doubt, but that's what the report said.) They said a big point of these reports of light-colored objects was that any high-flying object will appear to be dark against the sky. For this reason the UFO's couldn't be real.

I suggest that the next time you are outdoors and see a bomber go over at high altitude you look at it closely. Unless it's painted a dark color it won't look dark.

The U.S. Weather Bureau wrote an extremely compre-hensive and interesting report on all types of lightning. It was included in the Grudge Report but contained a note: "None of the recorded incidents appear to have been lightning."

There was one last appendix. It was entitled "Summary of the Evaluation of Remaining Reports." What the title meant was, We have 23 per cent of the reports that we can't explain but we have to explain them because we don't believe in flying saucers. This appendix contribu-ted greatly to the usage of the analogy to the Dark Ages, the age of "intellectual stagnation."

This appendix was important—it was the meat of the

whole report. Every UFO sighting had been carefully checked, and those with answers had been sifted out. Then the ones listed in "Summary of the Evaluation of Remaining Reports" should be the best UFO reports— the ones with no answers.

This was the appendix that the newsmen grabbed at when the Grudge Report was released. It contained the big story. But if you'll check back through old newspaper files you will hardly find a mention of the Grudge Report.

I was told that reporters just didn't believe it when I tried to find out why the Grudge Report hadn't been mentioned in the newspapers. I got the story from a newspaper correspondent in Washington whom I came to know pretty well and who kept me filled in on the latest UFO scuttlebutt being passed around the Washington press circles. He was one of those humans who had a brain like a filing cabinet; he could remember everything about everything. UFO's were a hobby of his. He remembered when the Grudge Report came out; in fact, he'd managed to get a copy of his own. He said the report had been quite impressive, but only in its ambiguousness, illogical reasoning, and very apparent effort to write off all UFO reports at any cost. He, personally, thought that it was a poor attempt to put out a "fake"

*report, full of misleading information, to cover up the
real story. Others, he told me, just plainly and simply
didn't know what to think—they were confused.*

And they had every right to be confused.

*As an example of the way that many of the better
reports of the 1947-49 period were "evaluated" let's
take the report of a pilot who tangled with a UFO near
Washington, D.C., on the night of November 18, 1948.*

*At about 9:45 EST I noticed a light moving generally
north to south over Andrews AFB. It appeared to be
one continuous, glowing white light. I thought it was an
aircraft with only one landing light so I moved in closer
to check, as I wanted to get into the landing pattern. I
was well above landing traffic altitude at this time. As I
neared the light I noticed that it was not another airplane. Just then it began to take violent evasive action so I
tried to close on it. I made first contact at 2,700 feet over
the field. I switched my navigation lights on and off but
got no answer so I went in closer—but the light quickly
flew up and over my airplane. I then tried to close again
but the light turned. I tried to turn inside of its turn
and, at the same time, get the light between the moon
and me, but even with my flaps lowered I couldn't turn
inside the light. I never did manage to get into a position*

*where the light was silhouetted against the moon.
I chased the light up and down and around for about 10
minutes, then as a last resort I made a pass and turned
on my landing lights. Just before the object made a final
tight turn and headed for the coast I saw that it was a
dark gray oval-shaped object, smaller than my T-6. I
couldn't tell if the light was on the object or if the whole
object had been glowing.*

*Two officers and a crew chief, a master sergeant, com-
pletely corroborated the pilot's report. They had been
standing on the flight line and had witnessed the entire
incident.*

*The Air Weather Service, who had been called in as
experts on weather balloons, read this report. They said,
"Definitely not a balloon." Dr. Hynek said, "No astronomical explanation." It wasn't another airplane and it
wasn't a hallucination.*

*But Project Grudge had an answer, it was a weather
balloon. There was no explanation as to why they had so
glibly reversed the decision of the Air Weather Service.*

There was an answer for every report.

From the 600 pages of appendixes, discussions of the

appendixes, and careful studies of UFO reports, it was concluded that:

1. Evaluation of reports of unidentified flying objects constitute no direct threat to the national security of the United States.

2. Reports of unidentified flying objects are the result of:

a. A mild form of mass hysteria or "war nerves."

b. Individuals who fabricate such reports to perpetrate a hoax or seek publicity.

c. Psychopathological persons.

d. Misidentification of various conventional objects.

It was recommended that Project Grudge be "reduced in scope" and that only "those reports clearly indicating realistic technical applications" be sent to Grudge. There was a note below these recommendations. It said, "It is readily apparent that further study along present lines would only confirm the findings presented herein."

Somebody read the note and concurred because with the completion and approval of the Grudge Report, Project

Grudge folded. People could rant and rave, see flying saucers, pink elephants, sea serpents, or Harvey, but it was no concern of ATIC's.

CHAPTER 6

The Presses Roll—The Air Force Shrugs

The Grudge Report was supposedly not for general distribution. A few copies were sent to the Air Force Press Desk in the Pentagon and reporters and writers could come in and read it. But a good many copies did get into circulation. The Air Force Press Room wasn't the best place to sit and study a 600-page report, and a quick glance at the report showed that it required some study—if no more than to find out what the authors were trying to prove—so several dozen copies got into circulation. I know that these "liberated" copies of the Grudge Report had been thoroughly studied because nearly every writer who came to ATIC during the time that I was in charge of Project Blue Book carried a copy.

Since the press had some questions about the motives behind releasing the Grudge Report, it received very little publicity while the writers put out feelers. Consequently in early 1950 you didn't read much about flying saucers.

Evidently certain people in the Air Force thought this lull in publicity meant that the UFO's had finally died because Project Grudge was junked. All the project files, hundreds of pounds of reports, memos, photos, sketches, and other assorted bits of paper were unceremoniously yanked out of their filing cabinets, tied up with string, and chucked into an old storage case. I would guess that many reports ended up as "souvenirs" because a year later, when I exhumed these files, there were a lot of reports missing.

About this time the official Air Force UFO project had one last post-death muscular spasm. The last bundle of reports had just landed on top of the pile in the storage case when ATIC received a letter from the Director of Intelligence of the Air Force. In official language it said, "What gives?" There had been no order to end Project Grudge. The answer went back that Project Grudge had not been disbanded; the project functions had been transferred and it was no longer a "special" project. From now on UFO reports would be processed through normal intelligence channels along with other intelligence reports.

To show good faith ATIC requested permission to issue a new Air Force-wide bulletin which was duly mimeographed and disseminated. In essence it said that Air Force Headquarters had directed ATIC to continue to collect and evaluate reports of unidentified flying objects. It went on to explain that most UFO reports were trash. It pointed out the findings of the Grudge Report in such strong language that by the time the recipient of the bulletin had finished reading it, he would be ashamed to send in a report. To cinch the deal the bulletins must have been disseminated only to troops in Outer Mongolia because I never found anyone in the field who had ever received a copy.

As the Air Force UFO-investigating activity dropped to nil, the press activity skyrocketed to a new peak. A dozen people took off to dig up their own UFO stories and to draw their own conclusions.

After a quiet January, True again clobbered the reading public. This time it was a story in the March 1950 issue and it was entitled, "How Scientists Tracked Flying Saucers." It was written by none other than the man who was at that time in charge of a team of Navy scientists at the super hush-hush guided missile test and development area, White Sands Proving Ground, New Mexico. He was Commander R. B. McLaughlin, an Annapolis graduate and a Regular Navy officer. His story had been cleared by the military and was in absolute, 180-degree, direct contradiction to every press release that had been made by the military in the past two years. Not only did the commander believe that he had proved that UFO's were real but that he knew what they were. "I am convinced," he wrote in the True article, "that it," referring to a UFO he had seen at White Sands, "was a flying saucer, and further, that these disks are spaceships from another planet, operated by animate, intelligent beings."

On several occasions during 1948 and 1949, McLaughlin or his crew at the White Sands Proving Ground had made good UFO sightings. The best one was made on April 24, 1949, when the commander's crew of engineers, scientists, and technicians were getting ready to launch one of the huge 100-foot-diameter skyhook balloons. It was 10:30 A.M. on an absolutely clear Sunday morning. Prior to the launching, the crew had sent up a small weather balloon to check the winds at lower levels. One man was watching the balloon through a theodolite, an instrument similar to a surveyor's transit built around a 25-power telescope, one man was holding a stop watch, and a third had a clipboard to record the measured data. The crew had tracked the balloon to about 10,000 feet when one of them suddenly shouted and pointed off to the left. The whole crew looked at the part of the sky where the man was excitedly pointing, and there was a UFO. "It didn't appear to be large," one of the scientists later said, "but it was plainly visible. It was easy to see that it was elliptical in shape and had a 'whitish-silver color.'" After taking a split second to realize what they were looking at, one of the men swung the theodolite around to pick up the object, and the timer reset his stop watch. For sixty seconds they tracked the UFO as it moved toward the east. In about fifty-five seconds it had dropped from an angle of elevation of 45 degrees to 25 degrees, then it zoomed upward and in a few seconds it was out of sight. The crew heard no sound and the New Mexico desert was so calm that day that they could have heard "a whisper a mile away."

When they reduced the data they had collected, McLaughlin and crew found out that the UFO had been traveling 4 degrees per second. At one time during the observed portion of its flight, the UFO had passed in front of a range of mountains that were visible to the observers. Using this as a check point, they estimated the size of the UFO to be 40 feet wide and 100 feet long, and they computed that the UFO had been at an altitude of 296,000 feet, or 56 miles, when they had first seen it, and that it was traveling 7 miles per second.

This wasn't the only UFO sighting made by White Sands scientists. On April 5, 1948, another team watched a UFO for several minutes as it streaked across the afternoon sky in a series of violent maneuvers. The disk-shaped object was about a fifth the size of a full moon.

On another occasion the crew of a C-47 that was tracking a skyhook balloon saw two similar UFO's come loping in from just above the horizon, circle the balloon, which was flying at just under 90,000 feet, and rapidly leave. When the balloon was recovered it was ripped.

I knew the two pilots of the C-47; both of them now believe in flying saucers. And they aren't alone; so do the people of the Aeronautical Division of General Mills who launch and track the big skyhook balloons. These scientists and engineers all have seen UFO's and they aren't their own balloons. I was almost tossed out of the General Mills offices into a cold January Minneapolis snowstorm for suggesting such a thing—but that comes later in our history of the UFO.

I don't know what these people saw. There has been a lot of interest generated by these sightings because of the extremely high qualifications and caliber of the obser-vers. There is some legitimate doubt as to the accuracy of the speed and altitude figures that McLaughlin's crew arrived at from the data they measured with their theodolite. This doesn't mean much, however. Even if they were off by a factor of 100 per cent, the speeds and altitudes would be fantastic, and besides they looked at the UFO through a 25-power telescope and swore that it was a flat, oval-shaped object. Balloons, birds, and airplanes aren't flat and oval-shaped.

*Astrophysicist Dr. Donald Menzel, in a book entitled
Flying Saucers, says they saw a refracted image of their
own balloon caused by an atmospheric phenomenon.
Maybe he is right, but the General Mills people don't
believe it. And their disagreement is backed up by years
of practical experience with the atmosphere, its tricks
and its illusions.*

*When the March issue of True magazine carrying
Commander McLaughlin's story about how the White
Sands Scientists had tracked UFO's reached the public, it
stirred up a hornets' nest. Donald Keyhoe's article in the
January True had converted many people but there were
still a few heathens. The fact that government scientists
had seen UFO's, and were admitting it, took care of
a large percentage of these heathens. More and more
people were believing in flying saucers.*

*The Navy had no comment to make about the sightings,
but they did comment on McLaughlin. It seems that
several months before, at the suggestion of a group of
scientists at White Sands, McLaughlin had carefully
written up the details of the sightings and forwarded
them to Washington. The report contained no personal opinions, just facts. The comments on McLaughlin's report had been wired back to White Sands from
Washington and they were, "What are you drinking out*

there?" A very intelligent answer—and it came from an admiral in the Navy's guided missile program.

By the time his story was published, McLaughlin was no longer at White Sands; he was at sea on the destroyer Bristol. Maybe he answered the admiral's wire.

The Air Force had no comment to make on McLaughlin's story. People at ATIC just shrugged and smiled as they walked by the remains of Project Grudge, and continued to "process UFO reports through regular intelligence channels."

In early 1950 the UFO's moved down to Mexico. The newspapers were full of reports. Tourists were bringing back more saucer stories than hand-tooled, genuine leather purses. Time reported that pickpockets were doing a fabulous business working the sky-gazing crowds that gathered when a plativolo was seen. Mexico's Department of National Defense reported that there had been some good reports but that the stories of finding crashed saucers weren't true.

On March 8 one of the best UFO sightings of 1950 took place right over ATIC.

About midmorning on this date a TWA airliner was

coming in to land at the Dayton Municipal Airport. As the pilot circled to get into the traffic pattern, he and his copilot saw a bright light hovering off to the southeast. The pilot called the tower operators at the airport to tell them about the light, but before he could say anything, the tower operators told him they were looking at it too. They had called the operations office of the Ohio Air National Guard, which was located at the airport, and while the tower operators were talking, an Air Guard pilot was running toward an F-51, dragging his parachute, helmet, and oxygen mask.

I knew the pilot, and he later told me, "I wanted to find out once and for all what these screwy flying saucer reports were all about."

While the F-51 was warming up, the tower operators called ATIC and told them about the UFO and where to look to see it. The people at ATIC rushed out and there it was—an extremely bright light, much brighter and larger than a star. Whatever it was, it was high because every once in a while it would be blanked out by the thick, high, scattered clouds that were in the area. While the group of people were standing in front of ATIC watching the light, somebody ran in and called the radar lab at Wright Field to see if they had any radar "on the air." The people in the lab said that they didn't have, but they could get operational in a hurry. They said they would search southeast of the field with their radar and suggested that ATIC send some people over. By the time the ATIC people arrived at the radar lab the radar was on the air and had a target in the same position as the light that everyone was looking at. The radar was also picking up the Air Guard F-51 and an F-51 that had been scrambled from Wright-Patterson. The pilots of the Air Guard '51 and the Wright-Patterson '51 could both see the UFO, and they were going after it. The master sergeant who was operating the radar called the F-51's on the radio, got them together and started to vector them toward the target. As the two airplanes climbed they kept up a continual conversation with the radar operator to make sure they were all after the same thing. For several minutes they could clearly see the UFO, but when they reached about 15,000 feet, the clouds moved in and they lost it. The pilots made a quick decision; since radar showed that they were getting closer to the target, they decided to spread out to keep from colliding with one another and to go up through the clouds. They went on instruments and in a few seconds they were in the cloud. It was much worse than they'd expected; the cloud was thick, and the airplanes were icing up fast. An F-51 is far from being a good instrument ship, but they stayed in their climb until radar called and said that they were close to the target; in fact, almost on it. The pilots had another hurried radio conference and decided that since the weather was so bad they'd better come down. If a UFO, or something, was in the clouds, they'd hit it before they could see it. So they made a wise decision; they dropped the noses of their airplanes and dove back down into the clear. They circled awhile but the clouds didn't break. In a few minutes the master sergeant on the radar reported that the target was fading fast. The F-51's went in and landed.

When the target faded on the radar, some of the people went outside to visually look for the UFO, but it was obscured by clouds, and the clouds stayed for an hour. When it finally did clear for a few minutes, the UFO was gone.

A conference was held at ATIC that afternoon. It included Roy James, ATIC's electronics specialist and expert on radar UFO's. Roy had been over at the radar lab and had seen the UFO on the scope but neither the F-51 pilots nor the master sergeant who operated the radar were at the conference. The records show that at this meeting a unanimous decision was reached as to the identity of the UFO's. The bright light was Venus since Venus was in the southeast during midmorning on March 8, 1950, and the radar return was caused by the ice-laden cloud that the F-51 pilots had encountered. Ice-laden clouds can cause a radar return. The group of intelligence specialists at the meeting decided that this was further proved by the fact that as the F-51's approached the center of the cloud their radar return appeared to approach the UFO target on the radarscope. They were near the UFO and near ice, so the UFO must have been ice.

The case was closed.

I had read the report of this sighting but I hadn't paid too much attention to it because it had been "solved." But one day almost two years later I got a telephone call at my office at Project Blue Book. It was a master sergeant, the master sergeant who had been operating the radar at the lab. He'd just heard that the Air Force was again seriously investigating UFO's and he wanted to see what had been said about the Dayton Incident. He came over, read the report, and violently disagreed with what had been decided upon as the answer. He said that he'd been working with radar before World War II; he'd helped with the operational tests on the first microwave warning radars developed early in the war by a group headed by Dr. Luis Alvarez. He said that what he saw on that radarscope was no ice cloud; it was some type of aircraft. He'd seen every conceivable type of weather target on radar, he told me; thunderstorms, ice-laden clouds, targets caused by temperature inversions, and

*the works. They all had similar characteristics—the tar-
get was "fuzzy" and varied in intensity. But in this case
the target was a good, solid return and he was convinced that it was caused by a good, solid object.*

*And besides, he said, when the target began to fade on
his scope he had raised the tilt of the antenna and the
target came back, indicating that whatever it was, it was
climbing. Ice-laden clouds don't climb, he commented
rather bitterly.*

*Nor did the pilot of one of the F-51's agree with the
ATIC analysis. The pilot who had been leading the
two-ship flight of F-51's on that day told me that what
he saw was no planet. While he and his wing man were
climbing, and before the clouds obscured it, they both
got a good look at the UFO, and it was getting bigger
and more distinct all the time. As they climbed, the light
began to take on a shape; it was definitely round. And if
it had been Venus it should have been in the same part
of the sky the next day, but the pilot said that he'd looked
and it wasn't there. The ATIC report doesn't mention
this point.*

*I remember asking him a second time what the UFO
looked like; he said, "huge and metallic"—shades of the
Mantell Incident.*

The Dayton Incident didn't get much of a play from the press because officially it wasn't an unknown and there's nothing intriguing about an ice cloud and Venus. There were UFO reports in the newspapers, however.

One story that was widely printed was about a sighting at the naval air station at Dallas, Texas. Just before noon on March 16, Chief Petty Officer Charles Lewis saw a disk-shaped UFO come streaking across the sky and buzz a high-flying B-36. Lewis first saw the UFO coming in from the north, lower than the B-36; then he saw it pull up to the big bomber as it got closer. It hovered under the B-36 for an instant, then it went speeding off and disappeared. When the press inquired about the incident, Captain M. A. Nation, commander of the air station, vouched for his chief and added that the base tower operators had seen and reported a UFO to him about ten days before.

This story didn't run long because the next day a bigger one broke when the sky over the little town of Farmington, New Mexico, about 170 miles northwest of Albuquerque, was literally invaded by UFO's. Every major newspaper carried the story. The UFO's had apparently been congregating over the four corners area for two days because several people had reported seeing UFO's on March 15 and 16. But the seventeenth was the big day, every saucer this side of Polaris must have made a successful rendezvous over Farmington, because on that day most of the town's 3,600 citizens saw the mass fly-by. The first reports were made at 10:15 A.M.; then for an hour the air was full of flying saucers. Estimates of the number varied from a conservative 500 to "thousands." Most all the observers said the UFO's were saucer-shaped, traveled at almost unbelievable speeds, and didn't seem to have any set flight path. They would dart in and out and seemed to avoid collisions only by inches. There was no doubt that they weren't hallucinations because the mayor, the local newspaper staff, ex-pilots, the highway patrol, and every type of person who makes up a community of 3,600 saw them.

I've talked to several people who were in Farmington and saw this now famous UFO display of St. Patrick's Day, 1950. I've heard dozens of explanations—cotton blowing in the wind, bugs' wings reflecting sunlight, a hoax to put Farmington on the map, and real honest-to-goodness flying saucers. One explanation was never publicized, however, and if there is an explanation, it is the best. Under certain conditions of extreme cold, probably 50 to 60 degrees below zero, the plastic bag of a skyhook balloon will get very brittle, and will take on the characteristics of a huge light bulb. If a sudden gust of wind or some other disturbance hits the balloon, it will shatter into a thousand pieces. As these pieces of plastic float down and are carried along by the wind, they could look like thousands of flying saucers.

On St. Patrick's Day a skyhook balloon launched from Holloman AFB, adjacent to the White Sands Proving Ground, did burst near Farmington, and it was cold enough at 60,000 feet to make the balloon brittle. True, the people at Farmington never found any pieces of plastic, but the small pieces of plastic are literally as light as feathers and could have floated far beyond the city.

The next day, on March 18, the Air Force, prodded by the press, shrugged and said, "There's nothing to it," but they had no explanation.

True magazine came through for a third time when their April issue, which was published during the latter part of March 1950, carried a roundup of UFO photos. They offered seven photos as proof that UFO's existed. It didn't take a photo-interpretation expert to tell that all seven could well be of doubtful lineage, nevertheless the collection of photos added fuel to the already smoldering fire. The U.S. public was hearing a lot about flying saucers and all of it was on the pro side. For somebody who didn't believe in the things, the public thought that the Air Force was being mighty quiet.

*The subject took on added interest on the night of March
26, when a famous news commentator said the UFO's
were from Russia. The next night Henry J. Taylor, in a
broadcast from Dallas, Texas, said that the UFO's were
Uncle Sam's own. He couldn't tell all he knew, but a flying saucer had been found on the beach near Galveston,
Texas. It had USAF markings.*

*Two nights later a Los Angeles television station cut into
a regular program with a special news flash; later in the
evening the announcer said they would show the first
photos of the real thing, our military's flying saucer. The
photos turned out to be of the Navy XF-5-U, a World
War II experimental aircraft that never flew.*

The public was now thoroughly confused.

*By now the words "flying saucer" were being batted
around by every newspaper reporter, radio and TV
newscaster, comedian, and man on the street. Some of
the comments weren't complimentary, but as Theorem
I of the publicity racket goes, "It doesn't make any difference what's said as long as the name's spelled right."*

*Early in April the publication that is highly revered by
so many, U.S. News and World Report, threw in their
lot. The UFO's belonged to the Navy. Up popped the old
non-flying XF-5-U again.*

Events drifted back to normal when Edward R. Murrow made UFO's the subject of one of his TV documentaries. He took his viewers around the U.S., talked to Kenneth Arnold, of original UFO fame, by phone and got the story of Captain Mantell's death from a reporter "who was there." Sandwiched in between accounts of actual UFO sightings were the pro and con opinions of top Washington brass, scientists, and the man on the street.

Even the staid New York Times, which had until now stayed out of UFO controversy, broke down and ran an editorial entitled, "Those Flying Saucers—Are They or Aren't They?"

All of this activity did little to shock the military out of their dogma. They admitted that the UFO investigation really hadn't been discontinued. "Any substantial reports of any unusual aerial phenomena would be processed through normal intelligence channels," they told the press.

Ever since July 4, 1947, ten days after the first flying saucer report, airline pilots had been reporting that they had seen UFO's. But the reports weren't frequent— maybe one every few months. In the spring of 1950 this changed, however, and the airline pilots began to make more and more reports—good reports. The reports went to ATIC but they didn't receive much attention. In a few instances there was a semblance of an investigation but it was halfhearted. The reports reached the newspapers too, and here they received a great deal more attention. The reports were investigated, and the stories checked and rechecked. When airline crews began to turn in one UFO report after another, it was difficult to believe the old "hoax, hallucination, and misidentification of known objects" routine. In April, May, and June of 1950 there were over thirty-five good reports from airline crews.

One of these was a report from a Chicago and Southern crew who were flying a DC-3 from Memphis to Little Rock, Arkansas, on the night of March 31. It was an exceptionally clear night, no clouds or haze, a wonderful night to fly. At exactly nine twenty-nine by the cockpit clock the pilot, a Jack Adams, noticed a white light off to his left. The copilot, G. W. Anderson, was looking at the chart but out of the corner of his eye he saw the pilot lean forward and look out the window, so he looked out too. He saw the light just as the pilot said, "What's that?"

The copilot's answer was classic: "No, not one of those things."

Both pilots had only recently voiced their opinions regarding the flying saucers and they weren't complimentary.

As they watched the UFO, it passed across the nose of their DC-3 and they got a fairly good look at it. Neither the pilot nor the copilot was positive of the object's shape because it was "shadowy" but they assumed it was disk-shaped because of the circular arrangement of eight or ten "portholes," each one glowing from a strong bluish-white light that seemed to come from the inside of whatever it was that they saw. The UFO also had a blinking white light on top, a fact that led many people to speculate that this UFO was another airliner. But this idea was quashed when it was announced that there were no other airliners in the area. The crew of the DC-3, when questioned on this possibility, were definite in their answers. If it had been another airplane, they could have read the number, seen the passengers, and darn near reached out and slugged the pilot for getting so close to them.

About a month later, over northern Indiana, TWA treated all the passengers of one of their DC-3 flights to a view of a UFO that looked like a "big glob of molten metal."

The official answer for this incident is that the huge

orange-red UFO was nothing more than the light from the many northern Indiana blast furnaces reflecting a haze layer. Could be, but the pilots say no.

There were similar sightings in North Korea two years later—and FEAF Bomber Command had caused a shortage of blast furnaces in North Korea.

UFO sightings by airline pilots always interested me as much as any type of sighting. Pilots in general should be competent observers simply because they spend a large part of their lives looking around the sky. And pilots do look; one of the first things an aviation cadet is taught is to "Keep your head on a swivel"; in other words, keep looking around the sky. Of all the pilots, the airline pilots are the cream of this group of good observers. Possibly some second lieutenant just out of flying school could be confused by some unusual formation of ground lights, a meteor, or a star, but airline pilots have flown thousands of hours or they wouldn't be sitting in the left seat of an airliner, and they should be familiar with a host of unusual sights.

One afternoon in February 1953 I had an opportunity to further my study of UFO sightings by airline pilots. I had been out at Air Defense Command Headquarters in Colorado Springs and was flying back East on a United Airlines DC-6. There weren't many passengers on the airplane that afternoon but, as usual, the captain came strolling back through the cabin to chat. When he got to me he sat down in the next seat. We talked a few minutes; then I asked him what he knew about flying saucers. He sort of laughed and said that a dozen people a week asked that question, but when I told him who I was and why I was interested, his attitude changed. He said that he'd never seen a UFO but he knew a lot of pilots on United who had. One man, he told me, had seen one several years ago. He'd reported it but he had been sloughed off like the rest. But he was so convinced that he'd seen something unusual that he'd gone out and bought a Leica camera with a 105-mm. telephoto lens, learned how to use it, and now he carried it religiously during his flights.

There was a lull in the conversation, then the captain said, "Do you really want to get an opinion about flying saucers?"

I said I did.

"O.K.," I remember his saying, "how much of a layover do you have in Chicago?"

I had about two hours.

"All right, as soon as we get to Chicago I'll meet you at Caffarello's, across the street from the terminal building. I'll see who else is in and I'll bring them along."

I thanked him and he went back up front.

I waited around the bar at Caffarello's for an hour. I'd just about decided that he wasn't going to make it and that I'd better get back to catch my flight to Dayton when he and three other pilots came in. We got a big booth in the coffee shop because he'd called three more off-duty pilots who lived in Chicago and they were coming over too. I don't remember any of the men's names because I didn't make any attempt to. This was just an informal bull session and not an official interrogation, but I really got the scoop on what airline pilots think about UFO's.

First of all they didn't pull any punches about what they thought about the Air Force and its investigation of UFO reports. One of the men got right down to the point: "If I saw a flying saucer flying wing-tip formation with me and could see little men waving—even if my whole load of passengers saw it—I wouldn't report it to the Air Force."

Another man cut in, "Remember the thing Jack Adams said he saw down by Memphis?"

I said I did.

"He reported that to the Air Force and some red-hot character met him in Memphis on his next trip. He talked to Adams a few minutes and then told him that he'd seen a meteor. Adams felt like a fool. Hell, I know Jack Adams well and he's the most conservative guy I know. If he said he saw something with glowing portholes, he saw something with glowing portholes—and it wasn't a meteor."

Even though I didn't remember the pilots' names I'll never forget their comments. They didn't like the way the Air Force had handled UFO reports and I was the Air Force's "Mr. Flying Saucer." As quickly as one of the pilots would set me up and bat me down, the next one grabbed me off the floor and took his turn. But I couldn't complain too much; I'd asked for it. I think that this group of seven pilots pretty much represented the feelings of a lot of the airline pilots. They weren't wide-eyed space fans, but they and their fellow pilots had seen something and whatever they'd seen weren't hallucinations, mass hysteria, balloons, or meteors.

Three of the men at the Caffarello conference had seen UFO's or, to use their terminology, they had seen something they couldn't identify as a known object. Two of these men had seen odd lights closely following their airplanes at night. Both had checked and double-checked with CAA, but no other aircraft was in the area. Both admitted, however, that they hadn't seen enough to class what they'd seen as good UFO sighting. But the third man had a lulu.

If I recall correctly, this pilot was flying for TWA. One day in March 1952 he, his copilot, and a third person who was either a pilot deadheading home or another crew member, I don't recall which, were flying a C-54 cargo airplane from Chicago to Kansas City. At about 2:30 P.M. the pilot was checking in with the CAA radio at Kirksville, Missouri, flying 500 feet on top of a solid overcast. While he was talking he glanced out at his No. 2 engine, which had been losing oil. Directly in line with it, and a few degrees above, he saw a silvery, disk-shaped object. It was too far out to get a really good look at it, yet it was close enough to be able definitely to make out the shape.

The UFO held its relative position with the C-54 for five or six minutes; then the pilot decided to do a little on-the-spot investigating himself. He started a gradual turn toward the UFO and for about thirty seconds he was getting closer, but then the UFO began to make a left turn. It had apparently slowed down because they were still closing on it.

*About this time the copilot decided that the UFO was
a balloon; it just looked as if the UFO was turning. The
pilot agreed halfway—and since the company wasn't
paying them to intercept balloons, they got back on
their course to Kansas City. They flew on for a few more
minutes with "the darn thing" still off to their left. If it
was a balloon, they should be leaving it behind, the pilot
recalled thinking to himself; if they made a 45-degree
right turn, the "balloon" shouldn't stay off the left wing;
it should drop 'way behind. So they made a 45-degree
right turn, and although the "balloon" dropped back a
little bit, it didn't drop back far enough to be a balloon.
It seemed to put on speed to try to make a turn outside
of the C-54's turn. The pilot continued on around until
he'd made a tight 360-degree turn, and the UFO had
followed, staying outside. They could not judge its speed,
not knowing how far away it was, but to follow even a
C-54 around in a 360-degree turn and to stay outside
all of the time takes a mighty speedy object.*

*This shot the balloon theory right in the head. After the
360-degree turn the UFO seemed to be gradually losing
altitude because it was getting below the level of the
wings. The pilot decided to get a better look. He asked
for full power on all four engines, climbed several thousand feet, and again turned into the UFO. He put the
C-54 in a long glide, headed directly toward it. As they
closed in, the UFO seemed to lose altitude a little faster*

and "sank" into the top of the overcast. Just as the C-54 flashed across the spot where the UFO had disappeared, the crew saw it rise up out of the overcast off their right wing and begin to climb so fast that in several seconds it was out of sight.

Both the pilot and copilot wanted to stay around and look for it but No. 2 engine had started to act up soon after they had put on full power for the climb, and they decided that they'd better get into Kansas City.

I missed my Dayton flight but I heard a good UFO story.

What had the two pilots and their passenger seen? We kicked it around plenty that afternoon. It was no balloon. It wasn't another airplane because when the pilot called Kirksville Radio he'd asked if there were any airplanes in the area. It might possibly have been a reflection of some kind except that when it "sank" into the overcast the pilot said it looked like something sinking into an overcast—it just didn't disappear as a reflection would. Then there was the sudden reappearance off the right wing. These are the types of things you just can't explain.

What did the pilots think it was? Three were sold that the UFO's were interplanetary spacecraft, one man was convinced that they were some U.S. "secret weapon," and three of the men just shook their heads. So did I. We all agreed on one thing—this pilot had seen something and it was something highly unusual.

The meeting broke up about 9:00 P.M. I'd gotten the personal and very candid opinion of seven airline captains, and the opinions of half a hundred more airline pilots had been quoted. I'd learned that the UFO's are discussed often. I'd learned that many airline pilots take UFO sightings very seriously. I learned that some believe they are interplanetary, some think they're a U.S. weapon, and many just don't know. But very few are laughing off the good sightings.

By May 1950 the flying saucer business had hit a new all-time peak.

The Air Force didn't take any side, they just shrugged. There was no attempt to investigate and explain the various sightings. Maybe this was because someone was afraid the answer would be "Unknown." Or maybe it was because a few key officers thought that the eagles or stars on their shoulders made them leaders of all men. If they didn't believe in flying saucers and said so, it would be like calming the stormy Sea of Galilee. "It's all a bunch of damned nonsense," an Air Force colonel who was controlling the UFO investigation said. "There's no such thing as a flying saucer." He went on to say that all people who saw flying saucers were jokers, crackpots, or publicity hounds. Then he gave the airline pilots who'd been reporting UFO's a reprieve. "They were just fatigued," he said. "What they thought were spaceships were windshield reflections."

This was the unbiased processing of UFO reports through normal intelligence channels.

But the U.S. public evidently had more faith in the "crackpot" scientists who were spending millions of the public's dollars at the White Sands Proving Grounds, in the "publicity-mad" military pilots, and the "tired, old" airline pilots, because in a nationwide poll it was found that only 6 per cent of the country's 150,697,361 people agreed with the colonel and said, "There aren't such things."

Ninety-four per cent had different ideas.

CHAPTER 7

The Pentagon Rumbles

On June 25, 1950, the North Korean armies swept down across the 38th parallel and the Korean War was on— the UFO was no longer a news item. But the lady, or gentleman, who first said, "Out of sight is out of mind," had never reckoned with the UFO.

On September 8, 1950, the UFO's were back in the news. On that day it was revealed, via a book entitled Behind the Flying Saucers, that government scientists had recovered and analyzed three different models of flying saucers. And they were fantastic—just like the book. They were made of an unknown super-duper metal and they were manned by little blue uniformed men who ate concentrated food and drank heavy water. The author of the book, Frank Scully, had gotten the story directly from a millionaire oilman, Silas Newton. Newton had in turn heard the story from an employee of his, a mysterious "Dr. Gee," one of the government scientists who had helped analyze the crashed saucers.

The story made news, Newton and "Dr. Gee" made fame, and Scully made money.

A little over two years later Newton and the man who was reportedly the mysterious "Dr. Gee" again made the news. The Denver district attorney's office had looked into the pair's oil business and found that the pockets they were trying to tap didn't contain oil. According to the December 6, 1952, issue of the Saturday Review, the D.A. had charged the two men with a $50,000 con game. One of their $800,000 electronic devices for their oil explorations turned out to be a $4.00 piece of war surplus junk.

Another book came out in the fall of 1950 when Donald Keyhoe expanded his original UFO story that had first appeared in the January 1950 issue of True magazine. Next to Scully's book Keyhoe's book was tame, but it convinced more people. Keyhoe had based his conjecture on fact, and his facts were correct, even if the conjecture wasn't.

Neither the seesaw advances and retreats of the United Nations troops in Korea nor the two flying saucer books seemed to have any effect on the number of UFO reports logged into ATIC, however. By official count, seventy-seven came in the first half of 1950 and seventy-five during the latter half. The actual count could have been more because in 1950, UFO reports were about as popular as sand in spinach, and I would, guess that at least a few wound up in the "circular file."

In early January 1951 I was recalled to active duty
and assigned to Air Technical Intelligence Center as an
intelligence officer. I had been at ATIC only eight and a
half hours when I first heard the words "flying saucer"
officially used. I had never paid a great deal of attention
to flying saucer reports but I had read a few—especially
those that had been made by pilots. I'd managed to collect some 2,000 hours of flying time and had seen many
odd things in the air, but I'd always been able to figure
out what they were in a few seconds. I was convinced
that if a pilot, or any crew member of an airplane, said
that he'd seen something that he couldn't identify he
meant it—it wasn't a hallucination. But I wasn't convinced that flying saucers were spaceships.

My interest in UFO's picked up in a hurry when I
learned that ATIC was the government agency that was
responsible for the UFO project. And I was really impressed when I found out that the person who sat three
desks down and one over from mine was in charge of the
whole UFO show. So when I came to work on my second
morning at ATIC and heard the words "flying saucer
report" being talked about and saw a group of people
standing around the chief of the UFO project's desk I
about sprung an eardrum listening to what they had to
say. It seemed to be a big deal—except that most of them
were laughing. It must be a report of hoax or hallucina-

tion, I remember thinking to myself, but I listened as one of the group told the others about the report.

The night before a Mid-Continent Airlines DC-3 was taxiing out to take off from the airport at Sioux City, Iowa, when the airport control tower operators noticed a bright bluish-white light in the west. The tower operators, thinking that it was another airplane, called the pilot of the DC-3 and told him to be careful since there was another airplane approaching the field. As the DC-3 lined up to take off, both the pilots of the airliner and the tower operators saw the light moving in, but since it was still some distance away the DC-3 was given permission to take off. As it rolled down the runway getting up speed, both the pilot and the copilot were busy, so they didn't see the light approaching. But the tower operators did, and as soon as the DC-3 was airborne, they called and told the pilot to be careful. The copilot said that he saw the light and was watching it. Just then the tower got a call from another airplane that was requesting landing instructions and the operators looked away from the light.

In the DC-3 the pilot and copilot had also looked away from the light for a few seconds. When they looked back, the bluish-white light had apparently closed in because it was much brighter and it was dead ahead. In a split second it closed in and flashed by their right wing—so close that both pilots thought that they would collide with it. When it passed the DC-3, the pilots saw more than a light—they saw a huge object that looked like the "fuselage of a B-29."

When the copilot had recovered he looked out his side window to see if he could see the UFO and there it was, flying formation with them. He yelled at the pilot, who leaned over and looked just in time to see the UFO disappear.

The second look confirmed the Mid-Continent crew's first impression—the object looked like a B-29 without wings. They saw nothing more, only a big "shadowy shape" and the bluish-white light—no windows, no exhaust.

The tower had missed the incident because they were landing the other airplane and the pilot and the copilot didn't have time to call them and tell them about what was going on. All the tower operators could say was that seconds after the UFO had disappeared the light that they had seen was gone.

When the airliner landed in Omaha, the crew filed a report that was forwarded to the Air Force. But this wasn't the only report that was filed; a full colonel from military intelligence had been a passenger on the DC-3. He'd seen the UFO too, and he was mighty impressed.

I thought that this was an interesting report and I wondered what the official reaction would be. The official reaction was a great big, deep belly laugh.

This puzzled me because I'd read that the Air Force was seriously investigating all UFO reports.

I continued to eavesdrop on the discussions about the report all day since the UFO expert was about to "investigate" the incident. He sent out a wire to Flight Service and found that there was a B-36 somewhere in the area of Sioux City at the time of the sighting, and from what I could gather he was trying to blame the sighting on the B-36. When Washington called to get the results of the analysis of the sighting, they must have gotten the B-36 treatment because the case was closed.

I'd only been at ATIC two days and I certainly didn't class myself as an intelligence expert, but it didn't take an expert to see that a B-36, even one piloted by an experienced idiot, could not do what the UFO had done—buzz a DC-3 that was in an airport traffic pattern.

I didn't know it at the time but a similar event had occurred the year before. On the night of May 29, 1950, the crew of an American Airlines DC-6 had just taken off from Washington National Airport, and they were about seven miles west of Mount Vernon when the copilot suddenly looked out and yelled, "Watch it— watch it." The pilot and the engineer looked out to see a bluish-white light closing in on them from dead ahead. The pilot racked the DC-6 up in a tight right turn while the UFO passed by on the left "from eleven to seven o'clock" and a little higher than the airliner. During this time the UFO passed between the full moon and DC-6 and the crew could see the dark silhouette of a "wingless B-29." Its length was about half the diameter of the full moon, and it had a blue flame shooting out the tail end.

Seconds after the UFO had passed by the DC-6, the copilot looked out and there it was again, apparently flying formation off their right wing. Then in a flash of blue flame it was gone—streaking out ahead of the airliner and making a left turn toward the coast.

The pilot of the DC-6, who made the report, had better than 15,000 hours' flying time.

I didn't hear anything about UFO's, or flying saucers, as they were then known, for several weeks but I kept them

in mind and one day I asked one of the old hands at
ATIC about them—specifically I wanted to know about
the Sioux City Incident. Why had it been sloughed off
so lightly? His answer was typical of the official policy
at that time. "One of these days all of these crazy pilots
will kill themselves, the crazy people on the ground will
be locked up, and there won't be any more flying saucer
reports."

But after I knew the people at ATIC a little better,
I found that being anti-saucer wasn't a unanimous
feeling. Some of the intelligence officers took the UFO
reports seriously. One man, who had been on Project
Sign since it was organized back in 1947, was convinced
that the UFO's were interplanetary spaceships. He had
questioned the people in the control tower at Godman
AFB when Captain Mantell was killed chasing the UFO,
and he had spent hours talking to the crew of the DC-3
that was buzzed near Montgomery, Alabama, by a
"cigar-shaped UFO that spouted blue flame." In essence,
he knew UFO history from A to Z because he had "been
there."

I think that it was this controversial thinking that first
aroused my interest in the subject of UFO's and led me
to try to sound out a few more people.

The one thing that stood out to me, being unindoctri-nated in the ways of UFO lore, was the schizophrenic approach so many people at ATIC took. On the surface they sided with the belly-laughers on any saucer issue, but if you were alone with them and started to ridicule the subject, they defended it or at least took an active interest. I learned this one day after I'd been at ATIC about a month.

A belated UFO report had come in from Africa. One of my friends was reading it, so I asked him if I could take a look at it when he had finished. In a few minutes he handed it to me.

When I finished with the report I tossed it back on my friend's desk, with some comment about the whole world's being nuts. I got a reaction I didn't expect; he wasn't so sure the whole world was nuts—maybe the nuts were at ATIC. "What's the deal?" I asked him. "Have they really thoroughly checked out every report and found that there's nothing to any of them?"

He told me that he didn't think so, he'd been at ATIC a long time. He hadn't ever worked on the UFO project, but he had seen many of their reports and knew what they were doing. He just plain didn't buy a lot of their explanations. "And I'm not the only one who thinks this," he added.

"Then why all of the big show of power against the UFO reports?" I remember asking him.

"The powers-that-be are anti-flying saucer," he answered about half bitterly, "and to stay in favor it behooves one to follow suit." As of February 1951 this was the UFO project.

The words "flying saucer" didn't come up again for a month or two. I'd forgotten all about the two words and was deeply engrossed in making an analysis of the performance of the Mig-15. The Mig had just begun to show up in Korea, and finding out more about it was a hot project.

Then the words "flying saucer" drifted across the room once more. But this time instead of belly laughter there was a note of hysteria.

It seems that a writer from Life magazine was doing some research on UFO's and rumor had it that Life was thinking about doing a feature article. The writer had gone to the Office of Public Information in the Pentagon and had inquired about the current status of Project Grudge. To accommodate the writer, the OPI had sent a wire out to ATIC: What is the status of Project Grudge?

Back went a snappy reply: Everything is under control; each new report is being thoroughly analyzed by our experts; our vast files of reports are in tiptop shape; and in general things are hunky-dunky. All UFO reports are hoaxes, hallucinations, and the misidentification of known objects.

Another wire from Washington: Fine, Mr. Bob Ginna of Life is leaving for Dayton. He wants to check some reports.

Bedlam in the raw.

Other magazines had printed UFO stories, and other reporters had visited ATIC, but they had always stayed in the offices of the top brass. For some reason the name Life, the prospects of a feature story, and the feeling that this Bob Ginna was going to ask questions caused sweat to flow at ATIC.

Ginna arrived and the ATIC UFO "expert" talked to him. Ginna later told me about the meeting. He had a long list of questions about reports that had been made over the past four years and every time he asked a question, the "expert" would go tearing out of the room to try to find the file that had the answer. I remember that day people spent a lot of time ripping open bundles of files and pawing through them like a bunch of gophers. Many times, "I'm sorry, that's classified," got ATIC out of a tight spot.

Ginna, I can assure you, was not at all impressed by the "efficiently operating UFO project." People weren't buying the hoax, hallucination, and misidentification stories quite as readily as the Air Force believed.

Where it started or who started it I don't know, but about two months after the visit from Life's representative the official interest in UFO's began to pick up. Lieutenant Jerry Cummings, who had recently been recalled to active duty, took over the project.

Lieutenant Cummings is the type of person who when given a job to do does it. In a few weeks the operation of the UFO project had improved considerably. But the project was still operating under political, economic, and manpower difficulties. Cummings' desk was right across from mine, so 1 began to get a UFO indoctrination via bull sessions. Whenever Jerry found a good report in the pile—and all he had to start with was a pile of papers and files—he'd toss it over for me to read.

Some of the reports were unimpressive, I remember. But a few were just the opposite. Two that I remember Jerry's showing me made me wonder how the UFO's could be sloughed off so lightly. The two reports involved movies taken by Air Force technicians at White Sands Proving Ground in New Mexico.

The guided missile test range at White Sands is fully instrumented to track high, fast-moving objects—the guided missiles. Located over an area of many square miles there are camera stations equipped with cinetheodolite cameras and linked together by a telephone system.

On April 27, 1950, a guided missile had been fired, and as it roared up into the stratosphere and fell back to earth, the camera crews had recorded its flight. All the crews had started to unload their cameras when one of them spotted an object streaking across the sky. By April 1950 every person at White Sands was UFO-conscious, so one member of the camera crew grabbed a telephone headset, alerted the other crews, and told them to get pictures. Unfortunately only one camera had film in it, the rest had already been unloaded, and before they could reload, the UFO was gone. The photos from the one station showed only a smudgy dark object. About all the film proved was that something was in the air and whatever it was, it was moving.

Alerted by this first chance to get a UFO to "run a measured course," the camera crews agreed to keep a sharper lookout. They also got the official O.K. to "shoot" a UFO if one appeared.

Almost exactly a month later another UFO did appear, or at least at the time the camera crews thought that it was a UFO. This time the crews were ready—when the call went out over the telephone net that a UFO had been spotted, all of the crews scanned the sky. Two of the crews saw it and shot several feet of film as the shiny, bright object streaked across the sky.

As soon as the missile tests were completed, the camera crews rushed their film to the processing lab and then took it to the Data Reduction Group. But once again the UFO had eluded man because there were apparently two or more UFO's in the, sky and each camera station had photographed a separate one. The data were no good for triangulation.

The records at ATIC didn't contain the analysis of these films but they did mention the Data Reduction Group at White Sands. So when I later took over the UFO investigation I made several calls in an effort to run down the actual film and the analysis. The files at White Sands, like all files, evidently weren't very good, because the original reports were gone. I did contact a major who was very co-operative and offered to try to find the people who had worked on the analysis of the film. His report, after talking to two men who had done the analysis, was what I'd expected —nothing concrete except that the UFO's were unknowns. He did say that by putting a correction factor in the data gathered by the two cameras they were able to arrive at a rough estimate of speed, altitude, and size. The UFO was "higher than 40,000 feet, traveling over 2,000 miles per hour, and it was over 300 feet in diameter." He cautioned me, however, that these figures were only estimates, based on the possibly erroneous correction factor; therefore they weren't proof of anything—except that something was in the air.

The people at White Sands continued to be on the alert for UFO's while the camera stations were in operation because they realized that if the flight path of a UFO could be accurately plotted and timed it could be positively identified. But no more UFO's showed up.

One day Lieutenant Cummings came over to my desk and dropped a stack of reports in front of me. "All radar reports," he said, "and I'm getting more and more of them every day."

Radar reports, I knew, had always been a controversial point in UFO history, and if more and more radar reports were coming in, there was no doubt that an already controversial issue was going to be compounded.

To understand why there is always some disagreement whenever a flying saucer is picked up on radar, it is necessary to know a little bit about how radar operates.

Basically radar is nothing but a piece of electronic equipment that "shouts" out a radio wave and "listens" for the echo. By "knowing" how fast the radio, or radar, wave travels and from which direction the echo is coming, the radar tells the direction and distance of the object that is causing the echo. Any "solid" object like an airplane, bird, ship, or even a moisture-laden cloud can cause a radar echo. When the echo comes back to the radar set, the radar operator doesn't have to listen for it and time it because this is all done for him by the radar set and he sees the "answer" on his radarscope—a kind of a round TV screen. What the radar operator sees is a bright dot, called a "blip" or a "return." The location of the return on the scope tells him the location of the object that was causing the echo. As the object moves through the sky, the radar operator sees a series of bright dots on his scope that make a track. On some radar sets the altitude of the target, the object causing the echo, can also be measured.

Under normal conditions the path that the radar waves take as they travel through the air is known. Normal conditions are when the temperature and relative humi-

dity of the air decrease with an increase in altitude. But sometimes a condition will occur where at some level, instead of the temperature and/or relative humidity decreasing with altitude, it will begin to increase. This layer of warm, moist air is known as an inversion layer, and it can do all kinds of crazy things to a radar wave. It can cause part of the radar wave to travel in a big arc and actually pick up the ground many miles away. Or it can cause the wave to bend down just enough to pick up trucks, cars, houses, or anything that has a surface perpendicular to the ground level.

One would immediately think that since the ground or a house isn't moving, and a car or truck is moving only 40, 50, or 60 miles an hour, a radar operator should be able to pick these objects out from a fast-moving target. But it isn't as simple as that. The inversion layer shimmers and moves, and one second the radar may be picking up the ground or a truck in one spot and the next second it may be picking up something in a different spot. This causes a series of returns on the scope and can give the illusion of extremely fast or slow speeds.

These are but a few of the effects of an inversion layer on radar. Some of the effects are well known, but others aren't. The 3rd Weather Group at Air Defense Command Headquarters in Colorado Springs has done a lot of work on the effects of weather on radar, and they have developed mathematical formulas for telling how favorable weather conditions are for "anomalous propagation," the two-bit words for false radar targets caused by weather.

The first problem in analyzing reports of UFO's being picked up on radar is to determine if the weather conditions are right to give anomalous propagation. This can be determined by putting weather data into a formula. If they are, then it is necessary to determine whether the radar targets were real or caused by the weather. This is the difficult job. In most cases the only answer is the appearance of the target on the radarscope. Many times a weather target will be a fuzzy and indistinct spot on the scope while a real target, an airplane for example, will be bright and sharp. This question of whether a target looked real is the cause of the majority of the arguments about radar-detected UFO's because it is up to the judgment of the radar operator as to what the target looked like. And whenever human judgment is involved in a decision, there is plenty of room for an argument.

All during the early summer of 1951 Lieutenant Cummings "fought the syndicate" trying to make the UFO respectable. All the time I was continuing to get my indoctrination. Then one day with the speed of a shotgun wedding, the long-overdue respectability arrived. The date was September 12, 1951, and the exact time was 3:04 P.M.

On this date and time a teletype machine at Wright-Patterson AFB began to chatter out a message. Thirty-six inches of paper rolled out of the machine before the operator ripped off the copy, stamped it Operational Immediate, and gave it to a special messenger to deliver to ATIC. Lieutenant Cummings got the message. The report was from the Army Signal Corps radar center at Fort Monmouth, New Jersey, and it was red-hot.

The incident had started two days before, on September 10, at 11:10 A.M., when a student operator was giving a demonstration to a group of visiting brass at the radar school. He demonstrated the set under manual operation for a while, picking up local air traffic, then he announced that that he would demonstrate automatic tracking, in which the set is put on a target and follows it without help from the operator. The set could track objects flying at jet speeds.

The operator spotted an object about 12,000 yards southeast of the station, flying low toward the north. He tried to switch the set to automatic tracking. He failed, tried again, failed again. He turned to his audience of VIPs, embarrassed.

"It's going too fast for the set," he said. "That means it's
going faster than a jet!"

A lot of very important eyebrows lifted. What flies faster
than a jet?

The object was in range for three minutes and the operator kept trying, without success, to get into automatic
track. The target finally went off the scope, leaving the
red-faced operator talking to himself.

The radar technicians at Fort Monmouth had checked
the weather—there wasn't the slightest indication of an
inversion layer.

Twenty-five minutes later the pilot of a T-33 jet trainer,
carrying an Air Force major as passenger and flying
20,000 feet over Point Pleasant, New Jersey, spotted
a dull silver, disklike object far below him. He described it as 30 to 50 feet in diameter and as descending
toward Sandy Hook from an altitude of a mile or so. He
banked the T-33 over and started down after it. As he
shot down, he reported, the object stopped its descent,
hovered, then sped south, made a 120-degree turn, and
vanished out to sea.

The Fort Monmouth Incident then switched back to the
radar group. At 3:15 P.M. they got an excited, almost

*frantic call from headquarters to pick up a target high
and to the north—which was where the first "faster-
than-a-jet" object had vanished—and to pick it up in
a hurry. They got a fix on it and reported that it was
traveling slowly at 93,000 feet. They also could see it
visually as a silver speck.*

What flies 18 miles above the earth?

*The next morning two radar sets picked up another
target that couldn't be tracked automatically. It would
climb, level off, climb again, go into a dive. When it
climbed it went almost straight up.*

*The two-day sensation ended that afternoon when the
radar tracked another unidentified slow-moving object
and tracked it for several minutes.*

*A copy of the message had also gone to Washington.
Before Jerry could digest the thirty-six inches of facts,
ATIC's new chief, Colonel Frank Dunn, got a phone call.
It came from the office of the Director of Intelligence of
the Air Force, Major General (now Lieutenant General)
C. P. Cabell. General Cabell wanted somebody from
ATIC to get to New Jersey—fast—and find out what was
going on. As soon as the reports had been thoroughly
investigated, the general said that he wanted a complete*

personal report. Nothing expedites like a telephone call from a general officer, so in a matter of hours Lieutenant Cummings and Lieutenant Colonel N. R. Rosengarten were on an airliner, New Jersey-bound.

The two officers worked around the clock interrogating the radar operators, their instructors, and the technicians at Fort Monmouth. The pilot who had chased the UFO in the T-33 trainer and his passenger were flown to New York, and they talked to Cummings and Rosengarten. All other radar stations in the area were checked, but their radars hadn't picked up anything unusual.

At about 4:00 A.M. the second morning after they had arrived, the investigation was completed, Cummings later told. He and Lieutenant Colonel Rosengarten couldn't get an airliner out of New York in time to get them to the Pentagon by 10:00 A.M., the time that had been set up for their report, so they chartered an airplane and flew to the capital to brief the general. General Cabell presided over the meeting, and it was attended by his entire staff plus Lieutenant Cummings, Lieutenant Colonel Rosengarten, and a special representative from Republic Aircraft Corporation. The man from Republic supposedly represented a group of top U.S. industrialists and scientists who thought that there should be a lot more sensible answers coming from the Air Force regarding the UFO's. The man was at the meeting at the personal request of a general officer.

Every word of the two-hour meeting was recorded on a wire recorder. The recording was so hot that it was later destroyed, but not before I had heard it several times. I can't tell everything that was said but, to be conservative, it didn't exactly follow the tone of the official Air Force releases—many of the people present at the meeting weren't as convinced that the "hoax, hallucination, and misidentification" answer was quite as positive as the Grudge Report and subsequent press releases made out.

Toward the end of the two-hour conference a general asked Lieutenant Cummings to review the activity of the UFO investigation for the past year and a half. Maybe it was just a lack of sleep, or maybe it was just Cummings, but the general got the straight answer—for all practical purposes the project was dead. Then Cummings proceeded to elaborate on the details, the attitude at ATIC, the opposition to his reorganizing the project, and the methods of processing reports. Lieutenant Cummings didn't miss a point. He later told me that all of the generals and about three fourths of the full colonels present at the meeting turned the shade of purple normally associated with rage while a sort of sickly grin graced the faces of the remaining few. Then one of the generals on the purple-faced team glared at the sickly-grin team and cut loose.

The first thing the general wanted to know was, "Who in hell has been giving me these reports that every decent flying saucer sighting is being investigated?"

Then others picked up the questioning.

"What happened to those two reports that General sent in from Saudi Arabia? He saw those two flying saucers himself."

"And who released this big report, anyway?" another person added, picking up a copy of the Grudge Report and slamming it back down on the table.

Lieutenant Cummings and Lieutenant Colonel Rosengarten came back to ATIC with orders to set up a new project and report back to General Cabell when it was ready to go. But Cummings didn't get a chance to do much work on the new revitalized Project Grudge—it was to keep the old name—because in a few days he was a civilian. He'd been released from active duty because he was needed back at Cal Tech, where he'd been working on an important government project before his recall to active duty.

The day after Cummings got his separation orders, Lieutenant Colonel Rosengarten called me into his office. The colonel was chief of the Aircraft and Missiles branch and one of his many responsibilities was Project Grudge. He said that he knew that I was busy as group leader of my regular group but, if he gave me enough people, could I take Project Grudge? All he wanted me to do was to get it straightened out and operating; then I could go back to trying to outguess the Russians. He threw in a few comments about the good job I'd done straightening out other fouled-up projects. Good old "Rosy." With my ego sufficiently inflated, I said yes.

On many later occasions, when I'd land at home in Dayton just long enough for a clean clothes resupply, or when the telephone would ring at 2:00 A.M. to report a new "hot" sighting and wake up the baby, Mrs. Ruppelt and I have soundly cussed my ego.

I had had the project only a few days when a minor flurry of good UFO reports started. It wasn't supposed to happen because the day after I'd taken over Project Grudge I'd met the ex-UFO "expert" in the hall and he'd nearly doubled up with laughter as he said something about getting stuck with Project Grudge. He predicted that I wouldn't get a report until the newspapers began to play up flying saucers again. "It's all mass hysteria," he said.

The first hysterical report of the flurry came from the Air Defense Command. On September 23, 1951, at seven fifty-five in the morning, two F-86's on an early patrol were approaching Long Beach, California, coming in on the west leg of the Long Beach Radio range. All of a sudden the flight leader called his ground controller—high at twelve o'clock he and his wing man saw an object. It was in a gradual turn to its left, and it wasn't another airplane. The ground controller checked his radars but they had nothing, so the ground controller called the leader of the F-86's back and told him to go after the object and try to identify it. The two airplanes started to climb.

By this time the UFO had crossed over them but it was still in a turn and was coming back. Several times they tried to intercept, but they could never climb up to it. Once in a while, when they'd appear to be getting close, the UFO would lazily move out of range by climbing slightly. All the time it kept orbiting to the left in a big, wide circle. After about ten minutes the flight leader told the ground controller, who had been getting a running account of the unsuccessful intercept, that their fuel was low and that they'd have to break off soon. They'd gotten a fairly good look at the UFO, the flight leader told the ground controller, and it appeared to be a silver airplane with highly swept-back wings. The controller acknowled-

ged the message and said that he was scrambling all his alert airplanes from George AFB. Could the two F-86's stay in the area a few more minutes? They stayed and in a few minutes four more F-86's arrived. They saw the UFO immediately and took over.

The two F-86's with nearly dry tanks went back to George AFB.

For thirty more minutes the newly arrived F-86's worked in pairs trying to get up to the UFO's altitude, which they estimated to be 55,000 feet, but they couldn't make it. All the time the UFO kept slowly circling and speeding up only when the F-86's seemed to get too close. Then they began to run out of fuel and asked for permission to break off the intercept.

By this time one remaining F-86 had been alerted and was airborne toward Long Beach. He passed the four homeward-bound F-86's as he was going in, but by the time he arrived over Long Beach the UFO was gone.

All the pilots except one reported a "silver airplane with highly swept-back wings." One pilot said the UFO looked round and silver to him.

The report ended with a comment by the local intelli-

gence officer. He'd called Edwards AFB, the big Air Force test base north of Los Angeles, but they had nothing in the air. The officer concluded that the UFO was no airplane. In 1951 nothing we had would fly higher than the F-86.

This was a good report and I decided to dig in. First I had some more questions I wanted to ask the pilots. I was just in the process of formulating this set of questions when three better reports came in. They automatically got a higher priority than the Long Beach Incident.

CHAPTER 8

The Lubbock Lights, Unabridged

When four college professors, a geologist, a chemist, a physicist, and a petroleum engineer, report seeing the same UFO's on fourteen different occasions, the event can be classified as, at least, unusual. Add the facts that hundreds of other people saw these UFO's and that they were photographed, and the story gets even better. Add a few more facts—that these UFO's were picked up on radar and that a few people got a close look at one of them, and the story begins to convince even the most ardent skeptics.

This was the situation the day the reports of the Lubbock Lights arrived at ATIC. Actually the Lubbock Lights, as Project Blue Book calls them, involved many widespread reports. Some of these incidents are known to the public, but the ones that added the emphasis and intrigue to the case and caused hundreds of hours of time to be spent analyzing the reports have not been told before. We collected all of these reports under the one title because there appeared to be a tie-in between them.

The first word of the sightings reached ATIC late in Sep-

*tember 1951, when the mail girl dropped letters into my
"in" basket. One of the letters was from Albuquerque,
New Mexico, one was from a small town in Washington
State, where I knew an Air Defense Command radar
station was located, and, the other from Reese AFB at
Lubbock, Texas.*

*I opened the Albuquerque letter first. It was a report
from 34th Air Defense at Kirtland AFB. The report said
that on the evening of August 25, 1951, an employee
of the Atomic Energy Commission's supersecret Sandia
Corporation and his wife had seen a UFO. About dusk
they were sitting in the back yard of their home on the
outskirts of Albuquerque. They were gazing at the night
sky, commenting on how beautiful it was, when both of
them were startled at the sight of a huge airplane flying
swiftly and silently over their home. The airplane had
been in sight only a few seconds but they had gotten a
good look at it because it was so low. They estimated 800
to 1,000 feet. It was the shape of a "flying wing" and one
and a half times the size of a B-36. The wing was sharply swept back, almost like a V. Both the husband and
wife had seen B-36's over their home many times. They
couldn't see the color of the UFO but they did notice that
there were dark bands running across the wing from
front to back. On the aft edge of the wings there were six
to eight pairs of soft, glowing, bluish lights. The aircraft
had passed over their house from north to south.*

The report went on to say that an investigation had been made immediately. Since the object might have been a conventional airplane, air traffic was checked. A commercial airlines Constellation was 50 miles west of Albuquerque and an Air Force B-25 was south of the city, but there had been nothing over Albuquerque that evening. The man's background was checked. He had a "Q" security clearance. This summed up his character, oddballs don't get "Q" clearances. No one else had reported the UFO, but this could be explained by the fact the AEC employee and his wife lived in such a location that anything passing over their home from north to south wouldn't pass over or near very many other houses. A sketch of the UFO was enclosed in the report.

I picked up the letter from Lubbock next. It was a thick report, and from the photographs that were attached, it looked interesting. I thumbed through it and stopped at the photos. The first thing that struck me was the similarity between these photos and the report I'd just read. They showed a series of lights in a V shape, very similar to those described as being on the aft edge of the "flying wing" that was reported from Albuquerque. This was something unique, so I read the report in detail.

On the night of August 25, 1951, about 9:20 P.M., just twenty minutes after the Albuquerque sighting, four college professors from Texas Technological College at Lubbock had observed a formation of soft, glowing, bluish-green lights pass over their home. Several hours later they saw a similar group of lights and in the next two weeks they saw at least ten more. On August 31 an amateur photographer had taken five photos of the lights. Also on the thirty-first two ladies had seen a large "aluminum-colored," "pear-shaped" object hovering near a road north of Lubbock. The report went into the details of these sightings and enclosed a set of the photos that had been taken.

This report, in itself, was a good UFO report, but the similarity to the Albuquerque sighting, both in the description of the object and the time that it was seen, was truly amazing.

I almost overlooked the report from the radar station because it was fairly short. It said that early on the morning of August 26, only a few hours after the Lubbock sighting, two different radars had shown a target traveling 900 miles per hour at 13.000 feet on a northwesterly heading. The target had been observed for six minutes and an F-86 jet interceptor had been scrambled but by the time the F-86 had climbed into the air the target was gone. The last paragraph in the report was rather curt and to the point. It was apparently in anticipation of the

*comments the report would draw. It said that the target
was not caused by weather. The officer in charge of the
radar station and several members of his crew had been
operating radar for seven years and they could recognize
a weather target. This target was real.*

*I quickly took out a map of the United States and drew
in a course line between Lubbock and the radar station.
A UFO flying between these two points would be on a
northwesterly heading and the times it was seen at the
two places gave it a speed of roughly 900 miles per hour.*

*This was by far the best combination of UFO reports I'd
ever read and I'd read every one in the Air Force's files.*

*The first thing I did after reading the reports was to rush
a set of the Lubbock photos to the intelligence officer
of the 34th Air Division in Albuquerque. I asked him
to show the photos to the AEC employee and his wife
without telling them what they were. I requested an
answer by wire. Later the next day I received my answer: "Observers immediately said that this is what they
saw on the night of 25 August. Details by airmail." The
details were a sketch the man and his wife had made
of a wing around the photo of the Lubbock Lights. The
number of lights in the photo and the number of lights
the two observers had seen on the wing didn't tally, but*

they explained this by saying that they could have been wrong in their estimate.

The next day I flew to Lubbock to see if I could find an answer to all of these mysterious happenings.

I arrived in Lubbock about 5:00 P.M. and contacted the intelligence officer at Reese AFB. He knew that I was on my way and had already set up a meeting with the four professors. Right after dinner we met them.

if a group had been hand-picked to observe a UFO, we couldn't have picked a more technically qualified group of people. They were:

Dr. W. I. Robinson, Professor of Geology.

Dr. A. G. Oberg, Professor of Chemical Engineering.

Professor W. L. Ducker, Head of the Petroleum Engineering Department.

Dr. George, Professor of Physics.

This is their story:

On the evening of August 25 the four men were sitting

in Dr. Robinson's back yard. They were discussing micro-meteorites and drinking tea. They jokingly stressed this point. At nine-twenty a formation of lights streaked across the sky directly over their heads. It all happened so fast that none of them had a chance to get a good look. One of the men mentioned that he had always admonished his students for not being more observant; now he was in that spot. He and his colleagues realized they could remember only a few details of what they had seen. The lights were a weird bluish-green color and they were in a semicircular formation. They estimated that there were from fifteen to thirty separate lights and that they were moving from north to south. Their one wish at this time was that the lights would reappear. They did; about an hour later the lights went over again. This time the professors were a little better prepared. With the initial shock worn off, they had time to get a better look. The details they had remembered from the first flight checked. There was one difference; in this flight the lights were not in any orderly formation, they were just in a group.

The professors reasoned that if the UFO's appeared twice they might come back. Come back they did. The next night and apparently many times later, as the professors made twelve more observations during the next few weeks. For these later sightings they added two more people to their observing team.

Being methodical, as college professors are, they made every attempt to get a good set of data. They measured the angle through which the objects traveled and timed them. The several flights they checked traveled through 90 degrees of sky in three seconds, or 30 degrees per second. The lights usually suddenly appeared 45 degrees above the northern horizon, and abruptly went out 45 degrees above the southern horizon. They always traveled in this north-to-south direction. Outside of the first flight, in which the objects were in a roughly semicircular formation, in none of the rest of the flights did they note any regular pattern. Two or three flights were often seen in one night.

They had tried to measure the altitude, with no success. First they tried to compare the lights to the height of clouds but the clouds were never near the lights, or vice versa. Next they tried a more elaborate scheme. They measured off a base line perpendicular to the objects' usual flight path. Friends of the professors made up two teams. Each of the two teams was equipped with elevation-measuring devices, and one team was stationed at each end of the base line. The two teams were linked together by two-way radios. If they sighted the objects they would track and time them, thus getting the speed and altitude.

Unfortunately neither team ever saw the lights. But the lights never seemed to want to run the course. The wives of some of the watchers claimed to have seen them from their homes in the, city. This later proved to be a clue.

The professors were not the sole observers of the mysterious lights. For two weeks hundreds of other people for miles around Lubbock reported that they saw the same lights. The professors checked many of these reports against the times of the flights they had seen and recorded, and many checked out close. They attempted to question these observers as to the length of time they had seen the lights and angles at which they had seen them, but the professors learned what I already knew, people are poor observers.

Naturally there has been much discussion among the professors and their friends as to the nature of the lights. A few simple mathematical calculations showed that if the lights were very high they would be traveling very fast. The possibility that they were some natural phenomena was, of course, discussed and seriously considered. The professors did a lot of thinking and research and decided that if they were natural phenomena they were something altogether new. Dr. George, who has since died, studied the phenomena of the night sky during his years as a professor at the University of Alaska, and he had never seen or heard of anything like this before.

This was the professors' story. It was early in the morning when we returned to Reese AFB. I sat up a few more hours unsuccessfully trying to figure out what they had seen.

The next day I again met the intelligence officer and we went to talk to Carl Hart, Jr., the amateur photographer who had taken the pictures of the lights. Hart was a freshman at Texas Tech. His story was that on the night of August 31 he was lying in his bed in an upstairs room of the Hart home. He, like everyone else in Lubbock, had heard about the lights but he had never seen them. It was a warm night and his bed was pushed over next to an open window. He was looking out at the clear night sky, and had been in bed about a half hour, when he saw a formation of the lights appear in the north, cross an open patch of sky, and disappear over his house. Knowing that the lights might reappear as they had done in the past, he grabbed his loaded Kodak 35, set the lens and shutter at f 3.5 and one tenth of a second, and went out into the middle of the back yard. Before long his vigil was rewarded when the lights made a second pass. He got two pictures. A third formation went over a few minutes later and he got three more pictures. The next morning bright and early Hart said he took the roll of unexposed film to a friend who ran a photo-finishing shop. He explained that he did all of his film processing in this friend's lab. He told the friend about the pictures and they quickly developed them.

I stopped Hart at this point and asked why he didn't get more excited about what could be the biggest news photos of the century. He said that the lights had appeared to be so dim that he was sure he didn't have anything on the negatives; had he thought that he did have some good pictures he would have awakened his friend to develop the negatives right away.

When he developed the negatives and saw that they showed an image, his friend suggested that he call the newspaper. At first the paper wasn't interested but then they decided to run the photos. I later found out that they had done some checking of their own.

We went with Hart into his back yard to re-enact what had taken place. He described the lights as being the same dull, glowing bluish-green color as those seen by the professors. The formation was different, however. The lights Hart saw were always flying in a perfect V. He traced the path from where they appeared over some trees in the north, through an open patch of sky over the back yard, to a point where they disappeared over the house. From the flight path he pointed out, the lights had crossed about 120 degrees of open sky in four seconds. This 30-degree-per-second angular velocity corresponded to the professors' measured angular velocity.

We made arrangements to borrow Hart's negatives, thanked him for his information, and left.

Armed with a list of names of other observers of the mysterious lights, the intelligence officer and I started out to try to get a cross-section account of the other UFO sightings in the Lubbock area. All the stories about the UFO's were the same; various types of formations of dull bluish-green lights, generally moving north to south. A few people had variations. One lady saw a flying venetian blind and another a flying double boiler. One point of interest was that very few claimed to have seen the lights before reading the professors' story in the paper, but this could get back to the old question, "Do people look up if they have no reason to do so?"

We talked to observers in nearby towns. Their stories were the same. Two of them, tower operators at an airport, reported that they had seen the lights on several occasions.

It was in one of these outlying towns, Lamesa, that we talked to an old gentleman, about eighty years old, who gave us a good lead. He had seen the lights and he had identified them. Ever since he had read the story in the papers he had been looking. One evening he and his wife were in their yard looking for the lights. All of a sudden two or three appeared. They were in view for several seconds, then they were gone. In a few minutes the lights did a repeat performance. The man admitted he had been scared. He broke off his story of the lights and launched into his background as a native Texan, with range wars, Indians, and stagecoaches under his belt. What he was trying to point out was that despite the range wars, Indians, and stagecoaches, he had been scared. His wife had been scared too. We had some difficulty getting back to the lights but we finally made it. The third time they came around, he said, one of the lights emitted a sound. It said, "Plover." The old gentleman had immediately identified it as a plover, a water bird about the size of a quail. Later that night, and on several other occasions, they had seen the same thing. After a few more hair-raising but interesting stories of the old west Texas, we left.

Our next stop was the federal game warden's office in Lubbock. We got the low-down on plovers. We explained our interest and the warden was very helpful. He had been around west Texas all of his life so he was familiar with wildlife. The oily white breast of a plover could easily reflect light, but plovers usually didn't travel in more than pairs, or three at the most. He had never seen or heard of them traveling in a flock of fifteen to thirty but, of course, this wasn't impossible. Ducks, yes, but probably not plovers. He did say that for some unknown reason there were more than the usual number of plovers in the area that fall.

I was anxious to get the negatives that Hart had lent us back to the photo lab at Wright Field, but I had one more call to make. I wanted to talk to the two ladies who had seen a strange object hovering near their car, but I also wanted to write my report before I left Lubbock. Two Air Force special investigators from Reese AFB offered to talk to the ladies, so I stayed at the air base and finished my report.

That night when the investigators came back, I got the story. They had spent the whole day talking to the ladies and doing a little discreet checking into their backgrounds.

The two ladies, a mother and her daughter, had left their home in Matador, Texas, 70 miles northeast of Lubbock, about twelve-thirty P.M. on August 31. They were driving along in their car when they suddenly noticed "a pear-shaped" object about 150 yards ahead of them. It was just off the side of the road, about 120 feet in the air. It was drifting slowly to the east, "less than the speed required to take off in a Cub airplane." They drove on down the road about 50 more yards, stopped, and got out of the car. The object, which they estimated to be the size of a B-29 fuselage, was still drifting along slowly. There was no sign of any exhaust blast and they heard no noise, but they did see a "porthole" in the side of the object. In a few seconds the object began to pick up speed and rapidly climb out of sight. As it climbed it seemed to have a tight spiraling motion.

The investigation showed that the two ladies were "solid citizens," with absolutely no talents, or reasons, for fabricating such a story. The daughter was fairly familiar with aircraft. Her husband was an Air Force officer then in Korea, and she had been living near air bases for several years. The ladies had said that the object was "drifting" to the east, which possibly indicated that it was moving with the wind, but on further investigation it was found that it was moving into the wind.

The two investigators had worked all day and hadn't come up with the slightest indication of an answer.

This added the final section to my now voluminous report on the Lubbock affair.

The next morning as I rode to the airport to catch an

airliner back to Dayton I tried to put the whole puzzle together. It was hard to believe that all I'd heard was real. Did a huge flying wing pass over Albuquerque and travel 250 miles to Lubbock in about fifteen minutes? This would be about 900 miles per hour. Did the radar station in Washington pick up the same thing? I'd checked the distances on the big wall map in flight operations just before leaving Reese AFB. It was 1,300 miles from Lubbock to the radar site. From talking to people, we decided that the lights were apparently still around Lubbock at 11:20 P.M. and the radar picked them up just after midnight. They would have had to be traveling about 780 miles per hour. This was fairly close to the 900-mile-per-hour speed clocked by the two radars. The photos of the Lubbock Lights checked with the description of what the AEC employee and his wife had seen in Albuquerque. Nobody in Lubbock, however, had reported seeing a "flying wing" with lights. All of this was swimming around in my mind when I stepped out of the staff car at the Lubbock airport.

My plane had already landed so I checked in at the ticket counter, picked up a morning paper, and ran out and got into the airplane. I sat down next to a man wearing a Stetson hat and cowboy boots. I soon found out he was a retired rancher from Lubbock.

On the front page of the paper was an account of a large meteor that had flashed across New Mexico, west Texas, and Oklahoma the night before. According to the newspaper account, it was very spectacular and had startled a good many people in Lubbock. I was interested in the story because I had seen this meteor. It was a spectacular sight and I could easily understand how such things could be called UFO's. My seat partner must have noticed that I was reading the story of the meteor because he commented that a friend of his, the man who had brought him to the airport, had seen it. We talked about the meteor. This led to a discussion of other odd happenings and left a perfect opening for him to bring up the Lubbock Lights. He asked me if I'd heard about them. I said that I had heard a few vague stories. I hoped that this would stave off any detailed accounts of stories I had been saturated with during the past five days, but it didn't. I heard all the details all over again.

As he talked on, I settled back in my seat waiting for a certain thing to happen. Pretty soon it came. The rancher hesitated and the tone of his voice changed to a half-proud, half-apologetic tone. I'd heard this transition many times in the past few months; he was going to tell about the UFO that he had seen. He was going to tell how he had seen the bluish-green lights. I was wrong; what he said knocked me out of my boredom.

The same night that the college professors had seen their formation of lights his wife had seen something. Nobody in Lubbock knew about the story, not even their friends. He didn't want anyone to think he and his wife were "crazy." He was telling me only because I was a stranger. Just after dark his wife had gone outdoors to take some sheets off the clothesline. He was inside the house reading the paper. Suddenly his wife had rushed into the house, as he told the story, "as white as the sheets she was carrying." As close as he could remember, he said, this was about ten minutes before the professors made their first sighting. He stopped at this point to tell me about his wife, she wasn't prone to be "flighty" and she "never made up tales." This character qualification was also standard for UFO storytellers. The reason his wife was so upset was that she had seen a large object glide swiftly and silently over the house. She said it looked like "an airplane without a body." On the back edge of the wing were pairs of glowing bluish lights. The Albuquerque sighting! He said he didn't have any idea what his wife had seen but he thought that it was an interesting story.

It was an interesting story. It hit me right between the eyes. I knew the rancher and his wife couldn't have possibly heard the Albuquerque couple's story, only they and a few Air Force people knew about it. The chances of two

*identical stories being made up were infinitesimal, espe-
cially since neither of them fitted the standard Lubbock
Light description. I wondered how many other people in
Lubbock, Albuquerque, or anywhere in the Southwest
had seen a similar UFO during this period and hesitated
to mention it.*

*I tried to get a few more facts from the rancher but he'd
told me all he knew. At Dallas I boarded an airliner to
Dayton and he went on to Baton Rouge, never knowing
what he'd added to the story of the Lubbock Lights.*

*On the way to Dayton I figured out a plan of attack
on the thousands of words of notes I'd taken. The best
thing to do, I decided, was to treat each sighting in the
Lubbock Light series as a separate incident. All of them
seemed to be dependent upon each other for importance. If the objects that were reported in several of
the incidents could be identified, the rest would merely
become average UFO reports. The photographs taken by
Carl Hart, Jr., became number one on the agenda.*

*As soon as I reached Dayton I took Hart's negatives to
the Photo Reconnaissance Laboratory at Wright Field.
This laboratory, staffed by the Air Force's top photo-
graphy experts, did all of our analysis of photographs.
They went right to work on the negatives and soon had
a report.*

There had originally been five negatives, but when we asked to borrow them Hart could only produce four. The negatives were badly scratched and dirty because so many people had handled them, so it was difficult to tell the actual photographic images from the dust spots and scratches. The first thing that the lab did was to look at each spot on the negatives to see if it was an actual photographic image. They found that the photos showed an inverted V formation of lights. In each photo the individual image of a light was badly blurred due to motion of the camera, but by careful scrutiny of each blurred image they were able to determine that the original lights that Hart had photographed were circular, near pinpoint sources of light. Like a bright star, or a distant light bulb. Next they made enlargements from the negatives and carefully plotted the position of each light in the formation.

In each photograph the individual lights in the formation shifted position according to a definite pattern.

One additional factor that was brought out in the report was that although the photos were taken on a clear night no images of the stars could be found in the background. This proved one thing, the lights, which were overexposed in the photograph, were a great deal brighter than the stars, or the lights affected the film more than the light from the stars.

This was all that the photos showed. It was impossible to determine the size of each image of the group, speed, or altitude.

The next thing was to try to duplicate what Hart said he had done. I enlisted the aid of several friends and we tried to photograph a moving light. When we were talking to Hart in Lubbock, he had taken us to his back yard, where he had shot the pictures. He had traced the flight path of lights across the sky. We had him estimate the speed by following an imaginary flight of lights across the sky. It came out to about four seconds. We had a camera identical to the one that Hart had used and set up a light to move at the same speed as the UFO's had flown. We tried to take photographs. In four seconds we could get only two poor shots. These were badly blurred, much worse than Hart's, due to the one-tenth-of-a-second shutter speed. We repeated our experiment several times, each time with the same results. This made a lot of people doubt the authenticity of Hart's photos.

With the completed photo lab report in my hands, I was still without an answer. The report was interesting but didn't prove anything. All I could do was to get opinions from as qualified sources as I could find. A physiologist at the Aeromedical Laboratory knocked out the timing theory immediately by saying that if Hart had been excited he could have easily taken three photos in four seconds if we could get two in four seconds in our experiment. Several professional photographers, one of them a top Life photographer, said that if Hart was familiar with his camera and was familiar with panning action shots, his photos would have shown much less blur than ours. I recalled what I heard about Hart's having photographed sporting events for the Lubbock newspaper. This would have called for a good panning technique.

The photographs didn't tally with the description of the lights that the professors had seen; in fact, they were firmly convinced that they were of "home manufacture." The professors had reported soft, glowing lights yet the photos showed what should have been extremely bright lights. Hart reported a perfect formation while the professors, except for the first flight, reported an unorderly group. There was no way to explain this disagreement in the arrangement of the lights. Of course, it wasn't impossible that on the night that Hart saw the lights they were flying in a V formation. The first time the professors saw them they were flying in a semicircle.

The intensity of the lights was difficult to explain. Again I went to the people in the Photo Reconnaissance Laboratory. I asked them if there was any possible situation that could cause this. They said yes. An intensely bright *light source which had a color far over in the red end of the spectrum, bordering on infrared, could do it. The eye is not sensitive to such a light, it could appear dim to the eye yet be "bright" to the film. I asked them what kind of a light source would cause this. There were several things, if you want to speculate, they said, extremely high temperatures for one. But this was as far as they would go. We have nothing in this world that flies that appears dim to the eye yet will show bright on film, they said.*

This ended the investigation of the photographs, and the investigation ended at a blank wall. My official conclusion, which was later given to the press, was that "The photos were never proven to be a hoax but neither were they proven to be genuine." There is no definite answer.

The emphasis of the investigation was now switched to the professors' sighting. The meager amount of data that they had gathered seemed to be accurate but it was inconclusive as far as getting a definite answer was concerned. They had measured two things, how much of the sky the objects had crossed in a certain time and the angle from one side of the formation to the other. These figures didn't mean a great deal, however, since the altitude at which the formation of lights was flying was unknown. If you assumed that the objects were flying at

*an altitude of 10,000 feet you could easily compute that
they were traveling about 3,600 miles per hour, or five to
six times the speed of sound. The formation would have
been about 1,750 feet wide. If each light was a separate
object it could have been in the neighborhood of 100 feet
in diameter. These figures were only a guess since nobody knew if the lights were at, above, or below 10,000
feet. If they had been higher they would have been going
faster and have been larger. If lower than 10,000 feet,
slower and smaller.*

*The only solid lead that had developed while the Reese
AFB intelligence officer and I were investigating the professors' sightings was that the UFO's were birds reflecting
the city lights; specifically plover. The old cowboy from
Lamesa had described something identical to what the
professors described and they were plover. Secondly,
whenever the professors left the vicinity of their homes
to look for the lights they didn't see them, yet their wives,
who stayed at home, did see them. If the "lights" were
birds they would be flying low and couldn't be seen from
more than a few hundred feet. While in Lubbock I'd
noticed several main boulevards lighted with the bluish
mercury vapor lights. I called the intelligence officer at
Reese AFB and he airmailed me a city map of Lubbock
with the mercury-vapor-lighted streets marked. The place where the professors had made their observations was*

close to one of these streets. The big hitch in this theory was that people living miles from a mercury-vapor-lighted boulevard had also reported the lights. How many of these sightings were due to the power of suggestion and how many were authentic I didn't know. If I could have found out, it would have been possible to plot the sightings in Lubbock, and if they were all located close to the lighted boulevards, birds would be an answer. This, however, it was impossible to do.

The fact that the lights didn't make any perceivable sound seemed as if it might be a clue. Birds or light phenomena wouldn't make any sound, but how about some object of appreciable size traveling at or above the speed of sound? Jet airplanes don't fly as fast as the speed of sound but they make a horrible roar. Artillery shells, which are going much faster than aircraft, whine as they go through the air. I knew that a great deal of the noise from a jet is due to the heated air rushing out of the tail pipe, but I didn't know exactly how much of the noise this caused. If a jet airplane with a silent engine could be built, how much noise would it make? How far could it be heard? To get the answer I contacted National Advisory Committee for Aeronautics Laboratory at Langley AFB, a government agency which specializes in aeronautical research. They didn't know. Neither they nor anybody else had ever done any research on this question. Their opinion was that such an aircraft could not be heard 5,000 or 10,000 feet away. Aerodynamicists at Wright Field's Aircraft Laboratory agreed.

I called the Army's Ballistic Research Laboratories at Aberdeen Proving Grounds, Maryland, to find out why artillery shells whine. These people develop and test all kinds of shells so they would have an answer if anybody did. They said that the majority of the whine of an artillery shell is probably caused by the flat back end of the shell. If a perfectly streamlined shell could be used it would not have any perceivable whine.

What I found out, or didn't find out, about the sound of an object moving at several times the speed of sound was typical of nearly every question that came up regarding UFO's. We were working in a field where there were no definite answers to questions. In some instances we were getting into fields far advanced above the then present levels of research. In other instances we were getting into fields where no research had been done at all. It made the problem of UFO analysis one of getting opinions. All we could do was hope the opinions we were getting were the best.

My attempts to reach a definite conclusion as to what the professors had seen met another blank wall. I had no more success than I'd had trying to reach a conclusion on the authenticity of the photographs.

A thorough analysis of the reports of the flying wings seen by the retired rancher's wife in Lubbock and the AEC employee and his wife in Albuquerque was made. The story from the two ladies who saw the aluminum-colored pear-shaped object hovering near the road near Matador, Texas, was studied, checked, and rechecked. Another blank wall on all three of these sightings.

By the time I got around to working on the report from the radar station in Washington State, the data of the weather conditions that existed on the night of the sighting had arrived. I turned the incident folder over to the electronics specialists at ATIC. They made the analysis and determined that the targets were caused by weather, although it was a borderline case. They further surmised that since the targets had been picked up on two radars, if I checked I'd find out that the two targets looked different on the two radarscopes. This is a characteristic of a weather target picked up on radars operating on different frequencies. I did check. I called the radar station and talked to the captain who was in charge of the crew the night the target had been picked up.

*The target looked the same on both scopes. This was
one of the reasons it had been reported, the captain told
me. If the target hadn't been the same on both scopes,
he wouldn't have made the report since he would have
thought he had a weather target. He asked me what
ATIC thought about the sighting. I said that Captain James thought it was weather. Just before the long-distance
wires between Dayton and Washington melted, I caught
some comment about people sitting in swivel chairs
miles from the closest radarscope. . . . I took it that he
didn't agree the target was caused by weather. But that's
the way it officially stands today.*

*Although the case of the Lubbock Lights is officially
dead, its memory lingers on. There have never been
any more reliable reports of "flying wings" but lights
somewhat similar to those seen by the professors have
been reported. In about 70 per cent of these cases they
were proved to be birds reflecting city lights.*

*The known elements of the case, the professors' sigh-
tings and the photos, have been dragged back and forth
across every type of paper upon which written material
appears, from the cheapest, coarsest pulp to the slick Life
pages. Saucer addicts have studied and offered the case
as all-conclusive proof, with photos, that UFO's are interplanetary. Dr. Donald Menzel of Harvard studied the*

case and ripped the sightings to shreds in Look, Time, and his book, Flying Saucers, with the theory that the professors were merely looking at refracted city lights. But none of these people even had access to the full report. This is the first time it has ever been printed.

The only other people outside Project Blue Book who have studied the complete case of the Lubbock Lights were a group who, due to their associations with the government, had complete access to our files. And these people were not pulp writers or wide-eyed fanatics, they were scientists—rocket experts, nuclear physicists, and intelligence experts. They had banded together to study our UFO reports because they were convinced that some of the UFO's that were being reported were interplanetary spaceships and the Lubbock series was one of these reports.

The fact that the formations of lights were in different shapes didn't bother them; in fact, it convinced them all the more that their ideas of how a spaceship might operate were correct.

This group of scientists believed that the spaceships, or at least the part of the spaceship that came relatively close to the earth, would have to have a highly swept-back wing configuration. And they believed that for propulsion and control the craft had a series of small jet orifices all around its edge. Various combinations of these small jets would be turned on to get various flight attitudes. The lights that the various observers saw differed in arrangement because the craft was flying in different flight attitudes.

(Three years later the Canadian Government announced that this was exactly the way that they had planned to control the flying saucer that they were trying to build. They had to give up their plans for the development of the saucer-like craft, but now the project has been taken over by the U.S. Air Force.)

This is the complete story of the Lubbock Lights as it is carried in the Air Force files, one of the most interesting and most controversial collection of UFO sightings ever to be reported to Project Blue Book. Officially all of the sightings, except the UFO that was picked up on radar, are unknowns.

Personally I thought that the professors' lights might have been some kind of birds reflecting the light from mercury-vapor street lights, but I was wrong. They weren't birds, they weren't refracted light, but they weren't spaceships. The lights that the professors saw— the backbone of the Lubbock Light series—have been

*positively identified as a very commonplace and easily
explainable natural phenomenon.*

*It is very unfortunate that I can't divulge exactly the way
the answer was found because it is an interesting story
of how a scientist set up complete instrumentation to
track down the lights and how he spent several months
testing theory after theory until he finally hit upon the
answer. Telling the story would lead to his identity and,
in exchange for his story, I promised the man complete
anonymity. But he fully convinced me that he had the
answer, and after having heard hundreds of explanations of UFO's, I don't convince easily.*

*With the most important phase of the Lubbock Lights
"solved"—the sightings by the professors—the other
phases become only good UFO reports.*

CHAPTER 9

The New Project Grudge

While I was in Lubbock, Lieutenant Henry Metscher, who was helping me on Project Grudge, had been sorting out the many bits and pieces of information that Lieutenant Jerry Cummings and Lieutenant Colonel Rosengarten had brought back from Fort Monmouth, New Jersey, and he had the answers.

The UFO that the student radar operator had assumed to be traveling at a terrific speed because he couldn't lock on to it turned out to be a 400-mile-an-hour conventional airplane. He'd just gotten fouled up on his procedures for putting the radar set on automatic tracking. The sighting by the two officers in the T-33 jet fell apart when Metscher showed how they'd seen a balloon.

The second radar sighting of the series also turned out to be a balloon. The frantic phone call from headquarters requesting a reading on the object's altitude was to settle a bet. Some officers in headquarters had seen the balloon launched and were betting on how high it was.

The second day's radar sightings were caused by another

balloon and weather—both enhanced by the firm conviction that there were some mighty queer goings on over Jersey.

The success with the Fort Monmouth Incident had gone to our heads and we were convinced that with a little diligent digging we'd be knocking off saucers like an ace skeet-shooter. With all the confidence in the world, I attacked the Long Beach Incident, which I'd had to drop to go to Lubbock, Texas. But if saucers could laugh, they were probably zipping through the stratosphere chuckling to themselves, because there was no neat solution to this one.

In the original report of how the six F-86's chased the high-flying UFO over Long Beach, the intelligence officer who made the report had said that he'd checked all aircraft flights, therefore this wasn't the answer.

The UFO could have been a balloon, so I sent a wire to the Air Force weather detachment at the Long Beach Municipal Airport. I wanted the track of any balloon that was in the air at 7:55 A.M. on September 23, 1951.

While I was waiting for the answers to my two wires, Lieutenant Metscher and I began to sort out old UFO reports. It was a big job because back in 1949, when the *old Project Grudge had been disbanded, the files had just been dumped into storage bins. Hank and I now had four filing case drawers full of a heterogeneous mass of UFO reports, letters, copies of letters, and memos.*

But I didn't get to do much sorting because the mail girl brought in a copy of a wire that had just arrived. It was a report of a UFO sighting at Terre Haute, Indiana. I read it and told Metscher that I'd quickly whip out an answer and get back to helping him sort. But it didn't prove to be that easy.

The report from Terre Haute said that on October 9, a CAA employee at Hulman Municipal Airport had observed a silvery UFO. Three minutes later a pilot, flying east of Terre Haute, had seen a similar object. The report lacked many details but a few phone calls filled me in on the complete story.

At 1:43 P.M. on the ninth a CAA employee at the airport was walking across the ramp in front of the administration building. He happened to glance up at the sky—why, he didn't know—and out of the corner of his eye he caught a flash of light on the southeastern horizon. He stopped and looked at the sky where the flash of light had been but he couldn't see anything. He was just about to walk on when he noticed what he described as "a pinpoint" of light in the same spot where he'd seen the flash. In a second or two the "pinpoint" grew larger and it was obvious to the CAA man that something was approaching the airport at a terrific speed. As he watched, the object grew larger and larger until it flashed directly overhead and disappeared to the northwest. The CAA man said it all happened so fast and he was so amazed that he hadn't called anybody to come out of the nearby hangar and watch the UFO. But when he'd calmed down he remembered a few facts. The UFO had been in sight for about fifteen seconds and during this time it had passed from horizon to horizon. It was shaped like a "flattened tennis ball," was a bright silver color, and when it was directly overhead it was "the size of a 50-cent piece held at arm's length."

But this wasn't all there was to the report. A matter of minutes after the sighting a pilot radioed Terre Haute that he had seen a UFO. He was flying from Greencastle, Indiana, to Paris, Illinois, when just east of Paris he'd looked back and to his left. There, level with his airplane and fairly close, was a large silvery object, "like a flattened orange," hanging motionless in the sky. He looked at it a few seconds, then hauled his plane around in a tight left bank. He headed directly toward the UFO, but it suddenly began to pick up speed and shot off toward the northeast. The time, by the clock on his instrument pa-

*nel, was 1:45 P.M.—just two minutes after the sighting
at Terre Haute.*

*When I finished calling I got an aeronautical chart out
of the file and plotted the points of the sighting. The
CAA employee had seen the UFO disappear over the
northwestern horizon. The pilot had been flying from
Greencastle, Indiana, to Paris, Illinois, so he'd have been
flying on a heading of just a little less than 270 degrees,
or almost straight west. He was just east of Paris when
he'd first seen the UFO, and since he said that he'd looked back and to his left, the spot where he saw the UFO
would be right at a spot where the CAA man had seen
his UFO disappear. Both observers had checked their
watches with radio time just after the sightings, so there
couldn't be more than a few seconds' discrepancy. All I
could conclude was that both had seen the same UFO.*

*I checked the path of every balloon in the Midwest. I
checked the weather—it was a clear, cloudless day; I
had the two observers' backgrounds checked and I even
checked for air traffic, although I knew the UFO wasn't
an airplane. I researched the University of Dayton
library for everything on daylight meteors, but this was
no good. From the description the CAA employee gave,
what he'd seen had been a clear-cut, distinct, flattened
sphere, with no smoke trail, no sparks and no tail. A
daylight meteor, so low as to be described as "a 50-cent*

piece held at arm's length," would have had a smoke
trail, sparks, and would have made a roar that would
have jolted the Sphinx. This one was quiet. Besides, no
daylight meteor stops long enough to let an airplane
turn into it.

Conclusion: Unknown.

In a few days the data from the Long Beach Incident
came in and I started to put it together. A weather balloon had been launched from the Long Beach Airport,
and it was in the vicinity where the six F-86's had made
their unsuccessful attempt to intercept a UFO. I plotted
out the path of the balloon, the reported path of the
UFO, and the flight paths of the F-86's. The paths of the
balloon and the F-86's were accurate, I knew, because
the balloon was being tracked by radio fixes and the
F-86's had been tracked by radar. At only one point
did the paths of the balloon, UFO, and F-86's coinci-
de. When the first two F-86's made their initial visual
contact with the UFO they were looking almost directly
at the balloon. But from then on, even by altering the
courses of the F-86's, I couldn't prove a thing.

In addition, the weather observers from Long Beach
said that during the period that the intercept was taking
place they had gone outside and looked at their balloon;

*it was an exceptionally clear day and they could see it
at unusually high altitudes. They didn't see any F-86's
around it. And one stronger point, the balloon had burst
about ten minutes before the F-86's lost sight of the
UFO.*

*Lieutenant Metscher took over and, riding on his Fort
Monmouth victory, tried to show how the pilots had
seen the balloon. He got the same thing I did—nothing.*

*On October 27, 1951, the new Project Grudge was
officially established. I'd written the necessary letters and
had received the necessary endorsements. I'd estimated,
itemized, and justified direct costs and manpower. I'd
conferred, inferred, and referred, and now I had the
money to operate. The next step was to pile up all this
paper work as an aerial barrier, let the saucers crash
into it, and fall just outside the door.*

*I was given a very flexible operating policy for Project
Grudge because no one knew the best way to track down
UFO's. I had only one restriction and that was that I
wouldn't have my people spending time doing a lot of
wild speculating. Our job would be to analyze each and
every UFO report and try to find what we believed to
be an honest, unbiased answer. If we could not identify
the reported object as being a balloon, meteor, planet,
or one of half a hundred other common things that*

are sometimes called UFO's, we would mark the folder "Unknown" and file it in a special file. At some later date, when we built up enough of these "Unknown" reports, we'd study them.

As long as I was chief of the UFO project, this was our basic rule. If anyone became anti-flying saucer and was no longer capable of making an unbiased evaluation of a report, out he went. Conversely anyone who became a believer was through. We were too busy during the initial phases of the project to speculate as to whether the unknowns were spaceships, space monsters, Soviet weapons, or ethereal visions.

I had to let three people go for being too pro or too con.

By the latter part of November 1951 I knew most of what had taken place in prior UFO projects and what I expected to do. The people in Project Sign and the old Project Grudge had made many mistakes. I studied these mistakes and profited by them. I could see that my predecessors had had a rough job. Mine would be a little bit easier because of the pioneering they had done.

Lieutenant Metscher and I had sorted out all of the pre-1951 files, refiled them, studied them, and outlined the future course of the new Project Grudge.

When Lieut. Colonel Rosengarten and Lieutenant Cummings had been at the Pentagon briefing Major General Cabell on the Fort Monmouth Incidents, the general had told them to report back when the new project was formed and ready to go. We were ready to go, but before taking my ideas to the Pentagon, I thought it might be wise to try them out on a few other people to get their reaction. Colonel Frank Dunn, then chief of ATIC, liked this idea. We had many well-known scientists and engineers who periodically visited ATIC as consultants, and Colonel Dunn suggested that these people's opinions and comments would be valuable. For the next two weeks every visitor to ATIC who had a reputation as a scientist, engineer, or scholar got a UFO briefing.

Unfortunately the names of these people cannot be revealed because I promised them complete anonymity. But the list reads like a page from Great Men of Science.

Altogether nine people visited the project during this trial period. Of the nine, two thought the Air Force was wasting its time, one could be called indifferent, and six were very enthusiastic over the project. This was a shock to me. I had expected reactions that ranged from an extremely cold absolute zero to a mild twenty below. Instead I found out that UFO's were being freely and seriously discussed in scientific circles. The majority of the visitors thought that the Air Force had goofed on previous projects and were very happy to find out that the project was being re-established. All of the visitors, even the two who thought we were wasting our time, had good suggestions on what to do. All of them offered their services at any future time when they might be needed. Several of these people became very good friends and valuable consultants later on.

About two weeks before Christmas, in 1951, Colonel Dunn and I went to the Pentagon to give my report. Major General John A. Samford had replaced Major General Cabell as Director of Intelligence, but General Samford must have been told about the UFO situation because he was familiar with the general aspects of the problem. He had appointed his Assistant for Production, Brigadier General W. M. Garland, to ride herd on the project for him.

Colonel Dunn briefly outlined to General Samford what we planned to do. He explained our basic policy, that of setting aside the unknowns and not speculating on them, and he told how the scientists visiting ATIC had liked the plans for the new Project Grudge.
There was some discussion about the Air Force's and ATIC's responsibility for the UFO reports. General Garland stated, and it was later confirmed in writing,

*that the Air Force was solely responsible for investigating
and evaluating all UFO reports. Within the Air Force,
ATIC was the responsible agency. This in turn meant
that Project Grudge was responsible for all UFO reports
made by any branch of the military service. I started my
briefing by telling General Samford and his staff about
the present UFO situation.*

*The UFO reports had never stopped coming in since
they had first started in June 1947. There was some cor-
relation between publicity and the number of sightings,
but it was not an established fact that reports came in
only when the press was playing up UFO's. Just within
the past few months the number of good reports had
increased sharply and there had been no publicity.*

*UFO's were seen more frequently around areas vital to
the defense of the United States. The Los Alamos-Al-
buquerque area, Oak Ridge, and White Sands Proving
Ground rated high. Port areas, Strategic Air Command
bases, and industrial areas ranked next. UFO's had been
reported from every state in the Union and from every
foreign country. The U.S. did not have a monopoly.*

*The frequency of the UFO reports was interesting. Every
July there was a sudden increase in the number of
reports and July was always the peak month of the year.
Just before Christmas there was usually a minor peak.*

The Grudge Report had not been the solution to the UFO problem. It was true that a large percentage of the reports were due to the "misidentification of known objects"; people were seeing balloons, airplanes, planets, but this was not the final answer. There were a few hoaxes, hallucinations, publicity-seekers, and fatigued pilots, but reports from these people constituted less than 1 per cent of the total. Left over was a residue of very good and very "unexplainable" UFO sightings that were classified as unknown.

The quality of the reports was getting better, I told the officers; they contained more details that could be used for analysis and the details were more precise and accurate. But still they left much to be desired.

Every one of the nine scientists and engineers who had reviewed the UFO material at ATIC had made one strong point: we should give top priority to getting reasonably accurate measurements of the speed, altitude, and size of reported UFO's. This would serve two purposes. First, it would make it easy to sort out reports of common things, such as balloons, airplanes, etc. Second, and more important, if we could get even one fairly accurate measurement that showed that some object was traveling through the atmosphere at high speed, and that it wasn't a meteor, the UFO riddle would be much easier to solve.

I had worked out a plan to get some measured data, and I presented it to the group for their comments.

I felt sure that before long the press would get wind of the Air Force's renewed effort to identify UFO's. When this happened, instead of being mysterious about the whole thing, we would freely admit the existence of the new project, explain the situation thoroughly and exactly as it was, and say that all UFO reports made to the Air Force would be given careful consideration. In this way we would encourage more people to report what they were seeing and we might get some good data.

To further explain my point, I drew a sketch on a blackboard. Suppose that a UFO is reported over a fair-sized city. Now we may get one or two reports, and these reports may be rather sketchy. This does us no good—all we can conclude is that somebody saw something that he couldn't identify. But suppose fifty people from all over the city report the UFO. Then it would be profitable for us to go out and talk to these people, find out the time they saw the UFO, and where they saw it (the direction and height above the horizon) . Then we might be able to use these data, work out a triangulation problem, and get a fairly accurate measurement of speed, altitude, and size.

*Radar, of course, will give an accurate measurement
of speed and altitude, I pointed out, but radar is not
infallible. There is always the problem of weather. To get
accurate radar data on a UFO, it is always necessary to
prove that it wasn't weather that was causing the target.
Radar is valuable, and we wanted radar reports, I said,
but they should be considered only as a parallel effort
and shouldn't take the place of visual sightings.*

*In winding up my briefing, I again stressed the point
that, as of the end of 1951—the date of this briefing—
there was no positive proof that any craft foreign to
our knowledge existed. All recommendations for the
reorganization of Project Grudge were based solely
upon the fact that there were many incredible reports
of UFO's from many very reliable people. But they were
still just flying saucer reports and couldn't be considered
scientific proof.*

*Everyone present at the meeting agreed—each had read
or had been briefed on these incredible reports. In fact,
two of the people present had seen UFO's.*

*Before the meeting adjourned, Colonel Dunn had one
last question. He knew the answer, but he wanted it confirmed. "Does the United States have a secret weapon
that is being reported as a UFO?"*

The answer was a flat "No."

In a few days I was notified that my plan had been given the green light. I already had the plan written up in the form of a staff study so I sent it through channels for formal approval.

It had been obvious right from the start of the reorganization of Project Grudge that there would be questions that no one on my staff was technically competent to answer. To have a fully staffed project, I'd need an astronomer, a physicist, a chemist, a mathematician, a psychologist, and probably a dozen other specialists. It was, of course, impossible to have all of these people on my staff, so I decided to do the next best thing. I would set up a contract with some research organization who already had such people on their staff; then I would call on them whenever their services were needed.

I soon found a place that was interested in such a contract, and the day after Christmas, Colonel S. H. Kirkland, of Colonel Dunn's staff, and I left Dayton for a two-day conference with these people to outline what we wanted. Their organization cannot be identified by name because they are doing other highly secret work for the government. I'll call them Project Bear.

Project Bear is a large, well-known research organization in the Midwest. The several hundred engineers and scientists who make up their staff run from experts on soils to nuclear physicists. They would make these people available to me to assist Project Grudge on any problem that might arise from a UFO report. They did not have a staff astronomer or psychologist, but they agreed to get them for us on a subcontract basis. Besides providing experts in every field of science, they would make two studies for us; a study of how much a person can be expected to see and remember from a UFO sighting, and a statistical study of UFO reports. The end product of the study of the powers of observation of a UFO observer would be an interrogation form.

Ever since the Air Force had been in the UFO business, attempts had been made to construct a form that a person who had seen a UFO could fill out. Many types had been tried but all of them had major disadvantages. Project Bear, working with the psychology department of a university, would study all of the previous questionnaires, along with actual UFO reports, and try to come up with as near a perfect interrogation form as possible. The idea was to make the form simple and yet extract as much and as accurate data as possible from the observer.

The second study that Project Bear would undertake would be a statistical study of all UFO reports. Since 1947 the Air Force had collected about 650 reports, but if our plan to encourage UFO reports worked out the way we expected this number could increase tenfold. To handle this volume of reports, Project Bear said that they would set up a complete UFO file on IBM punch cards. Then if we wanted any bit of information from the files, it would be a matter of punching a few buttons on an IBM card-sorting machine, and the files would be sorted electronically in a few seconds. Approximately a hundred items pertaining to a UFO report would be put on each card. These items included everything from the time the UFO was seen to its position in the sky and the observer's personality. The items punched on the cards would correspond to the items on the questionnaires that Project Bear was going to develop.

Besides giving us a rapid method of sorting data, this IBM file would give us a modus operandi file. Our MO file would be similar to the MO files used by police departments to file the methods of operations of a criminal. Thus when we received a report we could put the characteristics of the reported UFO on an IBM punch card, put it into the IBM machine, and compare it with the characteristics of other sightings that had known solutions. The answer might be that out of the one hundred items on the card, ninety-five were identical to *previous UFO reports that ducks were flying over a city at night reflecting the city's lights.*

On the way home from the meeting Colonel Kirkland and I were both well satisfied with the assistance we believed Project Bear could give to Project Grudge.

In a few days I again left ATIC, this time for Air Defense Command Headquarters in Colorado Springs, Colorado. I wanted to find out how willing ADC was to help us and what they could do. When I arrived I got a thorough briefing on the operations of ADC and the promise that they would do anything they could to help solve the UFO riddle.

All of this co-operation was something that I hadn't expected. I'd been warned by the people who had worked on Project Sign and the old Project Grudge that everybody hated the word UFO—I'd have to fight for everything I asked for. But once again they were wrong. The scientists who visited ATIC, General Samford, Project Bear, and now Air Defense Command couldn't have been more co-operative. I was becoming aware that there was much wider concern about UFO reports than I'd ever realized before.

While I traveled around the United States getting the project set up, UFO reports continued to come in and all of them were good. One series of reports was especially good, and they came from a group of people who had had a great deal of experience watching things in the sky—the people who launch the big skyhook balloons for General Mills, Inc. The reports of what the General Mills people had seen while they were tracking their balloons covered a period of over a year. They had just sent them in because they had heard that Project Grudge was being reorganized and was taking a different view on UFO reports. They, like so many other reliable observers, had been disgusted with the previous Air Force attitude toward UFO reports, and they had refused to send in any reports. I decided that these people might be a good source of information, and I wanted to get further details on their reports, so I got orders to go to Minneapolis. A scientist from Project Bear went with me. We arrived on January 14, 1952, in the middle of a cold wave and a blizzard.

The Aeronautical Division of General Mills, Inc., of Wheaties and Betty Crocker fame, had launched and tracked every skyhook balloon that had been launched prior to mid-1952. They knew what their balloons looked like under all lighting conditions and they also knew meteorology, aerodynamics, astronomy, and they knew UFO's. I talked to these people for the better part of a full day, and every time I tried to infer that there might

*be some natural explanation for the UFO's I just about
found myself in a fresh snowdrift.*

*What made these people so sure that UFO's existed? In
the first place, they had seen many of them. One man
told me that one tracking crew had seen so many that
the sight of a UFO no longer even especially interested
them. And the things that they saw couldn't be explained.*

*For example: On January 16, 1951, two people from
General Mills and four people from Artesia, New Mexico, were watching a skyhook balloon from the Artesia
airport. They had been watching the balloon off and on
for about an hour when one of the group saw two tiny
specks on the horizon, off to the northwest. He pointed
them out to the others because two airplanes were expected into the airport, and he thought that these might
be the airplanes. But as they watched, the two specks
began to move in fast, and within a few seconds the observers could see that "the airplanes" were actually two
round, dull white objects flying in close formation. The
two objects continued to come in and headed straight
toward the balloon. When they reached the balloon they
circled it once and flew off to the northwest, where they
disappeared over the horizon. As the two UFO's circled
the balloon, they tipped on edge and the observers saw
that they were disk-shaped.*

*When the two UFO's were near the balloon, the obser-
vers also had a chance to compare the size of the UFO's
with the size of the balloon. If the UFO's were as close to
the balloon as they appeared to be they would have been
60 feet in diameter.*

*After my visit to General Mills, Inc., I couldn't help
remembering a magazine article I'd read about a year
before. It said that there was not a single reliable UFO
report that couldn't be attributed to a skyhook balloon.*

*I'd been back at ATIC only a few days when I found
myself packing up to leave again. This time it was for
New York. A high-priority wire had come into ATIC
describing how a Navy pilot had chased a UFO over
Mitchel AFB, on Long Island. It was a good report.*

*I remember the trip to New York because my train pas-
sed through Elizabeth, New Jersey, early in the morning,
and I could see the fires caused by an American Airlines
Convair that had crashed. This was the second of the
three tragic Elizabeth, New Jersey, crashes.*

*The morning before, on January 21, a Navy pilot had
taken off from Mitchel in a TBM. He was a lieutenant
commander, had flown in World War II, and was now
an engineer at the Navy Special Devices Center on Long*

Island. At nine-fifty he had cleared the traffic pattern and was at about 2,500 feet, circling around the airfield. He was southeast of the field when he first noticed an object below him and "about three runway lengths off the end of Runway 30." The object looked like the top of a parachute canopy, he told me; it was white and he thought he could see the wedges or panels. He said that he thought that it was moving across the ground a little bit too fast to be drifting with wind, but he was sure that somebody had bailed out and that he was looking at the top of his parachute. He was just ready to call the tower when he suddenly realized that this "parachute" was drifting across the wind. He had just taken off from Runway 30 and knew which direction the wind was blowing.

As he watched, the object, whatever it was (by now he no longer thought that it was a parachute), began to gradually climb, so he started to climb, he said, staying above and off to the right of the object. When the UFO started to make a left turn, he followed and tried to cut inside, but he overshot and passed over it. It continued to turn and gain speed, so he dropped the nose of the TBM, put on more power, and pulled in behind the object, which was now level with him. In a matter of seconds the UFO made a 180-degree turn and started to make a big swing around the northern edge of Mitchel

AFB. The pilot tried to follow, but the UFO had begun to accelerate rapidly, and since a TBM leaves much to be desired on the speed end, he was getting farther and farther behind. But he did try to follow it as long as he could. As he made a wide turn around the northern edge of the airfield he saw that the UFO was now turning south. He racked the TBM up into a tight left turn to follow, but in a few seconds the UFO had disappeared. When he last saw it, it had crossed the Long Island coast line near Freeport and it was heading out to sea.

When he finished his account of the chase, I asked the commander some specific questions about the UFO. He said that just after he'd decided that the UFO was not a parachute it appeared to be at an altitude of about 200 to 300 feet over a residential section. From the time it took it to cover a city block, he'd estimated that it was traveling about 300 miles an hour. Even when he pulled in behind the object and got a good look, it still looked like a parachute canopy—dome-shaped—white—and it had a dark undersurface. It had been in sight two and a half minutes.

He had called the control tower at Mitchel during the chase, he told me, but only to ask if any balloons had been launched. He thought that he might be seeing a balloon. The tower had told him that there was a balloon in the area.

Then the commander took out an aeronautical chart and drew in his flight path and the apparent path of the UFO for me. I think that he drew it accurately because he had been continually watching landmarks as he'd chased the UFO and was very careful as he drew the sketches on the map.

I checked with the weather detachment at Mitchel and they said that they had released a balloon. They had released it at nine-fifty and from a point southeast of the airfield. I got a plot of its path. Just as in the Long Beach Incident, where the six F-86's tried to intercept the UFO, the balloon was almost exactly in line with the spot where the UFO was first seen, but then any proof you might attempt falls apart. If the pilot knew where he was, and had plotted his flight path even semi-accurately, he was never over the balloon. Yet he was over the UFO. He came within less than 2,000 feet of the UFO when he passed over it; yet he couldn't recognize it as a balloon even though he thought it might be a balloon since the tower had just told him that there was one in the area. He said that he followed the UFO around the north edge of the airfield. Yet the balloon, after it was launched southeast of the field, continued on a southeast course and never passed north of the airfield.

But the biggest argument against the object's being a

balloon was the fact that the pilot pulled in behind it; it was directly off the nose of his airplane, and although he followed it for more than a minute, it pulled away from him. Once you line up an airplane on a balloon and go straight toward it you will catch it in a matter of seconds, even in the slowest airplane. There have been dogfights with UFO's where the UFO's turned out to be balloons, but the pilots always reported that the UFO "made a pass" at them. In other words, they rapidly caught up with the balloon and passed it. I questioned this pilot over and over on this one point, and he was positive that he had followed directly behind the UFO for over a minute and all the time it was pulling away from him.

This is one of the most typical UFO reports we had in our files. It is typical because no matter how you argue there isn't any definite answer. If you want to argue that the pilot didn't know where he was during the chase—that he was 3 or 4 miles from where he thought he was—that he never did fly around the northern edge of the field and get in behind the UFO—then the UFO could have been a balloon.

But if you want to believe that the pilot knew where he was all during the chase, and he did have several thousand hours of flying time, then all you can conclude is that the UFO was an unknown.

I think the pilot summed up the situation very aptly when he told me, "I don't know what it was, but I've never seen anything like it before or since—maybe it was a spaceship."
284

I went back to Dayton stumped—maybe it was a spaceship.

CHAPTER 10

Project Blue Book and the Big Build-Up

Just twenty minutes after midnight on January 22, 1952, nineteen and a half hours after the Navy lieutenant commander had chased the UFO near Mitchel AFB, another incident involving an airplane and something unknown was developing in Alaska. In contrast with the unusually balmy weather in New York, the temperature in Alaska that night, according to the detailed account of the incident we received at ATIC, was a miserable 47 degrees below zero. The action was unfolding at one of our northernmost radar outposts in Alaska. This outpost was similar to those you may have seen in pictures, a collection of low, sprawling buildings grouped around the observatory—like domes that house the antennae of the most modern radar in the world. The entire collection of buildings and domes are one color, solid white, from the plastering of ice and snow. The picture that the outpost makes could be described as fascinating, something out of a Walt Disney fantasy—but talk to somebody who's been there—it's miserable.

At 0020, twenty minutes after midnight, an airman watching one of the outpost's radarscopes saw a target

*appear. It looked like an airplane because it showed up
as a bright, distinct spot. But it was unusual because it
was northeast of the radar site, and very few airplanes
ever flew over this area. Off to the northeast of the station there was nothing but ice, snow, and maybe a few
Eskimos until you got to Russia. Occasionally a B-50
weather reconnaissance plane ventured into the area,
but a quick check of the records showed that none was
there on this night.*

*By the time the radar crew had gotten three good plots
of the target, they all knew that it was something unusual—it was at 23,000 feet and traveling 1,500 miles
an hour. The duty controller, an Air Force captain, was
quickly called; he made a fast check of the targets that
had now been put on the plotting board and called to a
jet fighter-interceptor base for a scramble.*

*The fighter base, located about 100 miles south of the
radar site, acknowledged the captain's call and in a
matter of minutes an F-94 jet was climbing out toward
the north.*

*While the F-94 was heading north, the radar crew at
the outpost watched the unidentified target. The bright
dots that marked its path had moved straight across the
radarscope, passing within about 50 miles of the site. It*

was still traveling about 1,500 miles an hour. The radar had also picked up the F-94 and was directing it toward its target when suddenly the unidentified target slowed down, stopped, and reversed its course. Now it was heading directly toward the radar station. When it was within about 30 miles of the station, the radar operator switched his set to a shorter range and lost both the F-94 and the unidentified target.

While the radar operator was trying to pick up the target again, the F-94 arrived in the area. The ground controller told the pilot that they had lost the target and asked him to cruise around the area to see if he and his radar operator could pick up anything on the F-94's radar. The pilot said he would but that he was having a little difficulty, was low on fuel, and would have to get back to his base soon. The ground controller acknowledged the pilot's message, and called back to the air base telling them to scramble a second F-94.

The first F-94 continued to search the area while the ground radar tried to pick up the target but neither could find it.

About this time the second F-94 was coming in, so the ground radar switched back to long range. In a minute they had both of the F-94's and the unidentified target

on their scope. The ground controller called the second
F-94 and began to vector him into the target.

The first F-94 returned to its base.

As both the second F-94 and the target approached the
radar site, the operator again switched to short range
and again he lost the jet and the target. He switched
back to long range, but by now they were too close to the
radar site and he couldn't pick up either one.

The pilot continued on toward where the unidentified
target should have been. Suddenly the F-94 radar operator reported a weak target off to the right at 28,000 feet.
They climbed into it but it faded before they could make
contact.

The pilot swung the F-94 around for another pass, and
this time the radar operator reported a strong return. As
they closed in, the F-94's radar showed that the target
was now almost stationary, just barely moving. The F-94
continued on, but the target seemed to make a sudden
dive and they lost it. The pilot of the jet interceptor
continued to search the area but couldn't find anything.
As the F-94 moved away from the radar station, it was
again picked up on the ground radar, but the unidentified target was gone.

A third F-94 had been scrambled, and in the meantime its crew took over the search. They flew around for about ten minutes without detecting any targets on their radar. They were making one last pass almost directly over the radar station when the radar operator in the back seat of the F-94 yelled over the interphone that he had a target on his scope. The pilot called ground radar, but by this time both the F-94 and the unidentified target were again too close to the radar station and they couldn't be picked up. The F-94 closed in until it was within 200 yards of the target; then the pilot pulled up, afraid he might collide with whatever was out in the night sky ahead of him. He made another pass, and another, but each time the bright spot on the radar operator's scope just stayed in one spot as if something were defiantly sitting out in front of the F-94 daring the pilot to close in. The pilot didn't take the dare. On each pass he broke off at 200 yards.

The F-94 crew made a fourth pass and got a weak return, but it was soon lost as the target seemed to speed away. Ground radar also got a brief return, but in a matter of seconds they too lost the target as it streaked out of range on a westerly heading.

As usual, the first thing I did when I read this report was to check the weather. But there was no weather report for this area that was detailed enough to tell whether a weather inversion could have caused the radar targets.

But I took the report over to Captain Roy James, anyway, in hopes that he might be able to find a clue that would identify the UFO.

Captain James was the chief of the radar section at ATIC. He and his people analyzed all our reports where radar picked up UFO's. Roy had been familiar with radar for many years, having set up one of the first stations in Florida during World War II, and later he took the first aircraft control and warning squadron to Saipan. Besides worrying about keeping his radar operating, he had to worry about the Japs' shooting holes in his antennae.

Captain James decided that this Alaskan sighting I'd just shown him was caused by some kind of freak weather. He based his analysis on the fact that the unknown target had disappeared each time the ground radar had been switched to short range. This, he pointed out, is an indication that the radar was picking up some kind of a target that was caused by weather. The same weather that caused the ground radar to act up must have caused false targets on the F-94's radar too, he continued. After all, they had closed to within 200 yards of what they were supposedly picking up; it was a clear moonlight night, yet the crews of the F-94's hadn't seen a thing.

Taking a clue from the law profession, he quoted a precedent. About a year before over Oak Ridge, Tennessee, an F-82 interceptor had nearly flown into the ground three times as the pilot attempted to follow a target that his radar operator was picking up. There was a strong inversion that night, and although the target appeared as if it were flying in the air, it was actually a ground target.

Since Captain James was the chief of the radar section and he had said "Weather," weather was the official conclusion on the report. But reports of UFO's' being picked up on radar are controversial, and some of the people didn't agree with James's conclusion.

A month or two after we'd received the report, I was out in Colorado Springs at Air Defense Command Headquarters. I was eating lunch in the officers' club when I saw an officer from the radar operations section at ADC. He asked me to stop by his office when I had a spare minute, and I said that I would. He said that it was important.

It was the middle of the afternoon before I saw him and found out what he wanted. He had been in Alaska on TDY when the UFO had been picked up at the outpost radar site. In fact, he had made a trip to both the radar site and the interceptor base just two days after the sighting, and he had talked about the sighting with the people who had seen the UFO on the radar. He wanted to know what we thought about it.

When I told him that the sighting had been written off as weather, I remember that he got a funny look on his face and said, "Weather! What are you guys trying to pull, anyway?"

It was obvious that he didn't agree with our conclusion. I was interested in learning what this man thought because I knew that he was one of ADC's ace radar trouble shooters and that he traveled all over the world, on loan from ADC, to work out problems with radars.

"From the description of what the targets looked like on the radarscopes, good, strong, bright images, I can't believe that they were caused by weather," he told me.

Then he went on to back up his argument by pointing out that when the ground radar was switched to short range both the F-94 and the unknown target disappea-

red. If just the unknown target had disappeared, then
it could have been weather. But since both disappeared,
very probably the radar set wasn't working on short
ranges for some reason. Next he pointed out that if there
was a temperature inversion, which is highly unlikely in
northern Alaska, the same inversion that would affect
the ground radar wouldn't be present at 25,000 feet or
above.

I told him about the report from Oak Ridge that Captain James had used as an example, but he didn't buy
this comparison. At Oak Ridge, he pointed out, that
F-82 was at only 4,000 feet. He didn't know how the
F-94's could get to within 200 yards of an object without
seeing it, unless the object was painted a dull black.

"No," he said, "I can't believe that those radar targets
were caused by weather. I'd be much more inclined to
believe that they were something real, something that we
just don't know about."

During the early spring of 1952 reports of radar sightings increased rapidly. Most of them came from the
Air Defense Command, but a few came from other
agencies. One day, soon after the Alaskan Incident, I
got a telephone call from the chief of one of the sections
of a civilian experimental radar laboratory in New

York State. The people in this lab were working on the development of the latest types of radar. Several times recently, while testing radars, they had detected unidentified targets. To quote my caller, "Some damn odd things are happening that are beginning to worry me." He went on to tell how the people in his lab had checked their radars, the weather, and everything else they could think of, but they could find absolutely nothing to account for the targets; they could only conclude that they were real. I promised him that his information would get to the right people if he'd put it in a letter and send it to ATIC. In about a week the letter arrived—hand-carried by no less than a general. The general, who was from Headquarters, Air Matériel Command, had been in New York at the radar laboratory, and he had heard about the UFO reports. He had personally checked into them because he knew that the people at the lab were some of the sharpest radar engineers in the world. When he found out that these people had already contacted us and had prepared a report for us, he offered to hand-carry it to Wright-Patterson.

I can't divulge how high these targets were flying or how fast they were going because it would give an indication of the performance of our latest radar, which is classified Secret. I can say, however, that they were flying mighty high and mighty fast.

*I turned the letter over to ATIC's electronics branch, and
they promised to take immediate action. They did, and
really fouled it up. The person who received the report
in the electronics branch was one of the old veterans of
Projects Sign and Grudge. He knew all about UFO's.
He got on the phone, called the radar lab, and told the
chief (a man who possibly wrote all of the textbooks this
person had used in college) all about how a weather
inversion can cause false targets on weather. He was
gracious enough to tell the chief of the radar lab to call if
he had any more "trouble."*

*We never heard from them again. Maybe they found
out what their targets were. Or maybe they joined ranks
with the airline pilot who told me that if a flying saucer
flew wing tip to wing tip formation with him, he'd never
tell the Air Force.*

*In early February I made another trip to Air Defense
Command Headquarters in Colorado Springs. This time
it was to present a definite plan of how ADC could assist
ATIC in getting better data on UFO's. I briefed General
Benjamin W. Chidlaw, then the Commanding General
of the Air Defense Command, and his staff, telling them
about our plan. They agreed with it in principle and
suggested that I work out the details with the Director of
Intelligence for ADC, Brigadier General W. M. Burgess.*

General Burgess designated Major Verne Sadowski of his staff to be the ADC liaison officer with Project Grudge.

This briefing started a long period of close co-operation between Project Grudge and ADC, and it was a pleasure to work with these people. In all of my travels around the government, visiting and conferring with dozens of agencies, I never had the pleasure of working with or seeing a more smoothly operating and efficient organization than the Air Defense Command. General Chidlaw and General Burgess, along with the rest of the staff at ADC, were truly great officers. None of them were believers in flying saucers, but they recognized the fact that UFO reports were a problem that must be considered. With technological progress what it is today, you can't afford to have anything in the air that you can't identify, be it balloons, meteors, planets or flying saucers.

The plan that ADC agreed to was very simple. They agreed to issue a directive to all of their units explaining the UFO situation and telling specifically what to do in case one was detected. All radar units equipped with radarscope cameras would be required to take scope photos of targets that fell into the UFO category—targets that were not airplanes or known weather phenomena. These photos, along with a completed technical ques-

tionnaire that would be made up at ATIC by Captain Roy James, would be forwarded to Project Grudge.

The Air Defense Command UFO directive would also clarify the scrambling of fighters to intercept a UFO. Since it is the policy of the Air Defense Command to establish the identity of any unidentified target, there were no special orders issued for scrambling fighters to try to identify reported UFO's. A UFO was something unknown and automatically called for a scramble. However, there had been some hesitancy on the part of controllers to send airplanes up whenever radar picked up a target that obviously was not an airplane. The directive merely pointed out to the controllers that it was within the scope of existing regulations to scramble on radar targets that were plotted as traveling too fast or too slow to be conventional airplanes. The decision to scramble fighters was still up to the individual controller, however, and scrambling on UFO's would be a second or third priority.

The Air Defense Command UFO directive did not mention shooting at a UFO. This question came up during our planning meeting at Colorado Springs, but, like the authority to scramble, the authority to shoot at anything in the air had been established long ago. Every ADC pilot knows the rules for engagement, the rules that tell

*him when he can shoot the loaded guns that he always
carries. If anything in the air over the United States
commits any act that is covered by the rules for engagement, the pilot has the authority to open fire.*

*The third thing that ADC would do would be to integra-
te the Ground Observer Corps into the UFO reporting
net. As a second priority, the GOC would report
UFO's—first priority would still be reporting aircraft.*

*Ever since the new Project Grudge had been organized,
we hadn't had to deal with any large-scale publicity
about UFO's. Occasionally someone would bring in a
local item from some newspaper about a UFO sighting,
but the sightings never rated more than an inch or two
column space. But on February 19, 1952, the calm was
broken by the story of how a huge ball of fire paced two
B-29's in Korea. The story didn't start a rash of reports
as the story of the first UFO sighting did in June 1947,
but it was significant in that it started a slow build-up of
publicity that was far to surpass anything in the past.*

*This Korean sighting also added to the growing official
interest in Washington. Almost every day I was getting
one or two telephone calls from some branch of the
government, and I was going to Washington at least
once every two weeks. I was beginning to spend as much*

*time telling people what was going on as I was doing
anything about it. The answer was to get somebody in
the Directorate of Intelligence in the Pentagon to act as a
liaison officer. I could keep this person informed and he
could handle the "branch office" in Washington. Colonel
Dunn bought this idea, and Major Dewey J. Fournet got
the additional duty of manager of the Pentagon branch.
In the future all Pentagon inquiries went to Major Fournet, and if he couldn't answer them he would call me.
The arrangement was excellent because Major Fournet
took a very serious interest in UFO's and could always
be counted on to do a good job.*

*Sometime in February 1952 I had a visit from two Roy-
al Canadian Air Force officers. For some time, I learned,
Canada had been getting her share of UFO reports. One
of the latest ones, and the one that prompted the visit
by the RCAF officers, occurred at North Bay, Ontario,
about 250 miles north of Buffalo, New York. On two
occasions an orange-red disk had been seen from a new
jet fighter base in the area.*

*The Canadians wanted to know how we operated. I gave
them the details of how we were currently operating
and how we hoped to operate in the future, as soon as
the procedures that were now in the planning stages
could be put into operation. We agreed to try to set up*

channels so that we could exchange information and tie in the project they planned to establish with Project Grudge.

Our plans for continuing liaison didn't materialize, but through other RCAF intelligence officers I found out that their plans for an RCAF-sponsored project failed. A quasi-official UFO project was set up soon after this, however, and its objective was to use instruments to detect objects coming into the earth's atmosphere. In 1954 the project was closed down because during the two years of operation they hadn't officially detected any UFO's. My sources of information stressed the word "officially."

During the time that I was chief of the UFO project, the visitors who passed through my office closely resembled the international brigade. Most of the visits were unofficial in the sense that the officers came to ATIC on other business, but in many instances the other business was just an excuse to come out to Dayton to get filled in on the UFO story. Two RAF intelligence officers who were in the U.S. on a classified mission brought six single-spaced typed pages of questions they and their friends wanted answered. On many occasions Air Force intelligence officers who were stationed in England, France, and Germany, and who returned to the U.S. on business, took back stacks of unclassified flying saucer stories. One civilian intelligence agent who frequently traveled between the U.S. and Europe also acted as the unofficial courier for a German group—transporting hot newspaper and magazine articles about UFO's that I'd collected. In return I received the latest information on European sightings—sightings that never were released and that we never received at ATIC through official channels.

Ever since the fateful day when Lieutenant Jerry Cummings dropped his horn-rimmed glasses down on his nose, tipped his head forward, peered at Major General Cabell over his glasses and, acting not at all like a first lieutenant, said that the UFO investigation was all fouled up, Project Grudge had been gaining prestige. Lieutenant Colonel Rosengarten's promise that I'd be on the project for only a few months went the way of all military promises. By March 1952, Project Grudge was no longer just a project within a group; we had become a separate organization, with the formal title of the Aerial Phenomena Group. Soon after this step-up in the chain of command the project code name was changed to Blue Book. The word "Grudge" was no longer applicable. For those people who like to try to read a hidden meaning into a name, I'll say that the code name Blue Book was derived from the title given to college tests. Both the tests and the project had an abundance of equally confusing questions.

Project Blue Book had been made a separate group because of the steadily increasing number of reports we were receiving. The average had jumped from about ten a month to twenty a month since December 1951. In March of 1952 the reports slacked off a little, but April was a big month. In April we received ninety-nine reports.

On April 1, Colonel S. H. Kirkland and I went to Los Angeles on business. Before we left ATIC we had made arrangements to attend a meeting of the Civilian Saucer Investigators, a now defunct organization that was very active in 1952.

They turned out to be a well-meaning but Don Quixote-type group of individuals. As soon as they outlined their plans for attempting to solve the UFO riddle, it was obvious that they would fail. Project Blue Book had the entire Air Force, money, and enthusiasm behind it and we weren't getting any answers yet. All this group had was the enthusiasm.

The highlight of the evening wasn't the Civilian Saucer Investigators, however; it was getting a chance to read Ginna's UFO article in an advance copy of Life magazine that the organization had obtained—the article written from the material Bob Ginna had been researching for over a year. Colonel Kirkwood took one long look at the article, sidled up to me, and said, "We'd better get back to Dayton quick; you're going to be busy." The next morning at dawn I was sound asleep on a United Airlines DC-6, Dayton-bound.

The Life article undoubtedly threw a harder punch at the American public than any other UFO article ever written. The title alone, "Have We Visitors from Outer Space?" was enough. Other very reputable magazines, such as True, had said it before, but coming from Life, it was different. Life didn't say that the UFO's were from outer space; it just said maybe. But to back up this "maybe," it had quotes from some famous people. Dr. Walther Riedel, who played an important part in the development of the German V-2 missile and is presently the director of rocket engine research for North American Aviation Corporation, said he believed that the UFO's were from outer space. Dr. Maurice Biot, one of the world's leading aerodynamicists, backed him up.

But the most important thing about the Life article was the question in the minds of so many readers: "Why was it written?" Life doesn't go blasting off on flights of space fancy without a good reason. Some of the readers saw a clue in the author's comments that the hierarchy of the Air Force was now taking a serious look at UFO reports.

"Did the Air Force prompt Life to write the article?" was the question that many people asked themselves.

When I arrived at Dayton, newspapermen were beating down the door. The official answer to the Life article was released through the Office of Public Information in the Pentagon: "The article is factual, but Life's conclusions are their own." In answer to any questions about the article's being Air Force-inspired, my weasel-worded answer was that we had furnished Life with some raw data on specific sightings.

My answer was purposely weasel-worded because I knew that the Air Force had unofficially inspired the Life article. The "maybe they're interplanetary" with the "maybe" bordering on "they are" was the personal opinion of several very high-ranking officers in the Pentagon—so high that their personal opinion was almost policy. I knew the men and I knew that one of them, a general, had passed his opinions on to Bob Ginna.

Oddly enough, the Life article did not cause a flood of reports. The day after the article appeared we got nine sightings, which was unusual, but the next day they dropped off again.

The number of reports did take a sharp rise a few days

later, however. The cause was the distribution of an order that completed the transformation of the UFO from a bastard son to the family heir. The piece of paper that made Project Blue Book legitimate was Air Force Letter 200-5, Subject: Unidentified Flying Objects. The letter, which was duly signed and sealed by the Secretary of the Air Force, in essence stated that UFO's were not a joke, that the Air Force was making a serious study of the problem, and that Project Blue Book was responsible for the study. The letter stated that the commander of every Air Force installation was responsible for forwarding all UFO reports to ATIC by wire, with a copy to the Pentagon. Then a more detailed report would be sent by airmail. Most important of all, it gave Project Blue Book the authority to directly contact any Air Force unit in the United States without going through any chain of command. This was almost unheard of in the Air Force and gave our project a lot of prestige.

The new reporting procedures established by the Air Force letter greatly aided our investigation because it allowed us to start investigating the better reports before they cooled off. But it also had its disadvantages. It authorized the sender to use whatever priority he thought the message warranted. Some things are slow in the military, but a priority message is not one of them. When it comes into the message center, it is delivered to the addressee immediately, and for some reason, all messages reporting UFO's seemed to arrive between midnight and 4:00 A.M. I was considered the addressee on all UFO reports. To complicate matters, the messages were usually classified and I would have to go out to the air base and personally sign for them.

One such message came in about 4:30 A.M. on May 8, 1952. It was from a CAA radio station in Jacksonville, Florida, and had been forwarded over the Flight Service teletype net. I received the usual telephone call from the teletype room at Wright-Patterson, I think I got dressed, and I went out and picked up the message. As I signed for it I remember the night man in the teletype room said, "This is a lulu, Captain."

It was a lulu. About one o'clock that morning a Pan-American airlines DC-4 was flying south toward Puerto Rico. A few hours after it had left New York City it was out over the Atlantic Ocean, about 600 miles off Jacksonville, Florida, flying at 8,000 feet. It was a pitch-black night; a high overcast even cut out the glow from the stars. The pilot and copilot were awake but really weren't concentrating on looking for other aircraft because they had just passed into the San Juan Oceanic Control Area and they had been advised by radio that there were no other airplanes in the area. The copilot was turning around to look at number four engine when he noticed a light up ahead. It looked like the taillight of another airplane. He watched it closely for a few seconds since no other airplanes were supposed to be in the area. He glanced out at number four engine for a few seconds, looked back, and he saw that the light was in about the same position as when he'd first seen it. Then he looked down at the prop controls, synchronized the engines, and looked up again. In the few seconds that he had glanced away from the light, it had moved to the right so that it was now directly ahead of the DC-4, and it had increased in size. The copilot reached over and slapped the pilot on the shoulder and pointed. Just at that instant the light began to get bigger and bigger until it was "ten times the size of a landing light of an airplane." It continued to close in and with a flash it streaked by the DC-4's left wing. Before the crew could react and say anything, two more smaller balls of fire flashed by. Both pilots later said that they sat in their seats for several seconds with sweat trickling down their backs.

It was one of these two pilots who later said, "Were you ever traveling along the highway about 70 miles an hour at night, have the car that you were meeting suddenly swerve over into your lane and then cut back so that you just miss it by inches? You know the sort of sick, empty feeling you get when it's all over? That's just the way we felt."

As soon as the crew recovered from the shock, the pilot picked up his mike, called Jacksonville Radio, and told them about the incident. Minutes later we had the report. The next afternoon Lieutenant Kerry Rothstien, who had replaced Lieutenant Metscher on the project, was on his way to New York to meet the pilots when they returned from Puerto Rico.

When Kerry talked to the two pilots, they couldn't add a great deal to their original story. Their final comment was the one we all had heard so many times, "I always thought these people who reported flying saucers were crazy, but now I don't know."

When Lieutenant Rothstien returned to Dayton he triple-checked with the CAA for aircraft in the area— but there were none. Could there have been airplanes in the area that CAA didn't know about? The answer was almost a flat "No." No one would fly 600 miles off the coast without filing a flight plan; if he got into trouble or went down, the Coast Guard or Air Rescue Service would have no idea where to look.

Kerry was given the same negative answer when he checked on surface shipping.

The last possibility was that the UFO's were meteors,

but several points in the pilots' story ruled these out. First, there was a solid overcast at about 18,000 feet. No meteor cruises along straight and level below 18,000 feet. Second, on only rare occasions have meteors been seen traveling three in trail. The chances of seeing such a phenomenon are well over one in a billion.

Some people have guessed that some kind of an atmospheric phenomenon can form a "wall of air" ahead of an airplane that will act as a mirror and that lights seen at night by pilots are nothing more than the reflection of the airplane's own lights. This could be true in some cases, but to have a reflection you must have a light to reflect. There are no lights on an airplane that even approach being "ten times the size of a landing light."

What was it? I know a colonel who says it was the same thing that the two Eastern Airlines' pilots, Clarence Chiles and John Whitted, saw near Montgomery, Alabama, on July 24, 1948, and he thinks that Chiles and Whitted saw a spaceship.

Reports for the month of April set an all-time high. These were all reports that came from military installations. In addition, we received possibly two hundred letters reporting UFO's, but we were so busy all we could do was file them for future reference.

In May 1952 I'd been out to George AFB in California investigating a series of sightings and was on my way home. I remember the flight to Dayton because the weather was bad all the way. I didn't want to miss my connecting flight in Chicago, or get grounded, because I had faithfully promised my wife that we would go out to dinner the night that I returned to Dayton. I'd called her from Los Angeles to tell her that I was coming in, and she had found a baby sitter and had dinner reservations. I hadn't been home more than about two days a week for the past three months, and she was looking forward to going out for the evening.

I reached Dayton about midmorning and went right out to the base. When I arrived at the office, my secretary was gone but there was a big note on my desk: "Call Colonel Dunn as soon as you get in."

I called Colonel Dunn; then I called my wife and told her to cancel the baby sitter, cancel the dinner reservations, and pack my other bag. I had to go to Washington.

While I'd been in California, Colonel Dunn had received a call from General Samford's office. It seems that a few nights before, one of the top people in the Central Intelligence Agency was having a lawn party at his home just outside Alexandria, Virginia. A number of notable personages were in attendance and they had seen a flying saucer. The report had been passed down to Air Force intelligence, and due to the quality of the brass involved, it was "suggested" that I get to Washington on the double and talk to the host of the party. I was at his office before 5:00 P.M. and got his report.

About ten o'clock in the evening he and two other people were standing near the edge of his yard talking; he happened to be facing south, looking off across the country-side. He digressed a bit from his story to explain that his home is on a hilltop in the country, and when looking south, he had a view of the entire countryside. While he was talking to the two other people he noticed a light approaching from the west. He had assumed it was an airplane and had casually watched it, but when the light got fairly close, the CIA man said that he suddenly realized there wasn't any sound associated with it. If it were an airplane it would have been close enough for him to hear even above the hum of the guests' conversations. He had actually quit talking and was looking at the light when it stopped for an instant and began to climb almost vertically. He said something to the other guests, and they looked up just in time to see the light finish its climb, stop, and level out. They all watched it travel level for a few seconds, then go into a nearly vertical dive, level out, and streak off to the east.

Most everyone at the party had seen the light before it disappeared, and within minutes several friendly arguments as to what it was had developed, I was told. One person thought it was a lighted balloon, and a retired general thought it was an airplane. To settle the arguments, they had made a few telephone calls. I might add that these people were such that the mention of their names on a telephone got quick results. Radar in the Washington area said that there had been no airplanes flying west to east south of Alexandria in the past hour. The weather station at Bolling AFB said that there were no balloons in the area, but as a double check the weather people looked at their records of high-altitude winds. It couldn't have been a balloon because none of the winds up to 65,000 feet were blowing from west to east—and to be able to see a light on a balloon, it has to be well below 65,000 feet; the man from CIA told me that they had even considered the possibility that the UFO was a meteor and that the "jump" had been due to some kind of an atmospheric distortion. But the light had been in sight too long to be a meteor. He added that an army chaplain and two teetotaler guests had also seen the light jump.

There wasn't much left for me to do when I finished talking to the man. He and his guests had already made all of the checks that I'd have made. All I could do was

*go back to Dayton, write up his report, and stamp it
"Unknown."*

*Back in March, when it had become apparent that the
press was reviving its interest in UFO's, I had suggested
that Project Blue Book subscribe to a newspaper clipping
service. Such a service could provide several things.
First, it would show us exactly how much publicity the
UFO's were getting and what was being said, and it
would give us the feel of the situation. Then it would
also provide a lot of data for our files. In many cases the
newspapers got reports that didn't go to the Air Force.
Newspaper reporters rival any intelligence officer when
it comes to digging up facts, and there was always the
possibility that they would uncover and print something
we'd missed. This was especially true in the few cases of
hoaxes that always accompany UFO publicity. Last, it
would provide us with material on which to base a study of the effect of newspaper publicity upon the number
and type of UFO reports.*

*Colonel Dunn liked the idea of the clipping service,
and it went into effect soon after the first publicity had
appeared. Every three or four days we would get an en-
velope full of clippings. In March the clipping service was
sending the clippings to us in letter-sized envelopes. The
envelopes were thin—maybe there would be a dozen or*

*so clippings in each one. Then they began to get thicker
and thicker, until the people who were doing the clipping
switched to using manila envelopes. Then the manila
envelopes began to get thicker and thicker. By May we
were up to old shoe boxes. The majority of the newspaper stories in the shoe boxes were based on material that
had come from ATIC.*

*All of these inquiries from the press were adding to
Blue Book's work load and to my problems. Normally a
military unit such as ATIC has its own public information officer, but we had none so I was it. I was being
quoted quite freely in the press and was repeatedly being
snarled at by someone in the Pentagon. It was almost a
daily occurrence to have people from the "puzzle palace"
call and indignantly ask, "Why did you tell them that?"
They usually referred to some bit of information that somebody didn't think should have been released. I finally
gave up and complained to Colonel Dunn. I suggested
that any contacts with the press be made through the
Office of Public Information in the Pentagon. These
people were trained and paid to do this job; I wasn't.
Colonel Dunn heartily agreed because every time I got
chewed out he at least got a dirty look.*

*Colonel Dunn called General Samford's office and they
brought in General Sory Smith of the Department of*

Defense, Office of Public Information. General Smith appointed a civilian on the Air Force Press Desk, Al Chop, to handle all inquiries from the press. The plan was that Al would try to get his answers from Major Dewey Fournet, Blue Book's liaison officer in the Pentagon, and if Dewey didn't have the answer, Al had permission to call me.

This arrangement worked out fine because Al Chop had been through previous UFO publicity battles when he was in the Office of Public Information at Wright Field.

The interest in the UFO's that was shown by the press in May was surpassed only by the interest of the Pentagon. Starting in May, I gave on the average of one briefing in Washington every two weeks, and there was always a full house. From the tone of the official comments to the public about UFO's, it would indicate that there wasn't a great deal of interest, but nothing could be further from the truth. People say a lot of things behind a door bearing a sign that reads "Secret Briefing in Progress."

After one of the briefings a colonel (who is now a brigadier general) presented a plan that called for using several flights of F-94C jet interceptors for the specific purpose of trying to get some good photographs of UFO's. The flight that he proposed would be an opera-

*tional unit with six aircraft—two would be on constant
alert. The F-94C's, then the hottest operational jet we
had, would be stripped of all combat gear to give them
peak performance, and they would carry a special
camera in the nose. The squadrons would be located
at places in the United States where UFO's were most
frequently seen.*

*The plan progressed to the point of estimating how soon
enough airplanes for two flights could be stripped, how
soon special cameras could be built, and whether or not
two specific Air Force bases in the U.S. could support the
units.*

*Finally the colonel's plan was shelved, but not because he
was considered to be crazy. After considerable study and
debate at high command level, it was decided that twelve F-94C's couldn't be spared for the job and it would
have been ineffective to use fewer airplanes.*

*The consideration that the colonel's plan received was an
indication of how some of the military people felt about
the importance of finding out exactly what the UFO's
really were. And in the discussions the words "interplanetary craft" came up more than once.*

Requests for briefings came even from the highest figure

in the Air Force, Thomas K. Finletter, then the Secretary for Air. On May 8, 1952, Lieutenant Colonel R. J. Taylor of Colonel Dunn's staff and I presented an hour-long briefing to Secretary Finletter and his staff. He listened intently and asked several questions about specific sightings when the briefing was finished. If he was at all worried about the UFO's he certainly didn't show it. His only comment was, "You're doing a fine job, Captain. It must be interesting. Thank you."

Then he made the following statement for the press:

"No concrete evidence has yet reached us either to prove or disprove the existence of the so-called flying saucers. There remain, however, a number of sightings that the Air Force investigators have been unable to explain. As long as this is true, the Air Force will continue to study flying saucer reports."

In May 1952, Project Blue Book received seventy-nine UFO reports compared to ninety-nine in April. It looked as if we'd passed the peak and were now on the downhill side. The 178 reports of the past two months, not counting the thousand or so letters that we'd received directly from the public, had piled up a sizable backlog since we'd had time to investigate and analyze only the better reports. During June we planned to clear out the backlog, and then we could relax.

But never underestimate the power of a UFO. In June the big flap hit—they began to deliver clippings in big cardboard cartons.

CHAPTER 11

The Big Flap

In early June 1952, Project Blue Book was operating according to the operational plan that had been set up in January 1952. It had taken six months to put the plan into effect, and to a person who has never been indoctrinated into the ways of the military, this may seem like a long time. But consult your nearest government worker and you'll find that it was about par for the red tape course.

We had learned early in the project that about 60 per cent of the reported UFO's were actually balloons, airplanes, or astronomical bodies viewed under unusual conditions, so our operational plan was set up to quickly weed out this type of report. This would give us more time to concentrate on the unknown cases.

To weed out reports in which balloons, airplanes, and astronomical bodies were reported as UFO's, we utilized a flow of data that continually poured into Project Blue Book. We received position reports on all flights of the big skyhook balloons and, by merely picking up the telephone, we could get the details about the flight of any other research balloon or regularly scheduled weather balloon in the United States. The location of aircraft in an area where a UFO had been reported was usually checked by the intelligence officer who made the report, but we double-checked his findings by requesting the location of flights front CAA and military air bases. Astronomical almanacs and journals, star charts, and data that we got from observatories furnished us with clues to UFO's that might be astronomical bodies. All of our investigations in this category of report were double-checked by Project Bear's astronomer.

Then we had our newspaper clipping file, which gave us many clues. Hydrographic bulletins and Notams (notices to airmen), published by the government, sometimes gave us other clues. Every six hours we received a complete set of weather data. A dozen or more other sources of data that might shed some light on a reported UFO were continually being studied.

To get all this information on balloons, aircraft, astronomical bodies, and what have you, I had to co-ordinate Project Blue Book's operational plan with the Air Force's Air Weather Service, Flight Service, Research and Development Command, and Air Defense Command with the Navy's Office of Naval Research, and the aerology branch of the Bureau of Aeronautics; and with the Civil

Aeronautics Administration, Bureau of Standards, several astronomical observatories, and our own Project Bear. Our entire operational plan was similar to a Model A Ford I had while I was in high school—just about the time you would get one part working, another part would break down.

When a report came through our screening process and still had the "Unknown" tag on it, it went to the MO file, where we checked its characteristics against other reports. For example, on May 25 we had a report from Randolph AFB, Texas. It went through the screening process and came out "Unknown"; it wasn't a balloon, airplane, or astronomical body. So then it went to the MO file. It was a flock of ducks reflecting the city lights. We knew that the Texas UFO's were ducks because our MO file showed that we had an identical report from Moorhead, Minnesota, and the UFO's at Moorhead were ducks.

Radar reports that came into Blue Book went to the radar specialists of ATIC's electronics branch.

Sifting through reams of data in search of the answers to the many reports that were pouring in each week required many hours of overtime work, but when a report came out with the final conclusion, "Unknown," we were sure that it was unknown.

To operate Project Blue Book, I had four officers, two airmen, and two civilians on my permanent staff. In addition, there were three scientists employed full time on Project Bear, along with several others who worked part time. In the Pentagon, Major Fournet, who had taken on the Blue Book liaison job as an extra duty, was now spending full time on it. If you add to this the number of intelligence officers all over the world who were making preliminary investigations and interviewing UFO observers, Project Blue Book was a sizable effort.

Only the best reports we received could be personally investigated in the field by Project Blue Book personnel. The vast majority of the reports had to be evaluated on the basis of what the intelligence officer who had written the report had been able to uncover, or what data we could get by telephone or by mailing out a questionnaire. Our instructions for "what to do before the Blue Book man arrives," which had been printed in many service publications, were beginning to pay off and the reports were continually getting more detailed.

The questionnaire we were using in June 1952 was the one that had recently been developed by Project Bear. Project Bear, along with psychologists from a midwestern university, had worked on it for five months. Many test models had been tried before it reached its final form —the standard questionnaire that Blue Book is using today.

It ran eight pages and had sixty-eight questions which were booby-trapped in a couple of places to give us a cross check on the reliability of the reporter as an observer. We received quite a few questionnaires answered in such a way that it was obvious that the observer was drawing heavily on his imagination.

From this standard questionnaire the project worked up two more specialized types. One dealt with radar sightings of UFO's, the other with sightings made from airplanes.

In Air Force terminology a "flap" is a condition, or situation, or state of being of a group of people characterized by an advanced degree of confusion that has not quite yet reached panic proportions. It can be brought on by any number of things, including the unexpected visit of an inspecting general, a major administrative reorganization, the arrival of a hot piece of intelligence information, or the dramatic entrance of a well-stacked female into an officers' club bar.

In early June 1952 the Air Force was unknowingly in the initial stages of a flap—a flying saucer flap—the flying saucer flap of 1952. The situation had never been duplicated before, and it hasn't been duplicated since. All records for the number of UFO reports were not just broken, they were disintegrated. In 1948, 167 UFO reports had come into ATIC; this was considered a big year. In June 1952 we received 149. During the four years the Air Force had been in the UFO business, 615 reports had been collected. During the "Big Flap" our incoming-message log . showed 717 reports.

To anyone who had anything to do with flying saucers, the summer of 1952 was just one big swirl of UFO reports, hurried trips, midnight telephone calls, reports to the Pentagon, press interviews, and very little sleep.

If you can pin down a date that the Big Flap started, it would probably be about June 1.

It was also on June 1 that we received a good report of a UFO that had been picked up on radar. June 1 was a Sunday, but I'd been at the office all day getting ready to go to Los Alamos the next day. About 5:00 P.M. the telephone rang and the operator told me that I had a long-distance call from California. My caller was the chief of a radar test section for Hughes Aircraft Company in Los Angeles, and he was very excited about a UFO he had to report.

That morning he and his test crew had been checking out a new late-model radar to get it ready for some tests they planned to run early Monday morning. To see if their set was functioning properly, they had been tracking jets in the Los Angeles area. About midmorning, the Hughes test engineer told me, the jet traffic had begun to drop off, and they were about ready to close down their operation when one of the crew picked up a slow-moving target coming across the San Gabriel Mountains north of Los Angeles. He tracked the target for a few minutes and, from the speed and altitude, decided that it was a DC-3. It was at 11,000 feet and traveling about 180 miles an hour toward Santa Monica. The operator was about ready to yell at the other crew members to shut off the set when he noticed something mighty odd— there was a big gap between the last and the rest of the regularly spaced bright spots on the radarscope. The man on the scope called the rest of the crew in because DC-3's just don't triple their speed. They watched the target as it made a turn and started to climb over Los Angeles. They plotted one, two, three, and then four points during the target's climb; then one of the crew grabbed a slide rule. Whatever it was, it was climbing 35,000 feet per minute and traveling about 550 miles an hour in the process. Then as they watched the scope, the target leveled out for a few seconds, went into a high-speed dive, and again leveled out at 55,000 feet. When they lost the target, it was heading southeast somewhere near Riverside, California.

During the sighting my caller told me that when the UFO was only about ten miles from the radar site two of the crew had gone outside but they couldn't see anything. But, he explained, even the high-flying jets that they had been tracking hadn't been leaving vapor trails.

The first thing I asked when the Hughes test engineer finished his story was if the radar set had been working properly. He said that as soon as the UFO had left the scope they had run every possible check on the radar and it was O.K.

I was just about to ask my caller if the target might not have been some experimental airplane from Edwards AFB when he second-guessed me. He said that after sitting around looking at each other for about a minute, someone suggested that they call Edwards. They did, and Edwards' flight operations told them that they had nothing in the area.

I asked him about the weather. The target didn't look like a weather target was the answer, but just to be sure, the test crew had checked. One of his men was an

*electronics-weather specialist whom he had hired becau-
se of his knowledge of the idiosyncrasies of radar under
certain weather conditions. This man had looked into
the weather angle. He had gotten the latest weather data
and checked it, but there wasn't the slightest indication
of an inversion or any other weather that would cause a
false target.*

*Just before I hung up I asked the man what he thought
he and his crew had picked up, and once again I got
the same old answer: "Yesterday at this time any of us
would have argued for hours that flying saucers were a
bunch of nonsense but now, regardless of what you'll say
about what we saw, it was something damned real."*

*I thanked the man for calling and hung up. We couldn't
make any more of an analysis of this report than had
already been made, it was another unknown.*

*I went over to the MO file and pulled out the stack of
cards behind the tab "High-Speed Climb." There must
have been at least a hundred cards, each one representing a UFO report in which the reported object made a
high-speed climb. But this was the first time radar had
tracked a UFO during a climb.*

During the early part of June, Project Blue Book took

another jump up on the organizational chart. A year before the UFO project had consisted of one officer. It had
risen from the one-man operation to a project within
a group, then to a group, and now it was a section.
Neither Project Sign nor the old Project Grudge had
been higher than the project-within-a-group level. The
chief of a group normally calls for a lieutenant colonel,
and since I was just a captain this caused some conster-
nation in the ranks. There was some talk about putting
Lieutenant Colonel Ray Taylor of Colonel Dunn's staff
in charge. Colonel Taylor was very much interested in
UFO's; he had handled some of the press contacts prior
to turning this function over to the Pentagon and had
gone along with me on briefings, so he knew something
about the project. But in the end Colonel Donald Bower,
who was my division chief, decided rank be damned,
and I stayed on as chief of Project Blue Book.

The location within the organizational chart is always
indicative of the importance placed on a project. In
June 1952 the Air Force was taking the UFO problem
seriously. One of the reasons was that there were a lot of
good UFO reports coming in from Korea. Fighter pilots
reported seeing silver-colored spheres or disks on several
occasions, and radar in Japan, Okinawa, and in Korea
had tracked unidentified targets.

In June our situation map, on which we kept a plot of all of our sightings, began to show an ever so slight trend toward reports beginning to bunch up on the east coast. We discussed this build-up, but we couldn't seem to find any explainable reason for it so we decided that we'd better pay special attention to reports coming from the eastern states.

I had this build-up of reports in mind one Sunday night, June 15 to be exact, when the OD at ATIC called me at home and said that we were getting a lot of reports from Virginia. Each report by itself wasn't too good, the OD told me, but together they seemed to mean something. He suggested that I come out and take a look at them— so I did.

Individually they weren't too good, but when I lined them up chronologically and plotted them on a map they took the form of a hot report.

At 3:40 P.M. a woman at Unionville, Virginia, had reported a "very shiny object" at high altitude.

At 4:20 P.M. the operators of the CAA radio facility at Gordonsville, Virginia, had reported that they saw a "round, shiny object." It was southeast of their station, or directly south of Unionville.

At 4:25 P.M. the crew of an airliner northwest of Richmond, Virginia, reported a "silver sphere at eleven o'clock high."

At 4:43 P.M. a Marine pilot in a jet tried to intercept a "round shiny sphere" south of Gordonsville.

At 5:43 P.M. an Air Force T-33 jet tried to intercept a "shiny sphere" south of Gordonsville. He got above 35,000 feet and the UFO was still far above him.

At 7:35 P.M. many people in Blackstone, Virginia, about 80 miles south of Gordonsville, reported it. It was a "round, shiny object with a golden glow" moving from north to south. By this time radio commentators in central Virginia were giving a running account of the UFO's progress.

At 7:59 P.M. the people in the CAA radio facility at Blackstone saw it. At 8:00 P.M. jets arrived from Langley AFB to attempt to intercept it, but at 8:05 P.M. it disappeared.

This was a good report because it was the first time we ever received a series of reports on the same object, and there was no doubt that all these people had reported the same object. Whatever it was, it wasn't moving too fast, because it had traveled only about 90 miles in four hours and twenty-five minutes. I was about ready to give up until morning and go home when my wife called. The local Associated Press man had called our home and she assumed that it was about this sighting. She had just said that I was out so he might not call the base. I decided that I'd better keep working so I'd have the answer in time to keep the story out of the papers. A report like this could cause some excitement.

The UFO obviously wasn't a planet because it was moving from north to south, and it was too slow to be an airplane. I called the balloon-plotting center at Lowry AFB, where the tracks of the big skyhook balloons are plotted, but the only big balloons in the air were in the western United States, and they were all accounted for.

It might have been a weather balloon. The wind charts showed that the high-altitude winds were blowing in different directions at different altitudes above 35,000 feet, so there was no one flow of air that could have brought a balloon in from a certain area, and I knew that the UFO had to be higher than 35,000 feet because the T-33 jet had been this high and the UFO was still above it. The only thing to do was to check with all of the weather stations in the area. I called Richmond, Roanoke, several places in the vicinity of Washington, D.C., and four or five other weather stations, but all of their balloons were accounted for and none had been anywhere close to the central part of Virginia.

A balloon can travel only so far, so there was no sense in checking stations too far away from where the people had seen the UFO, but I took a chance and called Norfolk; Charleston, West Virginia; Altoona, Pennsylvania; and other stations within a 150-mile radius of Gordonsville mid Blackstone. Nothing.

I still thought it might be a balloon, so I started to call more stations. At Pittsburgh I hit a lead. Their radiosonde balloon had gone up to about 60,000 feet and evidently had sprung a slow leak because it had leveled off at that altitude. Normally balloons go up till they burst at 80,000 or 90,000 feet. The weather forecaster at Pittsburgh said that their records showed they had lost contact with the balloon when it was about 60 miles southeast of their station. He said that the winds at 60,000 feet were constant, so it shouldn't be too difficult to figure out where the balloon went after they had lost it. Things must be dull in Pittsburgh at 2:00 A.M. on Monday mornings, because he offered to plot the course that the balloon probably took and call me back.

In about twenty minutes I got my call. It probably was their balloon, the forecaster said. Above 50,000 feet there was a strong flow of air southeast from Pittsburgh, and this fed into a stronger southerly flow that was paralleling the Atlantic coast just east of the Appalachian Mountains. The balloon would have floated along in this flow of air like a log floating down a river. As close as he could estimate, he said, the balloon would arrive in the Gordonsville-Blackstone area in the late afternoon or early evening. This was just about the time the UFO had arrived.

"Probably a balloon" was a good enough answer for me.

The next morning at 8:00 A.M., Al Chop called from the Pentagon to tell me that people were crawling all over his desk wanting to know about a sighting in Virginia.

The reports continued to come in. At Walnut Lake, Michigan, a group of people with binoculars watched a "soft white light" go back and forth across the western sky for nearly an hour. A UFO "paced" an Air Force B-25 for thirty minutes in California. Both of these happened on June 18, and although we checked and rechecked them, they came out as unknowns.

On June 19 radar at Goose AFB in Newfoundland

picked up some odd targets. The targets came across
the scope, suddenly enlarged, and then became smaller
again. One unofficial comment was that the object was
flat or disk-shaped, and that the radar target had gotten
bigger because the disk had banked in flight to present a
greater reflecting surface. ATIC's official comment was
weather.

Goose AFB was famous for unusual reports. In early
UFO history someone had taken a very unusual colored
photo of a "split cloud." The photographer had seen a
huge ball of fire streak down through the sky and pass
through a high layer of stratus clouds. As the fireball
passed through the cloud it cut out a perfect swath. The
conclusion was that the fireball was a meteor, but the
case is still one of the most interesting in the file because
of the photograph.

Then in early 1952 there was another good report from
this area. It was an unknown.

The incident started when the pilot of an Air Force C-54
transport radioed Goose AFB and said that at 10:42
P.M. a large fireball had buzzed his airplane. It had
come in from behind the C-54, and nobody had seen
it until it was just off the left wink. The fireball was so
big that the pilot said it looked as if it was only a few

hundred feet away. The C-54 was 200 miles southwest, coming into Goose AFB from Westover AFB, Massachusetts, when the incident occurred. The base officer-of-the-day, who was also a pilot, happened to be in the flight operations office at Goose when the message came in and he overheard the report. He stepped outside, walked over to his command car, and told his driver about the radio message, so the driver got out and both of them looked toward the south. They searched the horizon for a few seconds; then suddenly they saw a light closing in from the southwest. Within a second, it was near the airfield. It had increased in size till it was as big as a "golf ball at arm's length," and it looked like a big ball of fire. It was so low that both the OD and his driver dove under the command car because they were sure it was going to hit the airfield. When they turned and looked up they saw the fireball make a 90-degree turn over the airfield and disappear into the northwest. The time was 10:47 P.M.

The control tower operators saw the fireball too, but didn't agree with the OD and his driver on how low it was. They did think that it had made a 90-degree turn and they didn't think that it was a meteor. In the years they'd been in towers they'd seen hundreds of meteors, but they'd never seen anything like this, they reported.

And reports continued to pour into Project Blue Book. It was now not uncommon to get ten or eleven wires in one day. If the letters reporting UFO sightings were counted, the total would rise to twenty or thirty a day. The majority of the reports that came in by wire could be classified as being good. They were reports made by reliable people and they were full of details. Some were reports of balloons, airplanes, etc., but the percentage of unknowns hovered right around 22 per cent.

To describe and analyze each report, or even the unknowns, would require a book the size of an unabridged dictionary, so I am covering only the best and most representative cases.

One day in mid-June, Colonel Dunn called me. He was leaving for Washington and he wanted me to come in the next day to give a briefing at a meeting. By this time I was taking these briefings as a matter of course. We usually gave the briefings to General Garland and a general from the Research and Development Board, who passed the information on to General Samford, the Director of Intelligence. But this time General Samford, some of the members of his staff, two Navy captains from the Office of Naval Intelligence, and some people I can't name were at the briefing.

When I arrived in Washington, Major Fournet told me that the purpose of the meetings, and my briefing, was to try to find out if there was any significance to the almost alarming increase in UFO reports over the past few weeks.

By the time that everyone had finished signing into the briefing room in the restricted area of the fourth-floor "B" ring of the Pentagon, it was about 9:15 A.M. I started my briefing as soon as everyone was seated.

I reviewed the last month's UFO activities; then I briefly went over the more outstanding "Unknown" UFO reports and pointed out how they were increasing in number—breaking all previous records. I also pointed out that even though the UFO subject was getting a lot of publicity, it wasn't the scare-type publicity that had accompanied the earlier flaps—in fact, much of the present publicity was anti-saucer.

Then I went on to say that even though the reports we were getting were detailed and contained a great deal of good data, we still had no proof the UFO's were anything real. We could, I said, prove that all UFO reports were merely the misinterpretation of known objects if we made a few assumptions.

At this point one of the colonels on General Samford's staff stopped me. "Isn't it true," he asked, "that if you make a few positive assumptions instead of negative assumptions you can just as easily prove that the UFO's are interplanetary spaceships? Why, when you have to make an assumption to get an answer to a report, do you always pick the assumption that proves the UFO's don't exist?"

You could almost hear the colonel add, "O.K., so now I've said it."

For several months the belief that Project Blue Book was taking a negative attitude and the fact that the UFO's could be interplanetary spaceships had been growing in the Pentagon, but these ideas were usually discussed only in the privacy of offices with doors that would close tight.

No one said anything, so the colonel who had broken the ice plunged in. He used the sighting from Goose AFB, where the fireball had buzzed the C-54 and sent the OD and his driver belly-whopping under the command car as an example. The colonel pointed out that even though we had labeled the report "Unknown" it wasn't accepted as proof. He wanted to know why.

I said that our philosophy was that the fireball could have been two meteors: one that buzzed the C-54 and another that streaked across the airfield at Goose AFB. Granted a meteor doesn't come within feet of an airplane or make a 90-degree turn, but these could have been optical illusions of some kind. The crew of the C-54, the OD, his driver, and the tower operators didn't recognize the UFO's as meteors because they were used to seeing the normal "shooting stars" that are most commonly seen.

But the colonel had some more questions. "What are the chances of having two extremely spectacular meteors in the same area, traveling the same direction, only five minutes apart?"

I didn't know the exact mathematical probability, but it was rather small, I had to admit.

Then he asked, "What kind of an optical illusion would cause a meteor to appear to make a 90-degree turn?"

I had asked our Project Bear astronomer this same question, and he couldn't answer it either. So the only answer I could give the colonel was, "I don't know."

I felt as if I were on a witness stand being cross-exami-

ned, and that is exactly where I was, because the colonel cut loose.

"Why not assume a point that is more easily proved?" he asked. "Why not assume that the C-54 crew, the OD, his driver, and the tower operators did know what they were talking about? Maybe they had seen spectacular meteors during the hundreds of hours that they had flown at night and the many nights that they had been on duty in the tower. Maybe the ball of fire had made a 90-degree turn. Maybe it was some kind of an intelligently controlled craft that had streaked northeast across the Gulf of St. Lawrence and Quebec Province at 2,400 miles an hour.

"Why not just simply believe that most people know what they saw?" the colonel said with no small amount of sarcasm in his voice.

This last comment started a lively discussion, and I was able to retreat. The colonel had been right in a sense—we were being conservative, but maybe this was the right way to be. In any scientific investigation you always assume that you don't have enough proof until you get a positive answer. I don't think that we had a positive answer—yet.

*The colonel's comments split the group, and a hot
exchange of ideas, pros and cons, and insinuations that
some people were imitating ostriches to keep from facing
the truth followed.*

*The outcome of the meeting was a directive to take fur-
ther steps to obtain positive identification of the UFO's.
Our original idea of attempting to get several separate
reports from one sighting so we could use triangulation
to measure speed, altitude, and size wasn't working out.
We had given the idea enough publicity, but reports
where triangulation could be used were few and far
between. Mr. or Mrs. Average Citizen just doesn't look
up at the sky unless he or she sees a flash of light or
hears a sound. Then even if he or she does look up and
sees a UFO, it is very seldom that the report ever gets
to Project Blue Book. I think that it would be safe to
say that Blue Book only heard about 10 per cent of the
UFO's that were seen in the United States.*

*After the meeting I went back to ATIC, and the next day
Colonel Don Bower and I left for the west coast to talk
to some people about how to get better UFO data. We
brought back the idea of using an extremely long focal-
length camera equipped with a diffraction grating.*

The cameras would be placed at various locations

throughout the United States where UFO's were most frequently seen. We hoped that photos of the UFO's taken through the diffraction gratings would give us some proof one way or the other.

The diffraction gratings we planned to use over the lenses of the cameras were the same thing as prisms; they would split up the light from the UFO into its component parts so that we could study it and determine whether it was a meteor, an airplane, or balloon reflecting sunlight, etc. Or we might be able to prove that the photographed UFO was a craft completely foreign to our knowledge.

A red-hot, A-1 priority was placed on the camera project, and a section at ATIC that developed special equipment took over the job of obtaining the cameras, or, if necessary, having them designed and built.

But the UFO's weren't waiting around till they could be photographed. Every day the tempo and confusion were increasing a little more.

By the end of June it was very noticeable that most of the better reports were coming from the eastern United States. In Massachusetts, New Jersey, and Maryland jet fighters had been scrambled almost nightly for a week.

On three occasions radar-equipped F-94's had locked on aerial targets only to have the lock-on broken by the apparent violent maneuvers of the target.

By the end of June there was also a lull in the newspaper publicity about the UFO's. The forthcoming political conventions had wiped out any mention of flying saucers. But on July 1 there was a sudden outbreak of good reports. The first one came from Boston; then they worked down the coast.

About seven twenty-five on the morning of July 1 two F-94's were scrambled to intercept a UFO that a Ground Observer Corps spotter reported was traveling southwest across Boston. Radar couldn't pick it up so the two airplanes were just vectored into the general area. The F-94's searched the area but couldn't see anything. We got the report at ATIC and would have tossed it out if it hadn't been for other reports from the Boston area at that same time.

One of these reports came from a man and his wife at Lynn, Massachusetts, nine miles northeast of Boston. At seven-thirty they had noticed the two vapor trails from the climbing jet interceptors. They looked around the sky to find out if they could see what the jets were after and off to the west they saw a bright silver "cigar-shaped object about six times as long as it was wide" traveling southwest across Boston. It appeared to be traveling just a little faster than the two jets. As they watched they saw that an identical UFO was following the first one some distance back. The UFO's weren't leaving vapor trails but, as the man mentioned in his report, this didn't mean anything because you can get above the vapor trail level. And the two UFO's appeared to be at a very high altitude. The two observers watched as the two F-94's searched back and forth far below the UFO's.

Then there was another report, also made at seven-thirty. An Air Force captain was just leaving his home in Bedford, about 15 miles northwest of Boston and straight west of Lynn, when he saw the two jets. In his report he said that he, too, had looked around the sky to see if he could see what they were trying to intercept when off to the east he saw a "silvery cigar-shaped object" traveling south. His description of what he observed was almost identical to what the couple in Lynn reported except that he saw only one UFO.

When we received the report, I wanted to send someone up to Boston immediately in the hope of getting more data from the civilian couple and the Air Force captain; this seemed to be a tailor-made case for triangulation. But by July 1 we were completely snowed under with *reports, and there just wasn't anybody to send. Then, to complicate matters, other reports came in later in the day.*

Just two hours after the sighting in the Boston area Fort Monmouth, New Jersey, popped back into UFO history. At nine-thirty in the morning twelve student radar operators and three instructors were tracking nine jets on an SCR 584 radar set when two UFO targets appeared on the scope. The two targets came in from the northeast at a slow speed, much slower than the jets that were being tracked, hovered near Fort Monmouth at 50,000 feet for about five minutes, and then took off in a "terrific burst of speed" to the southwest.

When the targets first appeared, some of the class went outside with an instructor, and after searching the sky for about a minute, they saw two shiny objects in the same location as the radar showed the two unidentified targets to be. They watched the two UFO's for several minutes and saw them go zipping off to the southwest at exactly the same time that the two radar targets moved off the scope in that direction.

We had plotted these reports, the ones from Boston and the one from Fort Monmouth, on a map, and without injecting any imagination or wild assumptions, it looked as if two "somethings" had come down across Boston on a southwesterly heading, crossed Long Island, hovered for a few minutes over the Army's secret laboratories at Fort Monmouth, then proceeded toward Washington. In a way we half expected to get a report from Washington. Our expectations were rewarded because in a few hours a report arrived from that city.

A physics professor at George Washington University reported a "dull, gray, smoky-colored" object which hovered north northwest of Washington for about eight minutes. Every once in a while, the professor reported, it would move through an arc of about 15 degrees to the right or left, but it always returned to its original position. While he was watching the UFO he took a 25-cent piece out of his pocket and held it at arm's length so that he could compare its size to that of the UFO. The UFO was about half the diameter of the quarter. When he first saw the UFO, it was about 30 to 40 degrees above the horizon, but during the eight minutes it was in sight it steadily dropped lower and lower until buildings in downtown Washington blocked off the view.

Besides being an "Unknown," this report was exceptionally interesting to us because the sighting was made from the center of downtown Washington, D.C. The professor reported that he had noticed the UFO when

*he saw people all along the street looking up in the air
and pointing. He estimated that at least 500 people were
looking at it, yet his was the only report we received.
This seemed to substantiate our theory that people
are very hesitant to report UFO's to the Air Force. But
they evidently do tell the newspapers because later
on we picked up a short account of the sighting in the
Washington papers. It merely said that hundreds of calls
had been received from people reporting a UFO.*

*When reports were pouring in at the rate of twenty or
thirty a day, we were glad that people were hesitant
to report UFO's, but when we were trying to find the
answer to a really knotty sighting we always wished that
more people had reported it. The old adage of having
your cake and eating it, too, held even for the UFO.*

*Technically no one in Washington, besides, of course,
Major General Samford and his superiors, had anything
to do with making policy decisions about the operation of Project Blue Book or the handling of the UFO
situation in general. Nevertheless, everyone was trying
to get into the act. The split in opinions on what to do
about the rising tide of UFO reports, the split that first
came out in the open at General Samford's briefing, was
widening every day. One group was getting dead-serious
about the situation. They thought we now had plenty of*

evidence to back up an official statement that the UFO's were something real and, to be specific, not something from this earth. This group wanted Project Blue Book to quit spending time investigating reports from the standpoint of trying to determine if the observer of a UFO had actually seen something foreign to our knowledge and start assuming that he or she had. They wanted me to aim my investigation at trying to find out more about the UFO. Along with this switch in operating policy, they wanted to clamp down on the release of information. They thought that the security classification of the project should go up to Top Secret until we had all of the answers, then the information should be released to the public. The investigation of UFO's along these lines should be a maximum effort, they thought, and their plans called for lining up many top scientists to devote their full time to the project. Someone once said that enthusiasm is infectious, and he was right. The enthusiasm of this group took a firm hold in the Pentagon, at Air Defense Command Headquarters, on the Research and Development Board, and many other agencies throughout the government. But General Samford was still giving the orders, and he said to continue to operate just as we had—keeping an open mind to any ideas.

After the minor flurry of reports on July 1 we had a short breathing spell and found time to clean up a sizable backlog of reports. People were still seeing UFO's but the frequency of the sighting curve was dropping steadily. During the first few days of July we were getting only two or three good reports a day.

On July 5 the crew of a non-scheduled airliner made page two of many newspapers by reporting a UFO over the AEC's supersecret Hanford, Washington, installation. It was a skyhook balloon. On the twelfth a huge meteor sliced across Indiana, southern Illinois, and Missouri that netted us twenty or thirty reports. Even before they had stopped coming in, we had confirmation from our astronomer that the UFO was a meteor.

But forty-two minutes later there was a sighting in Chicago that wasn't so easily explained.

According to our weather records, on the night of July 12 it was hot in Chicago. At nine forty-two there were at least 400 people at Montrose Beach trying to beat the heat. Many of them were lying down looking at the stars, so that they saw the UFO as it came in from the west northwest, made a 180-degree turn directly over their heads, and disappeared over the horizon. It was a "large red light with small white lights on the side," most of the people reported. Some of them said that it changed to a single yellow light as it made its turn. It was in sight about five minutes, and during this time no one reported hearing any sound.

One of the people at the beach was the weather officer from O'Hare International Airport, an Air Force captain. He immediately called O'Hare. They checked on balloon flights and with radar, but both were negative; radar said that there had been no aircraft in the area of Montrose Beach for several hours.

I sent an investigator to Chicago, and although he came back with a lot of data on the sighting, it didn't add up to be anything known.

The next day Dayton had its first UFO sighting in a long time when a Mr. Roy T. Ellis, president of the Rubber Seal Products Company, and many other people, reported a teardrop-shaped object that hovered over Dayton for several minutes about midnight. This sighting had an interesting twist because two years later I was in Dayton and stopped in at ATIC to see a friend who is one of the technical advisers at the center.

Naturally the conversation got around to the subject of UFO's, and he asked me if I remembered this specific sighting. I did, so he went on to say that he and his wife had seen this UFO that night but they had never told anybody. He was very serious when he admitted that he had no idea what it could have been. Now I'd heard this statement a thousand times before from other people, but coming from this person, it was really something because he was as anti-saucer as anyone I knew. Then he added, "From that time on I didn't think your saucer reporters were as crazy as I used to think they were."

The Dayton sighting also created quite a stir in the press. In conjunction with the sighting, the Dayton Daily Journal had interviewed Colonel Richard H. Magee, the Dayton-Oakwood civil defense director; they wanted to know what he thought about the UFO's. The colonel's answer made news: "There's something flying around in our skies and we wish we knew what it was."

When the story broke in other papers, the colonel's affiliation with civil defense wasn't mentioned, and he became merely "a colonel from Dayton." Dayton was quickly construed by the public to mean Wright-Patterson AFB and specifically ATIC. Some people in the Pentagon screamed while others gleefully clapped their hands. The gleeful handclaps were from those people who wanted the UFO's to be socially recognized, and they believed that if they couldn't talk their ideas into being they might be able to force them in with the help of this type of publicity.

The temporary lull in reporting that Project Blue Book had experienced in early July proved to be only the calm before the storm. By mid-July we were getting about twenty reports a day plus frantic calls from intelligence officers all over the United States as every Air Force installation in the U.S. was being swamped with reports. We told the intelligence officers to send in the ones that sounded the best.

The build-up in UFO reports wasn't limited to the United States—every day we would receive reports from our air attachés in other countries. England and France led the field, with the South American countries running a close third. Needless to say, we didn't investigate or evaluate foreign reports because we had our hands full right at home.

Most of us were putting in fourteen hours a day, six days a week. It wasn't at all uncommon for Lieutenant Andy Flues, Bob Olsson, or Kerry Rothstien, my investigators, to get their sleep on an airliner going out or coming back from an investigation. TWA airliners out of Dayton were more like home than home. But we hadn't seen anything yet.

All the reports that were coming in were good ones, ones with no answers. Unknowns were running about 40 per cent. Rumors persist that in mid-July 1952 the Air Force was braced for an expected invasion by flying saucers. Had these rumormongers been at ATIC in mid-July they would have thought that the invasion was already in full swing. And they would have thought that one of the beachheads for the invasion was Patrick AFB, the Air Force's Guided Missile Long-Range Proving Ground on the east coast of Florida.

On the night of July 18, at ten forty-five, two officers were standing in front of base operations at Patrick when they noticed a light at about a 45-degree angle from the horizon and off to the west. It was an amber color and "quite a bit brighter than a star." Both officers had heard flying saucer stories, and both thought the light was a balloon. But, to be comedians, they called to several more officers and airmen inside the operations office and told them to come out and "see the flying saucer." The people came out and looked. A few were surprised and took the mysterious light seriously, at the expense of considerable laughter from the rest of the group. The discussion about the light grew livelier and bets that it was a balloon were placed. In the meantime the light had drifted over the base, had stopped for about a minute, turned, and was now heading north. To settle the bet, one of the officers stepped into the base weather office to find out about the balloon. Yes, one was in the air and being tracked by radar, he was told. The weather officer said that he would call to find out exactly where it was. He called and found out that the weather balloon was being tracked due west of the base and that the light had gone out about ten minutes before. The officer went back outside to find that what was first thought to be a balloon was now straight north of the field and still lighted. To add to the confusion, a second amber light had appeared in the west about 20 degrees lower than where the first one was initially seen, and it was also heading north but at a much greater speed. In a few seconds the first light stopped and started moving back south over the base.

While the group of officers and airmen were watching the two lights, the people from the weather office came out to tell the UFO observers that the balloon was still traveling straight west. They were just in time to see a third light come tearing across the sky, directly overhead, from west to east. A weatherman went inside and called the balloon-tracking crew again—their balloon was still far to the west of the base.

Inside of fifteen minutes two more amber lights came in from the west, crossed the base, made a 180-degree turn over the ocean, and came back over the observers.

In the midst of the melee a radar set had been turned

on but it couldn't pick up any targets. This did, however, eliminate the possibility of the lights' being aircraft. They weren't stray balloons either, because the winds at all altitudes were blowing in a westerly direction. They obviously weren't meteors. They weren't searchlights on a haze layer because there was no weather conducive to forming a haze layer and there were no searchlights. They could have been some type of natural phenomenon, if one desires to take the negative approach. Or, if you take the positive approach, they could have been spaceships.

CHAPTER 12

What Are UFO's?

It was just a few minutes before midnight on January 28, 1953, when a message flashed into Wright-Patterson for Project Blue Book. It was sent "Operational Immediate," so it had priority handling; I was reading it by 12:30 A.M. A pilot had chased a UFO.

The report didn't have many details but it did sound good. It gave the pilot's name and said that he could be reached at Moody AFB. I put in a long-distance call, found the pilot, and flipped on my recorder so that I could get his story word for word.

He told me that he had been flying an F-86 on a "round-robin" navigation flight from Moody AFB to Lawson AFB to Robins AFB, then back to Moody—all in Georgia. At exactly nine thirty-five he was at 6,000 feet, heading toward Lawson AFB on the first leg of his flight. He remembered that he had just looked down and had seen the lights of Albany, Georgia; then he'd looked up again and seen this bright white light at "ten o'clock high." It was an unusually bright light, and he said that he thought this was why it was so noticeable among the stars. He flew on for a few minutes watching it as he passed over Albany. He decided that it must be an extremely bright star or another airplane—except it just didn't look right. It had too much of a definitely circular shape.

It was a nice night to fly and he had to get in so much time anyway, so he thought he'd try to get a little closer to it. If it was an airplane, chances were he could close in and if it was a star, he should be able to climb up to 30,000 feet and the light shouldn't change its relative position. He checked his oxygen supply, increased the r.p.m. of the engine, and started to climb. In three or four minutes it was obvious that he was getting above the light, and he watched it; it had moved in relation to the stars. It must be an airplane then, he'd decided—an airplane so far away that he couldn't see its red and green wing tip lights.

Since he'd gone this far, he decided that he'd get closer and make sure it was an airplane; so he dropped the nose of the F-86 and started down. As the needle on the machmeter nudged the red line, he saw that he was getting closer because the light was getting bigger, but still he couldn't see any lights other than the one big white one. Then it wasn't white any longer; it was changing color. In about a two-second cycle it changed from white to red, then back to white again. It went through this cycle two or three times, and then before he could realize what was going on, he told me, the light changed in shape to a perfect triangle. Then it split into two triangles, one above the other. By this time he had leveled off and wasn't closing in any more. In a flash the whole thing was gone. He used the old standard description for a disappearing UFO: "It was just like someone turning off a light—it's there, then it's gone."

I asked him what he thought he'd seen. He'd thought about flying saucers, he said, but he "just couldn't swallow those stories." He thought he had a case of vertigo and the more he thought about it, the surer he was that this was the answer. He'd felt pretty foolish, he told me, and he was glad that he was alone.

Up ahead he saw the sprawling lights of Fort Benning and Lawson AFB, his turning point on the flight, and he'd started to turn but then he'd checked his fuel. The climb had used up quite a bit, so he changed his mind about going to Robins AFB and started straight back to Moody.

He called in to the ground station to change his flight plan, but before he could say anything the ground radio operator asked him if he'd seen a mysterious light.

Well—he'd seen a light.

Then the ground operator proceeded to tell him that the UFO chase had been watched on radar. First the radar had the UFO target on the scope, and it was a UFO because it was traveling much too slowly to be an airplane. Then the radar operators saw the F-86 approach, climb, and make a shallow dive toward the UFO. At first the F-86 had closed in on the UFO, but then the UFO had speeded up just enough to maintain a comfortable lead. This went on for two or three minutes; then it had moved off the scope at a terrific speed. The radar site had tried to call him, the ground station told the F-86 pilot, but they couldn't raise him so the message had to be relayed through the tower.

Rack up two more points for the UFO—another unknown and another confirmed believer.

Two or three weeks after the meeting of the panel of scientists in Washington I received word that Project Blue Book would follow the recommendations that the panel had made. I was to start implementing the plan right away. Our proposal for setting up instruments had gone to the Pentagon weeks before, so that was already taken care of. We needed more people, so I drew up a new organizational cable that called for more investigators and analysts and sent it through to ATIC's personnel section.

About this time in the history of the UFO the first of a series of snags came up. The scientists had strongly recommended that we hold nothing back—give the public everything. Accordingly, when the press got wind of the Tremonton Movie, which up until this time had been a closely guarded secret, I agreed to release it for the newsmen to see. I wrote a press release which was O.K.'d by General Garland, then the chief of ATIC, and sent it to the Pentagon. It told what the panel had said about the movies, "until proved otherwise there is no reason why the UFO's couldn't have been sea gulls." Then the release went on to say that we weren't sure exactly what the UFO's were, the sea gull theory was only an opinion. When the Pentagon got the draft of the release they screamed, "No!" No movie for the press and no press release. The sea gull theory was too weak, and we had a new publicity policy as of now—don't say anything.

This policy, incidentally, is still in effect. The January 7, 1955, issue of the Air Force Information Services Letter said, in essence, people in the Air Force are talking too much about UFO's—shut up. The old theory that if you ignore them they'll go away is again being followed.

Inside of a month the UFO project took a few more hard jolts. In December of 1952 I'd asked for a transfer. I'd agreed to stay on as chief of Blue Book until the end of

February so that a replacement could be obtained and be broken in. But no replacement showed up. And none showed up when Lieutenant Rothstien's tour of active duty ended, when Lieutenant Andy Flues transferred to the Alaskan Air Command, or when others left. When I left the UFO project for a two-month tour of temporary duty in Denver, Lieutenant Bob Olsson took over as chief. His staff consisted of Airman First Class Max Futch. Both men were old veterans of the UFO campaign of '52, but two people can do only so much.

When I came back to ATIC in July 1953 and took over another job, Lieutenant Olsson was just getting out of the Air Force and A1/c Futch was now it. He said that he felt like the President of Antarctica on a non-expedition year. In a few days I again had Project Blue Book, as an additional duty this time, and I had orders to "build it up."

While I had been gone, our instrumentation plan had been rejected. Higher headquarters had decided against establishing a net of manned tracking stations, astronomical cameras tied in with radars, and our other proposed instrumentation. General Garland had argued long and hard for the plan, but he'd lost. It was decided that the cameras with diffraction gratings over the lenses, the cameras that had been under development for a year, would suffice.

The camera program had started out as a top-priority project, but it had lost momentum fast when we'd tested these widely publicized instruments and found that they wouldn't satisfactorily photograph a million-candle power flare at 450 yards. The cameras themselves were all right, but in combination with the gratings, they were no good. However, Lieutenant Olsson had been told to send them out, so he sent them out.

The first thing that I did when I returned to Project Blue Book was to go over the reports that had come in while I was away. There were several good reports but only one that was exceptional. It had taken place at Luke AFB, Arizona, the Air Force's advanced fighter-bomber school that is named after the famous "balloon buster" of World War I, Lieutenant Frank Luke, Jr. It was a sighting that produced some very interesting photographs.

There were only a few high cirrus clouds in the sky late on the morning of March 3 when a pilot took off from Luke in an F-84 jet to log some time. He had been flying F-51's in Korea and had recently started to check out in the jets. He took off, cleared the traffic pattern, and started climbing toward Blythe Radio, about 130 miles west of Luke. He'd climbed for several minutes and had just picked up the coded letters BLH that identified Blythe Radio when he looked up through the corner glass in

the front part of his canopy—high at about two o'clock
he saw what he thought was an airplane angling across
his course from left to right leaving a long, thin vapor
trail. He glanced down at his altimeter and saw that
he was at 23,000 feet. The object that was leaving the
vapor trail must really be high, he remembered thinking,
because he couldn't see any airplane at the head of it.
He altered his course a few degrees to the right so that
he could follow the trail and increased his rate of climb.
Before long he could tell that he was gaining on the
object, or whatever was leaving the vapor trail, because
he was under the central part of it. But he still couldn't
see any object. This was odd, he thought, because vapor
trails don't just happen; something has to leave them.
His altimeter had ticked off another 12,000 feet and he
was now at 35,000. He kept on climbing, but soon the
'84 began to mush; it was as high as it would go. The
pilot dropped down 1,000 feet and continued on—now
he was below the front of the trail, but still no airplane.
This bothered him too. Nothing that we have flies over
55,000 feet except a few experimental airplanes like the
D-558 or those of the ”X” series, and they don't stray far
from Edwards AFB in California. He couldn't be more
than 15,000 feet from the front of the trail, and you
can recognize any kind of an airplane 15,000 feet away
in the clear air of the substratosphere. He looked and
he looked and he looked. He rocked the F-84 back and

forth thinking maybe he had a flaw in the plexiglass of the canopy that was blinking out the airplane, but still no airplane. Whatever it was, it was darn high or darn small. It was moving about 300 miles an hour because he had to pull off power and "S" to stay under it.

He was beginning to get low on fuel about this time so he hauled up the nose of the jet, took about 30 feet of gun camera film, and started down. When he landed and told his story, the film was quickly processed and rushed to the projection room. It showed a weird, thin, forked vapor trail—but no airplane.

Lieutenant Olsson and Airman Futch had worked this one over thoroughly. The photo lab confirmed that the trail was definitely a vapor trail, not a freak cloud formation. But Air Force Flight Service said, "No other airplanes in the area," and so did Air Defense Command, because minutes after the F-84 pilot broke off contact, the "object" had passed into an ADIZ—Air Defense Identification Zone—and radar had shown nothing.

There was one last possibility: Blue Book's astronomer said that the photos looked exactly like a meteor's smoke trail. But there was one hitch: the pilot was positive that the head of the vapor trail was moving at about 300 miles an hour. He didn't know exactly how much ground he'd covered, but when he first picked up Blythe Radio he was on Green 5 airway, about 30 miles west of his base, and when he'd given up the chase he'd gotten another radio bearing, and he was now almost up to Needles Radio, 70 miles north of Blythe. He could see a lake, Lake Mojave, in the distance.

Could a high-altitude jet-stream wind have been blowing the smoke cloud? Futch had checked this—no. The winds above 20,000 feet were the usual westerlies and the jet stream was far to the north.

Several months later I talked to a captain who had been at Luke when this sighting occurred. He knew the F-84 pilot and he'd heard him tell his story in great detail. I won't say that he was a confirmed believer, but he was interested. "I never thought much about these reports before," he said, "but I know this guy well. He's not nuts. What do you think he saw?"

I don't know what he saw. Maybe he didn't travel as far as he thought he did. If he didn't, then I'd guess that he saw a meteor's smoke trail. But if he did know that he'd covered some 80 miles during the chase, I'd say that he saw a UFO—a real one. And I find it hard to believe that pilots don't know what they're doing.

During the summer of 1953, UFO reports dropped off considerably. During May, June, and July of 1952 we'd received 637 good reports. During the same months in 1953 we received only seventy-six. We had been waiting for the magic month of July to roll around again because every July there had been the sudden and unexplained peak in reporting; we wanted to know if it would happen again. It didn't—only twenty-one reports came in, to make July the lowest month of the year. But July did bring new developments.

Project Blue Book got a badly needed shot in the arm when an unpublicized but highly important change took place: another intelligence agency began to take over all field investigations.

Ever since I'd returned to the project, the orders had been to build it up—get more people—do what the panel recommended. But when I'd asked for more people, all I got was a polite "So sorry." So, I did the next best thing and tried to find some organization already in being which could and would help us. I happened to be expounding my troubles one day at Air Defense Command Headquarters while I was briefing General Burgess, ADC's Director of Intelligence, and he told me about his 4602nd Air Intelligence Squadron, a specialized intelligence unit that had recently become operational.

Maybe it could help—he'd see what he could work out, he told me.

Now in the military all commitments to do something carry an almost standard time factor. "I'll expedite it," means nothing will happen for at least two weeks. "I'll do it right away," means from a month to six weeks. An answer like, "I'll see what I can work out," requires writing a memo that explains what the person was going to see if he could work out and sealing it in a time capsule for preservation so that when the answer finally does come through the future generation that receives it will know how it all started. But I underestimated the efficiency of the Air Defense Command. Inside of two weeks General Burgess had called General Garland, they'd discussed the problem, and I was back in Colorado Springs setting up a program with Colonel White's 4602nd.

The 4602nd's primary function is to interrogate captured enemy airmen during wartime; in peacetime all that they can do is participate in simulated problems. Investigating UFO reports would supplement these problems and add a factor of realism that would be invaluable in their training. The 4602nd had field teams spread out all over the United States, and these teams could travel anywhere by airplane, helicopter, canoe, jeep, or skis on a minute's notice. The field teams had already established a working contact with the highway patrols, sheriffs' offices, police, and the other military in their respective areas, so they were in an excellent position to collect facts about a UFO report. Each member of the field teams had been especially chosen and trained in the art of interrogation, and each team had a technical specialist. We couldn't have asked for a better ally.

Project Blue Book was once more back in business. Until the formal paper work went through, our plan was that whenever a UFO report worth investigating came in we would call the 4602nd and they would get a team out right away. The team would make a thorough investigation and wire us their report. If the answer came back "Unknown," we would study the details of the sighting and, with the help of Project Bear, try to find the answer.

A few weeks after the final plans had been made with the 4602nd, I again bade farewell to Project Blue Book. In a simple ceremony on the poop deck of one of the flying saucers that I frequently have been accused of capturing, before a formation of the three-foot-tall green men that I have equally as frequently been accused of keeping prisoner, I turned my command over to A1/c Max Futch and walked out the door into civilian life with separation orders in hand.

The UFO's must have known that I was leaving because the day I found out that officers with my specialty, technical intelligence, were no longer on the critical list and that I could soon get out of the service, they really put on a show. The show they put on is still the best UFO report in the Air Force files.

I first heard about the sighting about two o'clock on the morning of August 13, 1953, when Max Futch called me from ATIC. A few minutes before a wire had come in carrying a priority just under that reserved for flashing the word the U.S. has been attacked. Max had been called over to ATIC by the OD to see the report, and he thought that I should see it. I was a little hesitant to get dressed and go out to the base, so I asked Max what he thought about the report. His classic answer will go down in UFO history, "Captain," Max said in his slow, pure Louisiana drawl, "you know that for a year I've read every flying saucer report that's come in and that I never really believed in the things." Then he hesitated and added, so fast that I could hardly understand him, "But you should read this wire." The speed with which he uttered this last statement was in itself enough to convince me. When Max talked fast, something was important.

A half hour later I was at ATIC—just in time to get a

call from the Pentagon. Someone else had gotten out of bed to read his copy of the wire.

I used the emergency orders that I always kept in my desk and caught the first airliner out of Dayton to Rapid City, South Dakota. I didn't call the 4602nd because I wanted to investigate this one personally. I talked to everyone involved in the incident and pieced together an amazing story.

Shortly after dark on the night of the twelfth, the Air Defense Command radar station at Ellsworth AFB, just east of Rapid City, had received a call from the local Ground Observer Corps filter center. A lady spotter at Black Hawk, about 10 miles west of Ellsworth, had reported an extremely bright light low on the horizon, off to the northeast. The radar had been scanning an area to the west, working a jet fighter in some practice patrols, but when they got the report they moved the sector scan to the northeast quadrant. There was a target exactly where the lady reported the light to be. The warrant officer, who was the duty controller for the night, told me that he'd studied the target for several minutes. He knew how weather could affect radar but this target was "well defined, solid, and bright." It seemed to be moving, but very slowly. He called for an altitude reading, and the man on the height-finding

*radar checked his scope. He also had the target—it was
at 16,000 feet.*

*The warrant officer picked up the phone and asked
the filter center to connect him with the spotter. They
did, and the two people compared notes on the UFO's
position for several minutes. But right in the middle of
a sentence the lady suddenly stopped and excitedly said,
"It's starting to move—it's moving southwest toward
Rapid."*

*The controller looked down at his scope and the target
was beginning to pick up speed and move southwest.
He yelled at two of his men to run outside and take a
look. In a second or two one of them shouted back that
they could both see a large bluish-white light moving
toward Rapid City. The controller looked down at his
scope—the target was moving toward Rapid City. As
all three parties watched the light and kept up a steady
cross conversation of the description, the UFO swiftly
made a wide sweep around Rapid City and returned to
its original position in the sky.*

*A master sergeant who had seen and heard the hap-
penings told me that in all his years of duty—combat
radar operations in both Europe and Korea—he'd
never been so completely awed by anything. When the*

warrant officer had yelled down at him and asked him what he thought they should do, he'd just stood there. "After all," he told me, "what in hell could we do—they're bigger than all of us."

But the warrant officer did do something. He called to the F-84 pilot he had on combat air patrol west of the base and told him to get ready for an intercept. He brought the pilot around south of the base and gave him a course correction that would take him right into the light, which was still at 16,000 feet. By this time the pilot had it spotted. He made the turn, and when he closed to within about 3 miles of the target, it began to move. The controller saw it begin to move, the spotter saw it begin to move and the pilot saw it begin to move—all at the same time. There was now no doubt that all of them were watching the same object.

Once it began to move, the UFO picked up speed fast and started to climb, heading north, but the F-84 was right on its tail. The pilot would notice that the light was getting brighter, and he'd call the controller to tell him about it. But the controller's answer would always be the same, "Roger, we can see it on the scope."

There was always a limit as to how near the jet could get, however. The controller told me that it was just as if the UFO had some kind of an automatic warning radar linked to its power supply. When something got too close to it, it would automatically pick up speed and pull away. The separation distance always remained about 3 miles.

The chase continued on north—out of sight of the lights of Rapid City and the base—into some very black night.

When the UFO and the F-84 got about 120 miles to the north, the pilot checked his fuel; he had to come back. And when I talked to him, he said he was damn glad that he was running out of fuel because being out over some mighty desolate country alone with a UFO can cause some worry.

Both the UFO and the F-84 had gone off the scope, but in a few minutes the jet was back on, heading for home. Then 10 or 15 miles behind it was the UFO target also coming back.

While the UFO and the F-84 were returning to the base—the F-84 was planning to land—the controller received a call from the jet interceptor squadron on the base. The alert pilots at the squadron had heard the conversations on their radio and didn't believe it. "Who's nuts up there?" was the comment that passed over the

*wire from the pilots to the radar people. There was an
F-84 on the line ready to scramble, the man on the
phone said, and one of the pilots, a World War II and
Korean veteran, wanted to go up and see a flying saucer.
The controller said, "O.K., go."*

*In a minute or two the F-84 was airborne and the
controller was working him toward the light. The pilot
saw it right away and closed in. Again the light began to
climb out, this time more toward the northeast. The pilot also began to climb, and before long the light, which
at first had been about 30 degrees above his horizontal
line of sight, was now below him. He nosed the '84 down
to pick up speed, but it was the same old story—as soon
as he'd get within 3 miles of the UFO, it would put on a
burst of speed and stay out ahead.*

*Even though the pilot could see the light and hear the
ground controller telling him that he was above it,
and alternately gaining on it or dropping back, he still
couldn't believe it—there must be a simple explanation.
He turned off all of his lights—it wasn't a reflection
from any of the airplane's lights because there it was.
A reflection from a ground light, maybe. He rolled the
airplane—the position of the light didn't change. A
star—he picked out three bright stars near the light and
watched carefully. The UFO moved in relation to the th-*

ree stars. Well, he thought to himself, if it's a real object out there, my radar should pick it up too; so he flipped on his radar-ranging gunsight. In a few seconds the red light on his sight blinked on—something real and solid was in front of him. Then he was scared. When I talked to him, he readily admitted that he'd been scared. He'd met MD 109's, FW 190's and ME 262's over Germany and he'd met MIG-15's over Korea but the large, bright, bluish-white light had scared him—he asked the controller if he could break off the intercept.

This time the light didn't come back.

When the UFO went off the scope it was headed toward Fargo, North Dakota, so the controller called the Fargo filter center. "Had they had any reports of unidentified lights?" he asked. They hadn't.

But in a few minutes a call came back. Spotter posts on a southwest-northeast line a few miles west of Fargo had reported a fast-moving, bright bluish-white light.

This was an unknown—the best.

The sighting was thoroughly investigated, and I could devote pages of detail on how we looked into every facet of the incident; but it will suffice to say that in every facet we looked into we saw nothing. Nothing but a big question mark asking what was it.

When I left Project Blue Book and the Air Force I severed all official associations with the UFO. But the UFO is like hard drink; you always seem to drift back to it. People I've met, people at work, and friends of friends are continually asking about the subject. In the past few months the circulation manager of a large Los Angeles newspaper, one of Douglas Aircraft Company's top scientists, a man who is guiding the future development of the supersecret Atlas intercontinental guided missile, a movie star, and a German rocket expert have called me and wanted to get together to talk about UFO's. Some of them had seen one.

I have kept up with the activity of the UFO and Project Blue Book over the past two years through friends who are still in intelligence. Before Max Futch got out of the Air Force and went back to law school he wrote to me quite often and a part of his letters were always devoted to the latest about the UFO's.

Then I make frequent business trips to ATIC, and I always stop in to see Captain Charles Hardin, who is now in charge of Blue Book, for a "What's new?" I always go to ATIC with the proper security clearances so I'm sure I get a straight answer to my question.

Since I left ATIC, the UFO's haven't gone away and neither has the interest. There hasn't been too much about them in the newspapers because of the present Air Force policy of silence, but they're with us. That the interest is still with us is attested to by the fact that in late 1953 Donald Keyhoe's book about UFO's, Flying Saucers from Outer Space, immediately appeared on best seller lists. The book was based on a few of our good UFO reports that were released to the press. To say that the book is factual depends entirely upon how one uses the word. The details of the specific UFO sightings that he credits to the Air Force are factual, but in his interpretations of the incidents he blasts way out into the wild blue yonder.

During the past two years the bulk of the UFO activity has taken place in Europe. I might add here that I have never seen any recent official UFO reports or studies from other countries; all of my information about the European Flap came from friends. But when these friends are in the intelligence branches of the U.S. Air Force, the RAF, and the Royal Netherlands Air Force, the data can be considered at least good.

The European Flap started in the summer of 1953, when reports began to pop up in England and France. Quality-wise these first reports weren't too good, however. But

*then, like a few reports that occurred early in the sta-
teside Big Flap of 1952, sightings began to drift in that
packed a bit of a jolt. Reports came in that had been
made by personal friends of the brass in the British and
French Air Forces. Then some of the brass saw them.
Corners of mouths started down.*

*In September several radar sites in the London area
picked up unidentified targets streaking across the city
at altitudes of from 44,000 to 68,000 feet. The crews who
saw the targets said, "Not weather," and some of these
crews had been through the bloody Battle of Britain.
They knew their radar.*

*In October the crew of a British European Airways
airliner reported that a "strange aerial object" had paced
their twin-engined Elizabethan for thirty minutes. Then
on November 3, about two-thirty in the afternoon,
radar in the London area again picked up targets. This
time two Vampire jets were scrambled and the pilots
saw a "strange aerial object." The men at the radar site
saw it too; through their telescope it looked like a "flat,
white-coloured tennis ball."*

*The flap continued into 1954. In January those people
who officially keep track of the UFO's pricked up their
ears when the report of two Swedish airline pilots came*

in. The pilots had gotten a good look before the UFO
had streaked into a cloud bank. It looked like a discus
with a hump in the middle.

On through the spring reports poured out of every country in Europe. Some were bad, some were good.

On July 3, 1954, at eight-fifteen in the morning, the captain, the officers and 463 passengers on a Dutch ocean
liner watched a "greenish-colored, saucer-shaped object
about half the size of a full moon" as it sped across the
sky and disappeared into a patch of high clouds.

There was one fully documented and substantiated case
of a "landing" during the flap. On August 25 two young
ladies in Mosjoen, Norway, made every major newspaper in the world when they encountered a "saucer-man."
They said that they were picking berries when suddenly
a dark man, with long shaggy hair, stepped out from
behind some bushes. He was friendly; he stepped right
up to them and started to talk rapidly. The two young
ladies could understand English but they couldn't understand him. At first they were frightened, but his smile
soon "disarmed" them. He drew a few pictures of flying
saucers and pointed up in the sky. "He was obviously
trying to make a point," one of the young ladies said.

A few days later it was discovered that the man from "outer space" was a lost USAF helicopter pilot who was flying with NATO forces in Norway.

As I've always said, "Ya gotta watch those Air Force pilots—especially those shaggy-haired ones from Brooklyn."

The reporting spread to Italy, where thousands of people in Rome saw a strange cigar-shaped object hang over the city for forty minutes. Newspapers claimed that Italian Air Force radar had the UFO on their scopes, but as far as I could determine, this was never officially acknowledged.

In December a photograph of two UFO's over Taormina, Sicily, appeared in many newspapers. The picture showed three men standing on a bridge, with a fourth running up with a camera. All were intently watching two disk-shaped objects. The photo looked good, but there was one flaw, the men weren't looking at the UFO's; they were looking off to the right of them. I'm inclined to agree with Captain Hardin of Blue Book—the photographer just fouled up on his double exposure.

Sightings spread across southern Europe, and at the end of October, the Yugoslav Government expressed official

*interest. Belgrade newspapers said that a "thoughtful
inquiry" would be set up, since reports had come from
"control tower operators, weather stations and hundreds
of farmers." But the part of the statement that swung the
most weight was, "Scientists in astronomical observatories have seen these strange objects with their own eyes."*

*During 1954 and the early part of 1955 my friends in
Europe tried to keep me up-to-date on all of the better
reports, but this soon approached a full-time job. Airline
pilots saw them, radar picked them up, and military
pilots chased them. The press took sides, and the controversy that had plagued the U.S. since 1947 bloomed
forth in all its confusion.*

*An ex-Air Chief Marshal in the RAF, Lord Dowding,
went to bat for the UFO's. The Netherlands Air Chief
of Staff said they can't be. Herman Oberth, the father
of the German rocket development, said that the UFO's
were definitely interplanetary vehicles.*

*In Belgium a senator put the screws on the Secretary
of Defense—he wanted an answer. The Secretary of
Defense questioned the idea that the saucers were "real"
and said that the military wasn't officially interested.
In France a member of parliament received a different
answer—the French military was interested. The French*

General Staff had set up a committee to study UFO
reports.

In Italy, Clare Boothe Luce, American Ambassador to
Italy, said that she had seen a UFO and had no idea
what it could be.

Halfway around the world, in Australia, the UFO's were
busy too. At Canberra Airport the pilot of an RAAF
Hawker Sea Fury and a ground radar station teamed
up to get enough data to make an excellent radar-visual
report.

In early 1955 the flap began to die down about as
rapidly as it had flared up, but it had left its mark—
many more believers. Even the highly respected British
aviation magazine, Aeroplane, had something to say.
One of the editors took a long, hard look at the over-all
UFO picture and concluded, "Really, old chaps—I don't
know."

Probably the most unique part of the whole European
Flap was the fact that the Iron Curtain countries were
having their own private flap. The first indications came
in October 1954, when Rumanian newspapers blamed
the United States for launching a drive to induce a "flying saucer psychosis" in their country. The next month

the Hungarian Government hauled an "expert" up in front of the microphone so that he could explain to the populace that UFO's don't really exist because, "all 'flying saucer' reports originate in the bourgeois countries, where they are invented by the capitalist warmongers with a view to drawing the people's attention away from their economic difficulties."

Next the U.S.S.R. itself took up the cry along the same lines when the voice of the Soviet Army, the newspaper Red Star, denounced the UFO's as, you guessed it, capitalist propaganda.

In 1955 the UFO's were still there because the day before the all-important May Day celebration, a day when the Soviet radio and TV are normally crammed with programs plugging the glory of Mother Russia to get the peasants in the mood for the next day, a member of the Soviet Academy of Sciences had to get on the air to calm the people's fears. He left out Wall Street and Dulles this time—UFO's just don't exist.

It was interesting to note that during the whole Iron Curtain Flap, not one sighting or complimentary comment about the UFO's was made over the radio or in the newspapers; yet the flap continued. The reports were obviously being passed on by word of mouth. This

*fact seems to negate the theory that if the newspaper re-
porters and newscasters would give up the UFO's would
go away. The people in Russia were obviously seeing
something.*

*While the European Flap was in progress, the UFO's
weren't entirely neglecting the United States. The number of reports that were coming into Project Blue Book
were below average, but there were reports. Many of
them would definitely be classed as good, but the best
was a report from a photo reconnaissance B-29 crew
that encountered a UFO almost over Dayton.*

*About 11:00 A.M. on May 24, 1954, an RB-29 equipped
with some new aerial cameras took off from Wright
Field, one of the two airfields that make up Wright-Patterson AFB, and headed toward the Air Force's photographic test range in Indiana. At exactly twelve noon
they were at 16,000 feet, flying west, about 15 miles
northwest of Dayton. A major, a photo officer, was in
the nose seat of the '29. All of the gun sights and the
bombsight in the nose had been taken out, so it was
like sitting in a large picture window—except you just
can't get this kind of a view anyplace else. The major
was enjoying it. He was leaning forward, looking down,
when he saw an extremely bright circular-shaped object
under and a little behind the airplane. It was so bright*

that it seemed to have a mirror finish. He couldn't tell how far below him it was but he was sure that it wasn't any higher than 6,000 feet above the ground, and it was traveling fast, faster than the B-29. It took only about six seconds to cross a section of land, which meant that it was going about 600 miles an hour.

The major called the crew and told them about the UFO, but neither the pilot nor the copilot could see it because it was now directly under the B-29. The pilot was just in the process of telling him that he was crazy when one of the scanners in an aft blister called in; he and the other scanner could also see the UFO.

Being a photo ship, the RB-29 had cameras—loaded cameras—so the logical thing to do would be to take a picture, but during a UFO sighting logic sometimes gets shoved into the background. In this case, however, it didn't, and the major reached down, punched the button on the intervalometer, and the big vertical camera in the aft section of the airplane clicked off a photo before the UFO sped away.

The photo showed a circular-shaped blob of light exactly as the major had described it to the RB-29 crew. It didn't show any details of the UFO because the UFO was too bright; it was completely overexposed on the negative.

The circular shape wasn't sharp either; it had fuzzy edges, but this could have been due to two things: its extreme brightness, or the fact that it was high, close to the RB-29, and out of focus. There was no way of telling exactly how high it was but if it were at 6,000 feet, as the major estimated, it would have been about 125 feet in diameter.

Working with people from the photo lab at Wright-Patterson, Captain Hardin from Project Blue Book carried out one of the most complete investigations in UFO history. They checked aircraft flights, rephotographed the area from high and low altitude to see if they could pick up something on the ground that could have been reflecting light, and made a minute ground search of the area. They found absolutely nothing that could explain the round blob of light, and the incident went down as an unknown.

Like all good "Unknown" UFO reports, there are as many opinions as to what the bright blob of light could have been as there are people who've seen the photo. "Some kind of light phenomenon" is the frequent opinion of those who don't believe. They point out that there is no shadow of any kind of a circular object showing on the ground—no shadow, nothing "solid." But if you care to take the time you can show that if the object, assuming that this is what it was, was above 4,000 feet the shadow would fall out of the picture.

Then all you get is a blank look from the light phenomenon theorists.

With the sighting from the RB-29 and the photograph, all of the other UFO reports that Blue Book has collected and all of those that came out of the European Flap, the big question—the key question—is: What have the last two years of UFO activity brought out? Have there been any important developments?

Some good reports have come in and the Air Force is sitting on them. During 1954 they received some 450 reports, and once again July was the peak month. In the first half of 1955 they had 189. But I can assure you that these reports add nothing more as far as proof is concerned. The quality of the reports has improved, but they still offer nothing more than the same circumstantial evidence that we presented to the panel of scientists in early 1953. There have been no reports in which the speed or altitude of a UFO has been measured, there have been no reliable photographs that show any details of a UFO, and there is no hardware. There is still no real proof.

So a public statement that was made in 1952 still holds true: "The possibility of the existence of interplanetary craft has never been denied by the Air Force, but UFO reports offer absolutely no authentic evidence that such interplanetary spacecraft do exist."

But with the UFO, what is lacking in proof is always made up for in opinions. To get a qualified opinion, I wrote to a friend, Frederick C. Durant. Mr. Durant, who is presently the director of a large Army Ordnance test station, is also a past president of the American Rocket Society and president of the International Astronautical Federation. For those who are not familiar with these organizations, the American Rocket Society is an organization established to promote interest and research in space flight and lists as its members practically every prominent scientist and engineer in the professional fields allied to aeronautics. The International Astronautical Federation is a world-wide federation of such societies.

Mr. Durant has spent many hours studying UFO reports in the Project Blue Book files and many more hours discussing them with scientists the world over—scientists who are doing research and formulating the plans for space flight. I asked him what he'd heard about the UFO's during the past several years and what he thought about them. This was his reply:

This past summer at the Annual Congress of the IAF at Innsbruck, as well as previous Congresses (Zurich, 1953, Stuttgart, 1952, and London, 1951), none of the delegates representing the rocket and space flight societies of all the countries involved had strong feelings on the subject of saucers. Their attitude was essentially the same as professional members of the American Rocket Society in this country. In other words, there appear to be no confirmed saucer fans in the hierarchy of the professional societies.

I continue to follow the subject of UFO's primarily because of my being requested for comment on the interplanetary flight aspects. My personal feelings have not changed in the past four years, although I continue to keep an objective outlook.

There are many other prominent scientists in the world whom I met while I was chief of Project Blue Book who, I'm sure, would give the same answer—they've not been able to find any proof, but they continue to keep an objective outlook. There are just enough big question marks sprinkled through the reports to keep their outlook objective.

I know that there are many other scientists in the world who, although they haven't studied the Air Force's

*UFO files, would limit their comment to a large laugh
followed by an "It can't be." But "It can't be's" are dang-
erous, if for no other reason than history has proved
them so.*

*Not more than a hundred years ago two members of the
French Academy of Sciences were unseated because they
supported the idea that "stones had fallen from the sky."
Other distinguished members of the French Academy
examined the stones, "It can't be—stones don't fall from
the sky," or words to that effect. "These are common
rocks that have been struck by lightning."*

*Today we know that the "stones from the sky" were
meteorites.*

*Not more than fifty years ago Dr. Simon Newcomb,
a world-famous astronomer and the first American
since Benjamin Franklin to be made an associate of the
Institute of France, the hierarchy of the world science,
said, "It can't be." Then he went on to explain that flight
without gas bags would require the discovery of some
new material or a new force in nature.*

*And at the same time Rear Admiral George W. Mel-
ville, then Chief Engineer for the U.S. Navy, said that
attempts to fly heavier-than-air vehicles was absurd.*

Just a little over ten years ago there was another "it can't be." Ex-President Harry S. Truman recalls in the first volume of the Truman Memoirs what Admiral William D. Leahy, then Chief of Staff to the President, had to say about the atomic bomb. "That is the biggest fool thing we have ever done," he is quoted as saying. "The bomb will never go off, and I speak as an expert in explosives."

Personally, I don't believe that "it can't be." I wouldn't class myself as a "believer," exactly, because I've seen too many UFO reports that first appeared to be unexplainable fall to pieces when they were thoroughly investigated. But every time I begin to get skeptical I think of the other reports, the many reports made by experienced pilots and radar operators, scientists, and other people who know what they're looking at. These reports were thoroughly investigated and they are still unknowns. Of these reports, the radar-visual sightings are the most convincing. When a ground radar picks up a UFO target and a ground observer sees a light where the radar target is located, then a jet interceptor is scrambled to intercept the UFO and the pilot also sees the light and gets a radar lock-on only to have the UFO almost impudently outdistance him, there is no simple answer. We have no aircraft on this earth that can at will so handily outdistance our latest jets.

The Air Force is still actively engaged in investigating UFO reports, although during the past six months there have been definite indications that there is a movement afoot to get Project Blue Book to swing back to the old Project Grudge philosophy of analyzing UFO reports—write them all off, regardless. But good UFO reports cannot be written off with such answers as fatigued pilots seeing a balloon or star; "green" radar operators with only fifteen years' experience watching temperature inversion caused blips on their radarscopes; or "a mild form of mass hysteria or war nerves." Using answers like these, or similar ones, to explain the UFO reports is an expedient method of getting the percentage of unknowns down to zero, but it is no more valid than turning the hands of a clock ahead to make time pass faster. Twice before the riddle of the UFO has been "solved," only to have the reports increase in both quantity and quality.

I wouldn't want to hazard a guess as to what the final outcome of the UFO investigation will be, but I am sure that within a few years there will be a proven answer. The earth satellite program, which was recently announced, research progress in the fields of electronics, nuclear physics, astronomy, and a dozen other branches of the sciences will furnish data that will be useful to the UFO investigators. Methods of investigating and analyzing UFO reports have improved a hundredfold since 1947 and they are continuing to be improved by the diligent work of Captain Charles Hardin, the present chief of Project Blue Book, his staff, and the 4602nd Air Intelligence Squadron. Slowly but surely these people are working closer to the answer—closer to the proof.

Maybe the final proven answer will be that all of the UFO's that have been reported are merely misidentified known objects. Or maybe the many pilots, radar specialists, generals, industrialists, scientists, and the man on the street who have told me, "I wouldn't have believed it either if I hadn't seen it myself," knew what they were talking about. Maybe the earth is being visited by interplanetary spaceships.

Only time will tell.

www.ingramcontent.com/pod-product-compliance
Lightning Source LLC
LaVergne TN
LVHW020312200726
843507LV00012B/2071